The Revolutionary Marxism
of Antonio Gramsci

Historical Materialism Book Series

The Historical Materialism Book Series is a major publishing initiative of the radical left. The capitalist crisis of the twenty-first century has been met by a resurgence of interest in critical Marxist theory. At the same time, the publishing institutions committed to Marxism have contracted markedly since the high point of the 1970s. The Historical Materialism Book Series is dedicated to addressing this situation by making available important works of Marxist theory. The aim of the series is to publish important theoretical contributions as the basis for vigorous intellectual debate and exchange on the left.

The peer-reviewed series publishes original monographs, translated texts, and reprints of classics across the bounds of academic disciplinary agendas and across the divisions of the left. The series is particularly concerned to encourage the internationalization of Marxist debate and aims to translate significant studies from beyond the English-speaking world.

For a full list of titles in the Historical Materialism Book Series available in paperback from Haymarket Books, visit:
www.haymarketbooks.org/category/hm-series

The Revolutionary Marxism
of Antonio Gramsci

Frank Rosengarten

Haymarket Books
Chicago, IL

First published in 2014 by Brill Academic Publishers, The Netherlands
© 2014 Koninklijke Brill NV, Leiden, The Netherlands

Published in paperback in 2015 by
Haymarket Books
P.O. Box 180165
Chicago, IL 60618
773-583-7884
www.haymarketbooks.org

ISBN: 978-1-60846-473-9

Trade distribution:
In the US, Consortium Book Sales, www.cbsd.com
In Canada, Publishers Group Canada, www.pgcbooks.ca
In the UK, Turnaround Publisher Services, www.turnaround-psl.com
In Australia, Palgrave Macmillan, www.palgravemacmillan.com.au
In all other countries, Publishers Group Worldwide, www.pgw.com

Cover design by Ragina Johnson.

This book was published with the generous support of
Lannan Foundation and the Wallace Global Fund.

Printed in Canada by union labor.

10 9 8 7 6 5 4 3 2 1

Library of Congress Cataloging-in-Publication data is available.

To John Cammett
In Memoriam

Contents

Part Three: Comparative Perspectives on Gramsci

Part Four: Two Protagonists of Gramsci Studies in the United States

Acknowledgments

I would like to acknowledge the special debt I owe to Peter D. Thomas, whose initiative was primarily responsible for the publication of this book of essays on Antonio Gramsci. I was fortunate to have Peter available to help me solve the problems that I encountered in bringing together essays that were written over a long span of time, from 1968 to 2012. I would also like to thank David Broder for his excellent comments, corrections and suggestions concerning the text of this book.

My thanks are due to three friends and colleagues with whom I have had illuminating discussions concerning the issues that I deal with in the present volume. They are Professors Joe Francese, Kate Crehan, and Ben Fontana, all of whom have offered me the benefit of their expertise through the years.

Professor Roberto Dainotto was indispensable to me for Chapter Nine on 'Gramsci in the Caribbean', which I presented at a Conference that Roberto, together with Professor Fredric Jameson, organised at Duke University in late April 2013.

Finally, it would be difficult for me to exaggerate the importance of the role that Joe Buttigieg has played not only in my own Gramsci studies, but in the work of scholars worldwide. Chapter Five of this book on Gramsci's analysis of Canto X of Dante's *Inferno* appeared first in the journal *Boundary 2*, of which Joe became an editor in the 1980s. Joe was elected first president of the International Gramsci Society in 1989; since that time, he has been a virtual roving ambassador of Gramsci studies, in which capacity he has used his organisational skills to promote all kinds of worthy initiatives, especially in Italy. The first three volumes of his projected five-volume English translation of Gramsci's *Prison Notebooks* have already appeared. They feature an impressive introduction and critical apparatus that all serious Gramsci scholars will need to consult.

Abbreviations

The following abbreviations are used in the text:

PCd'I   Partito Comunista d'Italia [Communist Party of Italy]
IGS   International Gramsci Society
JMIS   *Journal of Modern Italian Studies*
PCI   Partito Comunista Italiano [Italian Communist Party]
SSC   Socialist Scholars Conference

List of Permissions

The essays collected in this volume appeared originally in the following books and periodicals or were presented online or at conferences. They are listed in the order in which they appear in the present volume.

"The Gramsci-Trotsky Question: (1922–1932)," *Social Text*, Winter 1984/85. No. 11, pp. 65–95.

"Antonio Gramsci and the Italian Communist Press during the Fascist Era," taken from Part II of my book *The Italian Antifascist Press 1919–1945*, Cleveland: Case Western University Press, 1968, pp. 33–85.

"The Contemporary Relevance of Gramsci's Views on Italy's 'Southern Question'," *Perspectives on Gramsci – Politics, Culture and Social Theory*, ed. Joseph Francese, New York: 2009, pp. 134–144.

"Three Essays on Antonio Gramsci's *Letters from Prison*," *Italian Quarterly*, Summer/Fall 1984, Nos. 97–98, pp. 7–40.

"Gramsci's 'Little Discovery': Gramsci's Interpretation of Canto X of Dante's *Inferno*, *Boundary 2*, Vol. XIV, No. 3, Spring 1986, pp. 71–90.

"From 'Ploughman' to 'Fertiliser' of History: Gramsci as General Secretary of the Communist Party of Italy and Gramsci as Political Prisoner of the Fascist Régime," *Rivista di Studi Italiani*, June 1988, XVI, No. 1, pp. 39–56.

"Antonio Gramsci and C.L.R. James: Some Intriguing Similarities," is available on line at http://www.inernationalgramscisociety.org/resources/online_articles/rosengarten (2002)

"On the Qualities of Intellectuals: Antonio Gramsci, Edward Said, and Betty Friedan," *Italian Culture*, Vol. XXVIII, No. 7, September 2010, pp. 157–167.

"Gramsci in the Caribbean" was presented on April 20, 2013 at a Conference held at Duke University.

"Robert Dombroski's Critical Engagement with Marxism," *From Paradox to Parable – Essays in Memory of Robert S. Dombroski*, ed. Joseph Francese, New York: Bordighera Press, pp. 79–96.

"John Cammett's Writings on Antonio Gramsci and the PCI," *Journal of Modern Italian Studies*, Vol. 16 No. 2, March 2001, pp. 195–210.

Part One

Gramsci as Political Thinker and Activist

Introduction

Why Gramsci? And why Gramsci now? Each of the eleven chapters of this book addresses one or the other of these questions, but usually not directly and explicitly. That burden falls to the following introductory remarks.

If we look at the totality of Gramsci's intellectual production, from the articles he wrote as a young man for various socialist newspapers to the notebooks on which he laboured in prison, we are struck by their freshness and originality. Gramsci is never uninteresting; no matter what his subject, whether it be an Ibsen play or the relevance of Marxism to the study of history and politics, whether it be a debate over the methods and aims of education or the phenomenon of revolution, he approached his subjects in such a way as to leave his readers not only better informed, but above all challenged, stirred, and engaged. This is not merely a matter of Gramsci's style, although his prose is exceptionally incisive and free of verbiage. What especially distinguishes his writing is its mixture of spontaneity and rigour, of passion and restraint, rare combinations in one and the same individual.

One can speak, in Gramsci's case, of a 'heroic' effort to transcend the always difficult circumstances of his life, beginning with his early years in Sardinia to his arrival in Turin in 1911 as a scholarship student and later to the years when he was general secretary of the Communist Party of Italy [PCd'I] culminating in his arrest and imprisonment on 8 November 1926. His ideas and perspectives were honed in the crucible of hard struggles that exposed him to the vitriol and threats of his political enemies on an almost daily basis. Despite his diminutive stature and frequent ill-health, which was exacerbated by persistently penurious living conditions, he did not waver from his primary purpose, which was to help build an Italian society informed by socialist and democratic principles.

One of Gramsci's major contributions to modern socialist thought lies in the emphasis he placed on Marxism as a self-standing, independent, integrally coherent body of ideas free of supernaturalism and committed to translating the various strands of classical and Christian philosophy into historical-materialist terms. Like Marx himself, and like one of Marx's most fervent disciples in Italy, namely Antonio Labriola, Gramsci did his utmost to free Marxism of its idealist encrustations while, at the same time, recognising that human beings have spiritual as well as physical needs. This did not represent an evasion or softening of his materialist outlook. It signified his belief that unless Marxism took the full measure of humanity, unless it presented itself as a fulfilment – and not a negation – of the human need for community and meaning, it would remain at best on the margins of modern social life. Gramsci sought to move Marxist theory and practice, which he called 'the philosophy of praxis', away from the margins to the very centre of contemporary civilisation. It seems to me that he succeeded in doing precisely that, perhaps not in his own day, but certainly in the time since his death on 27 April 1937.

Indeed, in my view, Gramsci, while suffering a terrible defeat in his own time, emerged posthumously from that defeat and was responsible, as much as any other Marxist thinker, for reviving and nourishing interest in the relevance of Marxism to what Cesare Pavese called *il mestiere di vivere*, the demanding and tough 'business of living'. But it was Marxism not only as a repository of useful notions about economics and the nature of the capitalist system – as indispensable as these were to the cause of human liberation – but rather as a philosophy capable of interpreting human affairs in all their variety and complexity, that Gramsci tried to inculcate in his comrades and potential followers. Gramsci was a philosopher as well as a political activist, a 'democratic' philosopher, insofar as he saw his responsibility to be one of sharing his knowledge and insights with everyone irrespective of social class and educational attainment.

Gramsci's understanding of Marxism was at once practical and theoretical. This can be seen in many of his writings, two of which can serve as examples of what I mean. One belongs to a section of the *Prison Notebooks* that Quintin Hoare and Geoffrey Nowell Smith, following Gramsci's lead, call 'the philosophy of praxis'. The other comes from his prison letters, which are often brief but pithy disquisitions on serious questions that he liked to discuss with his correspondents.

One notices, for example, that under the sub-topic 'the study of philosophy', Gramsci takes philosophy out of the specialised workplace of the solitary intellectual and into the public arena. His aim was to remove the realm of ideas from the exclusive preserve of an intellectual or professional elite and, like Socrates, bring it down to earth where everyone interested could partake of its riches. He expounded his point of view on this and related questions in several passages that help to explain why Gramsci has been so central to almost all discussions of Marxism in the twentieth and twenty-first centuries. Here is one of the pages where he makes his own position quite clear:

The question posed here was the one we have already referred to, namely this: is a philosophical movement properly so called when it is devoted to creating a specialised culture among restricted intellectual groups, or rather when, and only when, in the process of elaborating a form of thought superior to 'common sense' and coherent on a scientific plane, it never forgets to remain in contact with the 'simple' and indeed finds in this contact the source of the problems it sets out to study and to resolve? Only by this contact does a philosophy become 'historical', purify itself of intellectualistic elements of an individual character and become 'a living force'.

A philosophy of praxis cannot but present itself at the outset in a polemical and critical guise, as superseding the existing mode of thinking and existing concrete thought (the existing cultural world). First of all, therefore, it must be a criticism of 'common sense', basing itself initially, however, on common sense in order to demonstrate that 'everyone' is a philosopher and that it is not a question of introducing from scratch a scientific form of thought into everyone's individual life, but of renovating and making 'critical' an already existing activity. It must then be a criticism of the philosophy of the intellectuals out of which the history of philosophy developed and which, in so far as it is a phenomenon of individuals (in fact it develops essentially in the activity of single particularly gifted individuals) can be considered as marking the common sense of the more educated strata of society but through them also of the people. Thus an introduction to the study of philosophy must expound in synthetic form the problems that have grown up in the process of the development of culture as a whole. The purpose of the synthesis must be to criticise the problems, to demonstrate their real value, if any, and the significance they have had as superseded links of an intellectual chain, and to determine what the new contemporary problems are and how the old problems should now be analysed.[1]

This passage – especially if read in conjunction with the pages that follow it a little later under the rubric 'problems of Marxism', where Gramsci links Marxism to the whole development of Western thought since the Renaissance – reveals the way in which he enlisted philosophy in the service of a larger and more far-reaching end, which was to establish the bases of a radically popular and democratic socio-political order. In this sense, for Gramsci, philosophy was one and only one expression of human intelligence, and was inextricably related to all other activities to which the human species devotes its time and energy. There is no mistaking the democratic origin of the perspective from which Gramsci wrote this section of the notebooks.

The other illustrative passage to which I referred above is taken from a prison letter that Gramsci wrote to his wife on 5 September 1932, about a year before he was transferred from prison to a hospital in Formia. The passage concerns the question of whether one could love yet not esteem a writer. This led Gramsci to make a value judgment about the Italian poet Giacomo Leopardi that I think also exemplifies, implicitly, Gramsci's

---

1. Gramsci 1971, pp. 330–1.

conception of Marxism as a philosophy of life, and not only as an analysis and clarification of capitalism. Here is the passage in question, all the more significant because of its spontaneity, as a reaction to something that his wife had said to him in her letter:

> Perhaps I made a distinction between aesthetic pleasure and the positive judgment of artistic beauty, that is, between a state of mind filled with enthusiasm for the work of art as such, and moral enthusiasm, that is, a feeling of participation in the artist's ideological world, a distinction that seems to me critically correct and necessary. I can admire Tolstoy's *War and Peace* aesthetically and not agree with the book's ideological substance; if the two aspects did coincide Tolstoy would be my *vademecum, le livre de chevet*. The same can be said for Shakespeare, for Goethe, and even for Dante. It would not be correct to say this for Leopardi, notwithstanding his pessimism. In Leopardi we find, in extremely dramatic form, the crisis of transition to modern man; the critical abandonment of all transcendental conceptions without having found a new moral and intellectual *ubi consistam*, which imparts the same certainty that has been forsaken.[2]

We can feel safe in saying that Gramsci's answer to the question *ubi consistam*, where do I stand, was Marxism, the philosophy of praxis, because it alone, in Gramsci's opinion, gave its adherents a comprehensive and coherent understanding of society and history, and of their place in it. Leopardi lacked the feeling of 'certainty' because he was unable to transcend his own philosophical pessimism. The other four writers that Gramsci mentioned in this letter could be said to have incorporated a coherent conception of life in their fictional and poetic writings, and were thus able, each in his own way, to give their readers a sense of completeness and resolution. Leopardi, on the other hand, had not been able to replace his pessimism with such a conception, which was precisely what made him the recognisably 'modern' and beloved poet that he was; a poet, that is, who spoke a language of yearning and regret, of hope and disappointment, of illusions and revelations that come for an instant and then fade away, swallowed up by the vast nothingness of the cosmos.

We should note, in this letter, Gramsci's insistence on speaking of a conception of life that was at once 'moral and intellectual' in nature. Marxism has not always or conventionally been understood this way. Yet, as I've already noted, Gramsci did see Marxism as much more than a critique of capitalism. It was also a bountiful source of insight into many different levels and aspects of human experience, one of which, he believed, was moral in nature. I think that much of Gramsci's appeal lies precisely in the fact that he reminds us that the human adventure is indelibly and necessarily marked by moral questions that have great influence on the decisions that individuals as well as societies and nations must make.

Closely connected to what I have just said about the way in which Gramsci interpreted Marxism was his tendency to see Marxism as still undergoing change and in need

---

2. Gramsci 1994, Vol. II, pp. 206–7.

of refinement and elaboration. It was not a worldview established once and for all, but rather a part of the historical process teeming with diverse elements, some congenial to the further development of a materialist conception of life and others incompatible with it. It was up to its exponents to make the right choices. In this sense, a modern political party aiming to lead masses of people had philosophical as well as practical tasks to accomplish.

One component of Gramsci's conception of life was his belief that political leaders aiming to diffuse their ideas among the masses of people and thereby influence the course of events must be prepared to take personal responsibility for their actions and, if necessary, pay the price that these actions may exact in the real world of clashing interests and ambitions. On a number of occasions, he exemplified this notion of leadership and responsibility in the figure of a ship's captain who must not abandon his post before making sure that his crew and passengers have reached safety or have found a means to escape harm. If a captain fails to do this, he violates a principle on which civilised co-existence ultimately depends. This principle is not merely economic and social in origin, but moral as well. It resides in the mind and spirit of human beings who, through eons of historical experience, have derived certain laws and principles that transcend the material dimension of things, no matter how important the latter may be; laws and principles that can never be discounted without at the same time destroying the fabric of social life.[3]

I once wrote a short essay on the events that led to Gramsci's arrest in which I raised the question of why he did not take effective measures to protect himself at a time when the Fascists were systematically cracking down on their opponents. I argued that one possible answer to this question lay in Gramsci's conviction that, just as a ship's captain in a moment of emergency evacuation must be the last to abandon ship, the leader of a political party must not seek safety until all of his comrades have done so. Such an attitude may seem naïve and even foolish to some, yet I believed that it would have been consistent with Gramsci's understanding of his role and responsibilities as leader of the Communist Party of Italy.

It was Gramsci's consciousness of moral responsibility that probably led him to become involved in politics in the first place. In his account of 'Western Marxism', Perry Anderson goes into considerable detail in order to explain why Gramsci is such a key figure. His importance does not lie only in the fact that he paid such close attention to the 'superstructural' dimensions of life, but also in the example he set of consistent personal involvement in struggle as a man of action, as someone who paid the price that his beliefs required of him. More perhaps than any of his distinguished Marxist

---

3. For an English translation of the passage in which Gramsci makes this judgment, see Derek Boothman's translation: Gramsci 1995, pp. lxxxv–lxxxvi.

contemporaries, Gramsci overcame what Anderson calls 'the structural divorce [of Western Marxism] from political practice'.[4]

Whether and to what extent this 'divorce' did in fact take place is open to debate, but there seems to be some basis for Anderson's perspective on successive generations of Marxists. He characterises the first 'classical' generation (Marx and Engels, followed by such figures as Lenin, Luxemburg, and Trotsky) as fully committed to living their ideas on a daily basis in the form of intense political engagement. The next generation, on the other hand (Lukács, Korsch, Benjamin, Marcuse), he describes as 'Western' Marxists interested primarily in theory and in promoting cultural and literary initiatives of various kinds. They were prolific writers and thinkers, but not men of action. Among this second group, only Gramsci, Anderson argues, was to the fullest extent both a theorist and an activist, deeply involved in cultural and intellectual enterprises yet always on the front line of political struggle.

Let me proceed now to an explanation of how and why I became involved in Gramsci studies, after which I will say a few words about the essays gathered in this volume.

My interest in Antonio Gramsci was sparked by John M. Cammett, author of the groundbreaking book *Antonio Gramsci and the Origins of Italian Communism* (1967). This was the first comprehensive, deeply researched book on Gramsci in the English language. John and I were fellow doctoral students at Columbia University in the mid-1950s, he in history and I in Italian. He had already chosen his thesis topic, which was on Gramsci as leader and theorist of the Turinese factory council movement from 1919 to 1924. John's enthusiastic accounts of the research that he had already completed on Gramsci, and the fact that we shared a strong admiration for the role played by the Italian Communist Party in the struggle against Fascism, led me to purchase several of the volumes of Gramsci's writings published by Einaudi from the late 1940s to the mid-1950s. Two of these made an especially strong impression on me: *Gli intellettuali e l'organizzazione della cultura* (1949) and *Il materialismo storico e la filosofia di Benedetto Croce* (1953). Both volumes were among the groundbreaking Italian-language anthologies of Gramsci's prison writings before the appearance in 1975 of the four-volume set of the *Quaderni del carcere* edited and annotated by Valentino Gerratana. As a student of modern and contemporary Italian literature, and as someone drawn to the socio-historical dimensions of literary scholarship, I read these books with a growing sense of excitement and discovery.

In the summer of 1956, while in Florence doing preliminary research for my doctoral dissertation on the novelist Vasco Pratolini, I had the good fortune to meet another pioneering figure in Gramsci studies, Louis Marks, who was putting the finishing touches on his anthology of Gramsci's prison notes. The anthology included several of the editorials

---

4. Anderson 1976, p. 29.

and articles Gramsci wrote for the newspaper *L'Ordine Nuovo* in the early 1920s, plus the complete text of Gramsci's last important essay before his imprisonment, *Some Aspects of the Southern Question*, written in October 1926. The book also included an excellent introduction by Marks.

More than three decades later, in the 1990s, I made the acquaintance of a third pioneer in Gramsci studies, Carl Marzani, who in 1957 translated and annotated a small paperback compilation of Gramsci's prison writings entitled *The Open Marxism of Antonio Gramsci*. Thus, all three of Gramsci's most assiduous translators and interpreters, at least in the English-language world, helped me find my own way as a critical reader of Gramsci's writings.

It would be hard for me to overestimate the importance that Gramsci has had in my own work. The only period over the past fifty-five years when Gramsci was not at the forefront of my attention was the 1970s, when I was carrying out research for a political biography of the anti-fascist jurist Silvio Trentin. But in that book as well I found it necessary to anchor some of my judgments in an ideological terrain that embraced both Trentin's militant revolutionary socialism and Gramsci's equally militant revolutionary communism. For this reason, in my introduction to *Silvio Trentin: From Interventionism to the Resistance* (1980), I pointed out that while there were ideological differences between Trentin and Gramsci concerning the meanings that they ascribed to the words socialism and democracy, Trentin had found tremendous value in Gramsci's life and thought.

My first readings of Gramsci were focused almost entirely on the *Prison Notebooks*. Only after several years did I realise that his personality and sensibilities also come vividly to life in his pre-prison critical and journalistic writings. It is in these early interventions into Italian political and cultural debates that we discover a human being amply endowed with insight into his own passions and motivations and capable of examining familiar problems in new and exciting ways. In the political and cultural commentary he wrote from 1913 to 1919, as a university student and then as a full-time propagandist and critic for the Italian Socialist Party, he produced a steady stream of commentary that we can read today with real pleasure and profit. Of these, the ones that stand out in my mind, and that are easily available in any one of several anthologies, are 'Socialism and Culture' (1916), 'Our Marx' (1918), 'Workers' Democracy' (1919), and 'The War in the Colonies' (1919).

In these articles, which Gramsci later (mistakenly) dismissed as mere journalistic effusions that were born and died in their moment, we are introduced to a man animated by a powerful desire to change the world for the better, eager to address the problems of education and personal development as they presented themselves to the working-class movement, possessed of a keen wit and a lucid, penetrating intelligence. Running through all of these writings is the red thread of self-awareness and self-discipline as the first and ineluctable responsibility of each and every member of a revolutionary political party. Here, for example, is how Gramsci defined 'culture' in 1916:

> The young student who knows a little Latin and history, the young lawyer who has been successful in wringing a scrap of paper called a degree out of the laziness and lackadaisical attitude of his professors – they end up seeing themselves as different from and superior to even the best skilled workman, who fulfills a precise and indispensable task in life and is a hundred times more valuable in his activity than they are in theirs. But this is not culture, but pedantry, not intelligence, but intellect, and it is absolutely right to react against it.
>
> Culture is something quite different. It is organization, discipline of one's inner self, a coming to terms with one's own personality; it is the attainment of a higher awareness, with the aid of which one succeeds in understanding one's historical value, one's own function in life, one's rights and obligations.[5]

The young man who wrote these lines was desperately poor and ill-clothed, stood four feet eleven inches in height, was hunch-backed, suffered from a nervous disorder, and lived alone in a small flat without reliable heating. We have a partial record of these years in Gramsci's angry letters to his father, whom he blamed for failing to send him the few extra lire he needed to cope with the bitter cold of a Turinese winter. Yet despite this deprivation, he was not only capable of articulating the ideas that mattered to him, but also of maintaining vital connections with other kindred spirits for needed examples and precedents. In 'Socialism and Culture', it is clear that the writer has internalised and made his own the spirit of Socrates, of the German Romantic poet Novalis, of the Italian philosopher Giambattista Vico, of the French novelist Romain Rolland. These same qualities are present in 'Our Marx', where Gramsci expounds basically the same point of view we find in 'Socialism and Culture' but this time concretely embedded in the figure of Karl Marx:

> Marx was great, his action was fecund, not because he invented from nothing, not because he extracted an *original* vision of history from his imagination, but because in him the fragmentary, the incomplete, the immature became maturity, system, awareness. His personal awareness can become everyone's, it has already become that of many people: because of this Marx is not just a scholar, he is a man of action; he is great and fecund in action as in thought, his books have transformed the world, just as they have transformed thought.
>
> Marx signifies the entry of intelligence into the history of humanity, the reign of awareness.[6]

These words were products of Gramsci's intellectual development mainly in the second decade of the twentieth century, but they also reveal his connection with the events that were unfolding in Russia and elsewhere as World War I drew to a close. His use of the word 'transformed' is a key indicator of his mentality at the time. News of the revolution

---

5. Gramsci 1988, p. 57.
6. Gramsci 1988, p. 36.

in Russia had for several years already become a beacon of hope for many European socialists. It was this revolution that gave Gramsci the confidence that he needed to carry on struggles in Italy: struggles that he correctly predicted would be fraught with difficulties. Indeed, his hopes and visions of a better time were destined to fail, and he died a prisoner of the régime whose incarnation in the person of Benito Mussolini he had warned his comrades about on more than one occasion. Yet what he was able to accomplish in these years and the legacy that he has left us remain very much alive today.

For reasons in part concerned with his conception of politics and culture as always dense and problematic in nature, and in part with the freshness and originality of his ideas, Gramsci has been relevant to many different kinds of people who, however, share an interest in advancing the socialist project theoretically and in practice. This can be seen in the growth of what amounts to a worldwide community of scholars who meet at regular intervals to discuss the meanings and implications of his writings.

To me one of the most memorable of these gatherings took place in Formia, Italy, from 25 to 28 October 1989, at which the International Gramsci Society (IGS) was founded. It was memorable because of the high quality of the papers presented there and because of the charged atmosphere in which it took place. Indeed, the Formia Conference could not have occurred at a more dramatic moment of postwar European history. The mood was tense and expectant from the outset because of one enormous fact: the growing unrest throughout the countries of Eastern Europe. It was clear that this reflected the loosening of dictatorial power in the Soviet Union, where since 1985 Mikhail Gorbachev had begun to effect far-reaching political and economic reforms that, as so often happens in this type of situation, had begun to move well beyond the initial demands of anti-government protesters. When the papers written by Elemer Kéri of Hungary and by Pavol Koprda and Marta Barova of Czechoslovakia were read to the general assembly (they were not present in person), almost without exception the reaction was one of strong support and solidarity with the people struggling for change in these two countries. Most of those present in Formia were old enough to remember earlier revolts and resistance against the existing régimes in the Soviet-dominated world: 1953 in East Germany, 1956 in Hungary, the 1970s and 1980s in Poland, and so on.

It was in this way that Gramsci's political and intellectual legacy became inextricably linked with the history of struggle and change in postwar Europe, a history in which Italian politics occupied a prominent place. In part because of his legacy, Italy had the largest and, electorally speaking, one of the most widely supported communist parties outside the Soviet Union. It had been Gramsci who named the main organ of the Communist Party of Italy L'Unità, a name he had borrowed from the united front policy that had been adopted at the Comintern congresses in 1921 and 1922 after it became clear that the revolution in Russia was not going to achieve quick victories in Europe, as both Lenin and Trotsky had hoped. On the contrary, what was waiting in the wings of the political stage in those years was the rising threat of right-wing reaction.

The reason that I mention this is to recall that no one at the Formia Conference felt uneasy about Gramsci's close attachment to the Russian Revolution and, implicitly at least, to the subsequent crises of 'actually existing socialism'. Of course, Gramsci did not have all the answers to the problems afflicting actually existing socialism. Yet it was felt by everyone present in Formia that he had valuable things to say about socialism and democracy that could shed light on the reasons for the breakdown of the socialist régimes in Eastern Europe. Moreover, everyone at Formia was aware that Gramsci was among the great losers of the early twentieth century; that his writings in the early 1920s, and above all his prison letters and notebooks, were the fruit of the defeat suffered by the working-class movement in the West led by the Socialist and Communist parties. Gramsci had the foresight and the intellectual resources to confront this crisis head on. He recognised that his own personal defeat and that of the party of which he was general secretary was but one episode in a world historical process that would be long and filled with unpredictable hazards and difficulties.

Looked at from our vantage point today, Gramsci's place among theorists of revolutionary Marxism takes on a distinct and controversial cast. He helped to theorise a type of political strategy that takes into account the diverse 'relations of force' existing in countries where the Marxist Left finds itself in prolonged contention for power with other well-established political formations. This kind of adaptability became a hallmark of the Italian Communist Party (PCI) after the end of World War II. For four decades, from the 1940s to the 1980s, the PCI succeeded in becoming a mass party rooted in the lives and fortunes of workers and, more generally, of ordinary people who were not necessarily affiliated with the Left but were open to a politics that challenged the hegemony of corporate capitalism. The fact that the PCI failed to maintain its unity and cohesion after the collapse of the Soviet Union does not invalidate Gramsci's political insights. Indeed, in my view, the current crisis of democratic governance in Italy only serves to highlight the soundness of his thinking. Without a strong unified party behind it, the Left in Italy has gone down to a humiliating defeat, from which it may take many years to recover.

The titles of each of this book's four sections refer as much to the type as to the themes and subject matter of the eleven essays. Chapter One deals with Gramsci's work as an activist and as a theorist of the Italian and international communist movements during Italy's tormented transition from liberalism to Fascism. The international ramifications of his political activities from the early 1920s to 1932 are at the core of this chapter. Chapters Two and Three are mainly concerned with Gramsci as a militant anti-fascist. But in all three of these chapters, I have made an effort to provide some insight into his activities before the onset of Fascism. Gramsci was a revolutionary well before Mussolini took power in October 1922. On the other hand, the rise and triumph of the Fascist régime compelled him to rethink some of his youthful political positions. He was further radicalised by Fascism, which compelled him to deepen his analysis of Italy's class structure and at the same time led him to reflect more systematically on several of the social and cultural problems that were later to occupy his attention in the *Prison Notebooks*.

The three essays in Part Two delve necessarily into psychological and literary-critical problems in a more focused way than do those of the other three sections. They all come to grips with Gramsci's prison experience from 1926 to his death in 1937. The brute reality of prolonged incarceration compelled him to monitor his own emotions, which he did in a typically painstaking manner, while at the same time he did his best to understand the people with whom he corresponded. The letters often make for painful reading, yet they are remarkably lively and revealing about aspects of Gramsci's personality that might otherwise have remained hidden from view. All three chapters on Gramsci's years in prison show him to have been an imaginative, creative, humorous person endowed with a remarkable sensitivity to the sensuous side of life.

Part Three looks at Gramsci in relation to other prominent personalities of the twentieth century who, to one degree or another, invite comparison with him for a number of reasons. Like Gramsci, C.L.R. James, to whom I devoted a study published in 2008, was an original thinker whose perspectives on history and political struggle were strongly influenced by his study of Marxism. Yet like Gramsci, James cannot be understood properly if we confine ourselves to his assimilation of Marxism. Other experiences played a part in making him the man and the thinker he was, not the least of which were his formative years spent in the multi-lingual, multi-racial, multi-cultural island of Trinidad. In any case, a comparative approach to these two seminal figures in the history of modern socialism and communism yields benefits, and I have tried to explicate these in Chapter Seven. Chapters Eight and Nine may be of some interest on account of their offbeat qualities. A comparison between Gramsci and Betty Friedan, for example, is not a common theme of Gramsci studies, while my brief consideration of Gramsci's critical fortunes in the islands of the Caribbean archipelago is still an under-explored subject. Quite surprisingly, in view of Cuba's long attempt to build a society on socialist foundations, relatively little seems to be known about Gramsci's critical reception in that country. My review of 'Gramsci in the Caribbean' is a small step toward remedying this deficiency.

Finally, the last two essays are my way of acknowledging the contributions to Gramsci studies made by two good friends who passed away over the past ten years. For Bob Dombroski, Gramsci served to stimulate and at times to guide him in a certain type of literary-historical inquiry, one motivated by a need to situate writers in their time and place but without reducing them to their origins and without forcing them into preconceived categories.

John Cammett spent a good part of his life devoted to Gramsci, beginning in the 1950s and ending after the turn of the twenty-first century. His critical and bibliographical work will be crucial to Gramsci studies for a long time.

I hope that this volume will give the reader already knowledgeable about Gramsci added appreciation of the qualities of his mind and spirit. I hope also that it will provide less informed readers with several entry points through which to approach Gramsci's ideas in a number of different fields, from Marxist theory to literary criticism, from political history to sociolinguistics, from education to folklore and religion. All of these areas of interest came into play in Gramsci's life as a man committed to the struggle for a new socialist society.

Chapter One
The Gramsci-Trotsky Question

Gramsci's reactions to the personality and political views of Leon Trotsky offer valuable insights into the history of the Third International from 1922 to 1932. The evidence of a Trotskyist influence on Gramsci is rather persuasive,[1] and sheds light on the encounter between the 'classical' (Trotsky) and 'Western' (Gramsci) traditions of revolutionary Marxism, to use Perry Anderson's terminology in *Considerations on Western Marxism*.[2]

Some of the recent scholarly work done on Gramsci, and a preponderance of the references to him that one comes across in left periodicals published during the last ten to fifteen years have tended to downplay his connections with the makers and events of the Bolshevik Revolution, and to privilege those aspects of his ideas that fit into the framework of what has been loosely called 'cultural radicalism'. Gramsci has become a kind of role model to many radical literary intellectuals, academic Marxists, and left-leaning social democrats.

No doubt, Gramsci has much to offer people interested in consciousness, subjectivity, and culture. But it should always be remembered that, for Gramsci, the study of how we understand phenomena and of how and why particular conceptions of the world are mediated by institutions and filter down into the consciousness of the masses was part of a larger enterprise whose aim was the socialist restructuring of capitalist society. His 'pessimism of the intellect', so

---

1. For some aspects of this essay, whose initial arguments reflect the time in which it was written (the early 1980s), I am especially indebted to Leonardo Rapone and Giancarlo Bergami.

2. Anderson calls Gramsci, Karl Korsch, and György Lukács 'the real originators of the whole pattern of Western Marxism'. See Anderson 1976, p. 29.

widespread today, was counterbalanced by an 'optimism of the will', which seems sorely lacking in the Left circles of the 1980s. Had Gramsci lived on into the 1960s and 1970s, perhaps he would have sympathised with the skepticism of New Left intellectuals today who ask 'What is socialism, anyway' or who are rereading Marx, Lenin, and Trotsky with the insights provided to them by Foucault and Derrida. It is not unreasonable to see Gramsci as, in some respects, a precursor of deconstructionism. One can accept the view of Gramsci as a thinker who provided a 'new and unique reformulation of Marxian theory'.[3] His reflections on the role of intellectuals in rationalising systems of political control and domination would be sufficient – even if he had not had anything else original to say – to make him attractive to the New Left. I would argue, however, that a balanced view of Gramsci requires that we not only acknowledge his contribution to current 'cultural radical' discourse, but that we also situate him unequivocally in the context of the revolutionary struggle to build a new society in accordance with the principles of socialist democracy. To remove him from the struggles and ferment of the 1920s is to neglect a decisive stage in his personal and political development. In Italy, Gramsci wrote in October 1924, the only battle cry that made sense was 'neither Fascism nor liberalism: Sovietism!'[4] This was the lesson he wanted to teach his co-militants and the Italian people who were being seduced in droves by the rhetoric of nationalism and Fascism.

None of the various contemporary appropriations of Gramsci are entirely convincing. New Left emphasis on the anti-authoritarian content of Gramsci's socialist project, to the exclusion of his tough-minded, resolute stands from 1917 to the 1930s in defence of the Bolshevik Revolution, is matched in its onesidedness by the arguments of Eurocommunists and groups to the left of Eurocommunism, including some Trotskyists. At the same time, I would say that orthodox, uncritical defenders of the present system in the Soviet Union are not entitled either to lay undisputed claim to Gramsci's ideas, since such defence implies a *forma mentis* that can reconcile rigid bureaucracy and intolerance of even loyal dissent (as in the case of Roy Medvedev) with socialist democracy. Gramsci did believe in unfettered discussion and debate of ideas, although he did not flinch from imposing restraints on openly counterrevolutionary propaganda.

James Joll makes this assertion:

> Gramsci not only suggested the possibility of a more humane and a more diversified form of Marxism than that used to justify the bureaucratic dictatorship and cruelty of the Soviet régime; he has also given indications of how a communist party in a liberal democratic state might actually hope to attain power.[5]

---

3. Piccone 1983, p. 197.
4. Gramsci 1971, pp. 542–4. The article appeared in the semi-clandestine *L'Unità* on 7 October 1924.
5. Joll 1978, p. 19.

This is correct, but with qualifications. For Gramsci a bureaucratic dictatorship was the antithesis of his conception of socialist democracy. It is also true, however, that he accepted the principle of the revolutionary dictatorship of the proletariat, and that he is not known to have ever repudiated the harsh and at times brutal measures taken by the young Soviet Republic against its real and presumed enemies. Gramsci's politics ought not to be arbitrarily softened in this manner.

Chantal Mouffe comes closer to the mark when she writes that 'the Gramscian conception of hegemony is not only compatible with pluralism, it implies it; but this is a pluralism which is always located within the hegemony of the working class'. Yet she pushes this point too far when she adds that Gramsci's strategy for change 'provides the basis for any real struggle for a democratic socialism'.[6] It is my view, as already indicated, that Gramsci's name should be associated with socialist democracy, not social democracy or democratic socialism.

Giorgio Napolitano, who in the 1970s was a leading Italian exponent of Eurocommunism,[7] was correct when he said, in commenting on the PCI's advance towards a new type of progressive democracy, that 'for his part, Gramsci in prison had done inspired work in the search for a road to socialism different from that travelled in Russia'.[8] True enough, except that it was not Gramsci, but Lenin and Trotsky, who originated the notion that the dense layers of civil society in the West would require a different road to socialism than that taken by the Russian Bolsheviks. This does not mean, of course, that Gramsci did not vastly enrich and expand the implications of what was still a rather crude formulation in the early 1920s. But I do not think that there is an unbroken continuity from Gramsci's view of the tasks and perspectives of socialism to the various policies pursued by the PCI since the 1940s that have moved from 'progressive democracy' under Togliatti to the 'historic compromise' and the 'democratic alternative' under Enrico Berlinguer. The merits of these PCI policies should be evaluated on their own terms, as responses to the postwar restoration in Europe of bourgeois-liberal institutions and of capitalist hegemony and counter-revolutionary ideology led by the United States.

It seems to me that, despite the partisan and mistaken claims made by both pro and anti-Gramscian Trotskyists, the most accurate assessment of where Gramsci belongs in the history of the European Left has been made by a Trotskyist and a leader of the Fourth International, Ernest Mandel. In answer to the question, 'Is Eurocommunism the executor of the testament of Antonio Gramsci?', Mandel writes:

> Although it must be acknowledged that there was an evolution in Gramsci's thought between the foundation of the *Ordine Nuovo* in 1919 and the drafting of his *Prison Notebooks*, there is not the slightest evidence that Gramsci ever abandoned the conception that the socialist revolution implies the destruction of the bourgeois state apparatus and

6. Mouffe 1979, p. 15.
7. Napolitano is currently President of Italy.
8. Hobsbawm and Napolitano 1977, p. 27.

the replacement of bourgeois-parliamentary democracy with socialist democracy based on democratically and freely elected workers' councils.[9]

In the following pages, I argue, with Mandel, that Gramsci's indebtedness to Trotsky exemplifies his mediating function between the 'classical' and 'western' traditions of Marxism. Gramsci's creative development of the Marxist method and his articulation of concepts that help to illuminate our contemporary situation do not owe their genesis to some mysterious visitation during his years in prison, but are rooted in the experiences he had as a leader of the Third International. The opportunity to study and then to participate directly in the unfolding process of the Bolshevik revolution gave Gramsci the impetus to develop some of the original interpretations of problems in politics and culture that are part of his legacy.

Gramsci and the leaders of the Bolshevik Revolution

In Gramsci's attitude towards Trotsky, one finds a web of contradictions and ambiguities that do not manifest themselves in his attitude towards the other leading figures of the Bolshevik Revolution. None of the ambivalences, none of the inconsistencies and changing interpretations that mark his responses to Trotsky and to Trotskyism appear in his many writings on Lenin. Walter Adamson has taken pains to analyse some of the differences between Gramsci's concept of the socialist revolution and that of Lenin, and has stressed Gramsci's belief 'in the capacity of and need for workers to define their socialist consciousness through production-based institutions of their own creation'.[10] Adamson thinks that the guiding role of the Communist Party was not as central to Gramsci's concept of revolution as it was to Lenin's. No doubt there were distinctive features in Gramsci's adaptation of Marxist and Leninist theory to Italian conditions. Nevertheless, it seems fair to say that, for Gramsci, Lenin was always the complete communist revolutionary, at once deeply rooted in the national traditions of the Russian people yet always aware of the international dimensions of the struggle to which he dedicated his life.

> Comrade Lenin [Gramsci wrote in *L'Ordine Nuovo* on 1 March 1924] was the initiator of a new process of historical development, but he accomplished this because he was also the exponent and the last most individualized embodiment of a process of development of past history, not only of Russia but of the entire world.[11]

This comment appeared in an article entitled 'Leader', written shortly after Lenin's death on 21 January 1924. In it, Gramsci expressed his unqualified approval of the methods and aims of the proletarian dictatorship established under Lenin's leadership in the new Soviet Republic.

---

9. Mandel 1978, p. 201.
10. Adamson 1980, p. 100.
11. Gramsci 1967, pp. 540–3. The article appeared originally in *L'Ordine Nuovo* of 1 March 1924.

Both before and after his imprisonment, Gramsci looked to Lenin as a model to emulate in his own efforts as a Communist Party organiser, strategist, and educator. Indeed, he felt that he had accomplished an indispensable task of theoretical and organisational work for the Communist Party of Italy when, in May 1925, he said that the Party had finally achieved a 'Leninist stabilisation' between the Left extremism of Amadeo Bordiga and the social-democratic leanings of Angelo Tasca.[12] Since Gramsci believed that all members of the Communist Party should cultivate moral rigour, intellectual discipline, and critical independence, and since his conception of democratic centralism was based on the integration of free and uninhibited discussion of all points of view into the decision-making process, there were bound to be some tensions in his attitude towards Stalin. On several occasions, Gramsci voiced his dismay at the intolerance and authoritarianism increasingly evident in the methods used by Stalin. In January 1924, for example, in a letter to his wife sent from Vienna to Moscow, he characterised Stalin's attacks on the Left Opposition as 'very irresponsible and dangerous'.[13]

Yet it must also be said that Gramsci never really called into question the legitimacy of Stalin's role as the political leader behind whom loyal communists throughout the world should align themselves in an indestructible phalanx. After Stalin gained ascendancy in the Russian Communist Party, whose unity Gramsci regarded as a precondition for the unity of the international Communist movement as a whole, his methods, even if at times repugnant, were in the final analysis accepted by Gramsci as necessary for the consolidation of the Soviet state and for the continued spread of the world socialist revolution. That there might have been an inherent incompatibility between Stalinism and the cause of world socialist revolution does not seem to have occurred to Gramsci until the early 1930s, when, according to a prison-mate at Turi di Bari, Ezio Riboldi, he began to suspect that 'Stalin was a Russian nationalist first, then a communist'.[14] But other remarks made by Gramsci to fellow communist prisoners in Turi, and several entries in the *Prison Notebooks* that deal with Stalin, suggest that even after his unofficial rejection of the Comintern's policies in the early 1930s, Gramsci continued to regard Stalin as the guardian of the régime that had arisen from the October Revolution. In sum, it is safe to say that, despite moments of doubt and dismay, Gramsci maintained a relatively constant and essentially supportive posture towards Stalin.[15]

Gramsci was in close personal contact with Karl Radek, Grigory Zinoviev, Nikolai Bukharin, and Lev Kamenev, for short but intense periods of work during the years 1922 and 1923. All four men were actively involved with the Italian question and strove to persuade the recalcitrant Italian delegation in Moscow to apply the directives concerned with the policy of the united front adopted by the Comintern – then under the presidency of Zinoviev – at the end of 1921. There were some tensions in Gramsci's

---

12. Gramsci 1971, pp. 62–74.
13. Fiori 1977, p. 193.
14. Riboldi 1964, p. 182.
15. Gramsci 1975, Vol. III, pp. 1728–9.

relationships with these men caused by misunderstandings and differences of opinion over procedural, organisational, and tactical matters. In the case of Bukharin, Gramsci objected quite strenuously to what he saw as the Russian thinker's failure to move beyond Marxism as a sociology and consequent inability to grasp the essentials of Marxism 'as a general philosophy' founded on a dialectical approach to history and to the role of political activity in history'.[16] The pages on Bukharin's *Popular Manual* in *The Prison Notebooks* make it clear that Gramsci judged the *Manual* to be a vulgarisation, not a popularisation, of Marxism. But this philosophical disagreement did not spill over into personal polemics, nor does one sense in the numerous pages of the *Notebooks* devoted to Bukharin any hesitation, uncertainty or ambivalence. To repeat what was said above: of the original group of Bolshevik leaders who made the October Revolution and laid the groundwork for the Third International from 1919 to 1923, Leon Trotsky was the only one who provoked in Gramsci a deeply contradictory reaction; the only thinker to whom he was indebted for certain elements of his own political and intellectual development, yet who appears in the *Prison Notebooks* in an almost entirely negative light; the one communist revolutionary whose brilliance and imperious personality may have interfered with the customary lucidity and cool rationality of Gramsci's judgments.

Gramsci's interaction with Trotsky in 1922 and 1923; his tentative defence in 1924 of some features of what had by then already become Trotskyism; his letter of early October 1926 to the Central Committee of the Russian Communist Party at the height of the prolonged and corrosive internal conflict between the Stalinist majority and the Left Opposition; and finally his retrospective oral and written comments on Trotsky and Trotskyism during his years in prison, are chapters of a dramatic story whose highlights will be discussed in the following pages.

The letter of early October 1926

Let us look first at Gramsci's attempt to serve as mediator and peacemaker in the ideological struggle that, since the latter months of 1923, was threatening to create a permanent schism between two groups at the highest echelons of power in Soviet Russia: the minority Left Opposition, led by Trotsky (in April 1926 Zinoviev and Kamenev joined forces with Trotsky in a broader coalition called the United Opposition) and the dominant majority group, headed by the Party's secretary, Joseph Stalin. Gramsci's attempt at mediation took the form of a letter[17] that he sent in early October 1926, on behalf of the Political Office of the Communist Party of Italy, to the Central Committee of the Russian Communist Party. To make sure that the letter arrived promptly at its destination, Gramsci mailed it to Palmiro Togliatti, who was then in Moscow representing

---

16. Adamson 1980, pp. 122–5.
17. For the content and political background of this letter, see Ferrata and Gallo, 1964, pp. 820–8; Berti 1967; Gramsci 1973, pp. 232–42.

the Communist Party of Italy on the Executive Committee of the Comintern. Togliatti replied to Gramsci's letter on 18 October. He told Gramsci that he had decided not to deliver the letter directly to the Russian Central Committee out of fear that a few of its remarks might exacerbate tensions at precisely the moment in which the Opposition had indicated its willingness to end all factionism. The essential thing, Togliatti said, was for the PCd'I to be unequivocal in its support of the Bolshevik majority and in its repudiation of the mistaken positions of the Trotskyists. For this reason, he had given the letter to Bukharin, who chose not to present it officially to the Party's Central Committee, as Gramsci had wished. Instead, he dispatched a prominent Swiss member of the Comintern, Jules Humbert-Droz, to Italy for the purpose of explaining to the Italian party leaders the 'true nature' of the issues involved in the fight between the majority group and the Opposition.

Whether Stalin ever read Gramsci's letter, or was even told of its point of view, is not entirely clear. In any case, Gramsci was angered by Togliatti's response, and on 26 October he said that he found Togliatti's line of reasoning unacceptable. After characterising Togliatti's letter of 18 October as 'tainted by bureaucratism', he stated that what was at stake in the Russian events was no longer the seizure and consolidation of power by the Bolsheviks, which was an accomplished fact, but the conviction, in the minds of the masses of people, that 'the proletariat, once power has been taken, *can build socialism*'. (Gramsci's emphasis) Disunity could only have the effect of undermining this conviction, even within the ranks of the Communist movement, many of whose segments, especially in the West, were still inexperienced, volatile, and in need of a firm grounding in the methodology of socialist revolution. It was for this reason, Gramsci said, that although he agreed with the 'indictment of the Opposition', he wished at the same time to help the Central Committee of the Russian Communist Party to regain its unity and international authority.[18]

What were the features of Gramsci's letter of early October that made Togliatti so uneasy and that, according to Giuseppe Berti, caused Bukharin and other Bolsheviks to suspect that the Italian Communist leadership was moving in a direction that would eventually take it into the camp of the Trotskyist opposition? Gramsci touches only superficially on the substantive issues at stake in the struggle between Trotsky and Stalin. He reveals his fundamental agreement with Stalin's argument that Trotskyism constituted a threat to the very core of Leninist doctrine, and that 'in the ideology and practice of the opposition bloc is being fully reborn the entire tradition of social democracy and syndicalism which has thus far prevented the Western proletariat from organizing itself into a ruling class'. Unexceptionable, from a Stalinist point of view, was Gramsci's assertion that Trotskyism tended to undermine the principle and the practice of the hegemony of the proletariat, and to weaken the alliance between workers and peasants forged in the course of decades of revolutionary struggle. To the extent that he was able to make

18. Gramsci 1978, pp. 426–8.

such statements, Gramsci was as prudently conformist and orthodox as his friend and comrade Togliatti. But the similarity between the two men ends there. Even as Gramsci blamed Trotsky and the other leaders of the Left Opposition for their divisive and intractable stance, he proceeded to make three points that reflected a conception of political method and a perspective on the recent history of the world Communist movement that did not fit easily into the established Stalinist framework. First, he expressed his conviction that the violent passions unleashed by the majority's determination to annihilate rather than reintegrate the Opposition had caused them to lose sight of the international ramifications of the questions being debated within the Central Committee of the Russian Communist Party. Second, he reminded his Russian comrades that Party unity and discipline were desirable ends if they were the fruit of persuasion and inner conviction, not when imposed 'mechanically' and with 'coercive pressures'. Third, Gramsci paid tribute to the Opposition leaders in a manner that suggests the presence within him of vivid personal memories and experiences as well as political motivations. Although conceding to the majority its claim that the Opposition was primarily responsible for the potentially irreparable schism menacing the Russian and therefore the world Communist Party, Gramsci forthrightly stated that 'Comrades Zinoviev, Trotsky, and Kamenev have contributed powerfully to educating us for the revolution, at times they have corrected us very energetically and severely, they have been our teachers'.

An ambiguous yet courageous letter, conciliatory and prudent on the one hand, bold and animated by a sense of fairness and justice on the other. Gramsci agreed that the Left Opposition had deviated sharply from Leninist policy, yet at the same time he let it be known that the very men who embodied that opposition had until quite recently been his mentors, his guides, his demanding teachers in the art and science of revolutionary politics. To understand at least in part some of the reasons underlying this juxtaposition of praise and blame, we have to go back to the years 1922 to 1924 and to focus on the interaction between Gramsci and the man who, on 25 October 1926, in the name of the Marxist-Leninist heritage, called Stalin 'the gravedigger of the revolution':[19] Leon Trotsky.

The interaction between Gramsci and Trotsky from 1922 to 1924

From late May 1922 to November 1923, Gramsci was in Moscow as a delegate to the Executive Committee of the Third International and as a member of various Commissions whose purpose was to examine specific organisational, political, and procedural problems, and to co-ordinate the struggles of national Communist Parties with the general strategic directives and policies of the Comintern. On 4 December 1923, he arrived in Vienna to take up a difficult series of assignments, among which was the establishment

---

19. Deutscher 1965, p. 296.

of a clandestine network to help Italian Communist émigrés find work abroad and prevent their dispersion; the maintenance of regular contacts with the Party in Italy, as well as with other Communist Parties, in order to facilitate a steady flow of information in both directions and above all to keep the Italians abreast of developments in Moscow; and the creation of new publishing and educational enterprises, the most important of which was the revival of the review *L'Ordine Nuovo*. This publication reappeared phoenix-like, under Gramsci's direction, on 1 March 1924. He remained in Vienna until 12 May 1924, when he returned to Italy to take his seat in the Chamber of Deputies after his victory in the political elections of 16 April.

The two years that Gramsci spent outside of Italy were crucial to his development as a party tactician and organiser, as a thinker on such questions as the relations between politics and culture, and as a human being with long-suppressed needs and desires that at last found gratification in his relationship with the Russian woman who was to become his wife and the mother of his two sons, Julca Schucht, whom he met while convalescing in a sanatorium outside of Moscow in September of 1922. In direct contact with the makers of the Russian Revolution, with members of the various foreign delegations to the Comintern, and, through Julca and other Russian friends, with the numerous cultural and literary groups that enjoyed an all too brief flowering in the early years of the Revolution, Gramsci was a witness to and a participant in a period of intense political and intellectual ferment in the Soviet Union. His stay in Moscow reinforced a conviction that he had formed some years earlier, that revolution was not so much an event as a process, that the elaboration of a new mode of thought and new social, economic, and political institutions would not crystallise as a result of the conquest of power by the working class but instead that this conquest would mark the beginning of a difficult and often painful experiment whose outcome was by no means predetermined by vast impersonal and objective forces.

Leon Trotsky played an important role in Gramsci's education as a Communist revolutionary who always saw his central objective as being that of 'forming cadres capable not only of taking power, but of being able to organize a new society'.[20]

The available evidence indicates that there are five areas in which Trotsky's influence made itself felt in Gramsci's development as both a theorist and as a practical tactician and party organiser. They are as follows: 1) the conceptualisation and application of the policy of the united front; 2) the analysis of the Fascist phenomenon as a highly particularised form of capitalist reaction whose most original and dangerous component was its ability to compete successfully with the working-class parties for the support of the disaffected petit-bourgeois masses; 3) the struggle on two fronts, waged simultaneously by Trotsky from 1923 on, against the growing bureaucratisation of the political system in the Soviet Union, especially as this tendency manifested itself in the Communist Party apparatus, and for the enlargement of inner-party proletarian democracy; 4) concern

---

20. Somai 1979, p. 153.

with the quality of culture, with the mores and customs of a civilisation undergoing radical transformation, and the defense of the integrity of literature and art against harassment by bureaucratised dogmatists disguised as proletarian moralists; 5) the idea that the socialist revolution as it unfolded in Russia was in some respects *sui generis*, and that for this reason Communist revolutionaries in the advanced capitalist countries of the West would have to confront a different set of tasks and perspectives in order eventually to take power.

The research of Gramsci and Trotsky scholars, and the testimony of some authoritative contemporaries, leave little room for doubt that there was a considerable amount of interaction between the two men in 1922 and 1923. Among Gramsci's first important writing projects after his arrival in Moscow was an essay on Italian futurism, dated 8 September 1922, which he wrote expressly for Trotsky, who was interested in taking a comparative look at the Italian and Russian futurist movements. Trotsky included Gramsci's essay in Section IV of his work *Literature and Revolution*, which appeared in late 1923.[21] In this connection Isaac Deutscher notes that 'during his stay in Moscow Gramsci enjoyed Trotsky's confidence',[22] and Valentino Gerratana observes that unlike his association with most other prominent Bolsheviks, Gramsci worked together with Trotsky not only on political matters but also 'in the area of cultural studies'.[23] In 1923, Trotsky devoted himself assiduously to cultural and literary problems. There is evidence, both in his correspondence and in several paragraphs of the *Prison Notebooks*, that Gramsci acquired from Trotsky a still keener appreciation than he had assimilated from an earlier exposure to Crocean philosophy of the fact that even in a revolutionary society, aesthetic values have a special place in the spectrum of human endeavours, and must not be indiscriminately confused with political values and aims, no matter how transcendently important the latter may be.

Perhaps 'collaboration' is not quite the appropriate term to describe the relationship between Gramsci and Trotsky with respect to cultural problems, but that Gramsci was aware of Trotsky's efforts in this area, and that he was in some measure influenced by the emphasis that Trotsky placed on the relative autonomy of the moral, intellectual, and artistic aspects of life *vis-à-vis* the political domain, cannot be seriously doubted. If we are not dealing with a clear-cut influence, then we must speak of a natural affinity, for the positions that Gramsci was to take on the relations between art and politics in the *Prison Notebooks* are, as noted by Massimo Salvadori,[24] Enrico Bogliolo,[25] and other scholars, remarkably similar to those taken by Trotsky in the years 1923 and 1924, when

---

21. A copy of the original Russian edition of this work, dated 8 September 1924, is available in the Slavic Division of the New York Public Library: pp. 120–2. It is often left out of translations of Trotsky's work.

22. Deutscher 1965, Vol. II, p. 185, n. 1.

23. Gramsci 1975, Vol. IV, p. 2651.

24. Salvadori 1970, pp. 293–4

25. Bogliolo 1977, pp. 20–1.

he was one of Russia's leading literary critics and led the campaign waged by some sections of the Soviet intelligentsia 'to reject party tutelage over science and art'.[26]

As far as the strictly political domain is concerned, the eyewitness accounts of several Italian Communists who were in Moscow in November and December of 1922 to attend the Fourth World Congress of the Comintern, and an almost word-for-word summary of a direct confrontation between Trotsky and Gramsci at a meeting of the Italian Commission on 15 November 1922, are further confirmation of the interaction that took place between the two men. The wording of some of these accounts leads one to believe that when Gramsci, in his letter of 14 October 1926 to the Central Committee of the Russian Communist Party, alluded to the fact that the three Opposition leaders – Zinoviev, Trotsky, and Kamenev – had on occasion 'corrected us very energetically and severely', it was Trotsky whom he had chiefly in mind.

Indeed, before Gramsci's arrival in the Soviet Union, other Italian Communists, notably Umberto Terracini, had already experienced the full force of Trotsky's imperious personality and penchant for acerbic polemics.[27] Camilla Ravera recalls two things about the encounters between Gramsci and Trotsky in the fall of 1922 that corroborate what Terracini has revealed about his earlier discussions with Trotsky in February 1922, at the first session of the Enlarged Executive Committee of the Comintern. She recalls that Trotsky, in Lenin's absence (due to illness) was inflexibly resolute in his efforts to break down the resistance of the Italians to the united front tactics approved at the Third World Congress of the Comintern held in the summer of 1921. During the Fourth World Congress, she said, Trotsky was busy trying to overcome the currents of left-wing intransigence in the French, Spanish, and Italian parties, but that he was especially hard in the stand he took as a member of the Italian commission against the positions taken by Amadeo Bordiga, the general secretary of the Italian party at that time and the exponent par excellence of a strategy that in April 1920 Lenin had called 'left-wing communism'.

In the autumn of 1922, Gramsci was still reluctant to separate himself ideologically from Bordiga. But at the same time Gramsci seemed, to Trotsky and other leaders of the Comintern, to be the man potentially best suited to pry the Italian party loose from the rigidities of 'sectarian politics' as practiced by Bordiga. For this reason, Gramsci became the main target of Trotsky's verbal assaults.

In Trotsky's opinion, the Italians underestimated the potentially mass appeal of Fascism, and, therefore, did not grasp the importance of basing anti-fascist and anti-capitalist tactics on the concept of a united front. As remembered by Ravera, 'in the weeks preceding the Fourth Congress Trotsky had long conversations with Gramsci about Fascism, about the dangers that Fascism represented, about the possibility of a Fascist coup d'état in Italy'.[28]

---

26. Deutscher 1965, p. xii.
27. Terracini 1967, pp. 18–20.
28. Ravera 1973, p. 129.

Nine years later, in *What Next? Vital Questions for the German Proletariat*, written in exile on the Turkish island of Prinkipo, Trotsky recalled that in the early 1920s, in the eyes of almost all the Italian Communists with whom he had spoken, Fascism appeared as simply another form of 'capitalist reaction' no worse and no different in nature from others that had manifested themselves periodically since the latter part of the nineteenth century. 'The particular traits of Fascism which spring from the mobilisation of the petit-bourgeoisie against the proletariat', Trotsky wrote, 'the Italian Communist Party was unable to discern. Italian comrades inform me that with the sole exception of Gramsci, the Communist Party wouldn't even allow the possibility of the Fascists' seizing power'.[29]

Ravera's portrait of Trotsky puts into sharp relief certain traits of character that could help to explain why, at a later date, Gramsci decided to take his distance from Trotsky, and to see him as a kind of incorrigible individualist whose actual behaviour belied his collectivist philosophy and collegial conception of decision-making:

> Trotsky's personality, as it had appeared in my mind from what I had heard and read about him, was not less distinctive in this direct encounter, to be sure, but different from what I had expected. Tall, erect, somewhat rigid in his posture and in the military uniform that he always wore, precise and sarcastically cutting in his speech, aristocratic by reason of a natural marked distinction and a permanent marked detachment, Trotsky appeared absolutely and inflexibly sure of himself: different in his aspect, his manners, from the other Bolsheviks.[30]

Ravera's portrait squares with what Lenin had said of Trotsky in his testament dictated in December 1922, that although he was 'the most able' of all the Party leaders, he was also possessed of 'excessive self-confidence' and had a tendency to oppose himself individualistically to the Central Committee. Gramsci had a high regard for individuality, but he loathed individualism and self-centredness, he was almost obsessive in his stress on the importance of party unity and discipline. As noted above, this may help to explain some of his judgments concerning Trotsky in later years. But we ought not to allow these personal traits and postures to obscure the more essential political content of their interaction at the Fourth World Congress. In this regard, Giuseppe Berti, who in 1922 and 1924 was a member of the Italian Communist Youth Federation and a delegate to the Comintern in that capacity, furnishes some useful information and insights.

In the summer of 1924, Berti was present at a conversation between Trotsky and Giacinto Menotti Serrati, leader of the 'Third Internationalist' wing of the Italian Socialist Party.[31] During that conversation, Berti recalls, Trotsky told Serrati that in the second

---

29. Trotsky 1932, p. 86.
30. Ravera 1973, p. 129.
31. The 'third internationalist' wing of the Italian Socialist Party fused with the Communist Party of Italy in August 1924, after two years of tortuous vacillation by both parties.

half of 1922, he had been active in the Italian Commission together with Zinoviev and Bukharin. What stood out in Trotsky's memory, says Berti, were the difficulties the Commission had encountered in its discussions with Gramsci. 'We had to press hard', Trotsky said, 'to convince him to take a combative position against Bordiga and I don't know whether we succeeded'. Berti adds that in 1924, 'Trotsky did not conceal the fact that in 1922 he had played a decisive role in the pressures exerted on Gramsci so that he would adopt a critical attitude towards Bordiga'.[32]

Let's look now at the one direct account we possess[33] of the session of the Italian commission held on 15 November 1922, during the Fourth World Congress, at which Gramsci and Trotsky clashed over aspects of the united front as applied to the political situation in Italy then dominated by the coming-to-power of Benito Mussolini. The importance of this clash of views lies in the fact that because of Lenin's illness and inability to take part in the daily business of the Congress, Trotsky had assumed the lion's share of responsibility for driving a wedge between left-wing Communists of Bordiga's type, who were inclined to rely on their own strength and to reject collaboration with other working-class parties and movements, except within labour unions, and Communists who were disposed to accept the postulates of the united front in a period characterised by retreat and retrenchment by the revolutionary forces. Thus, Trotsky's opinions carried great authority at this juncture. Gramsci, too, had considerable prestige both within his own party and in the ranks of the Comintern: with Egidio Gennari and Amadeo Bordiga, he was one of three Italian delegates elected to that body's Executive Committee at the Fourth World Congress, and was named as a candidate member of the Presidium.[34]

At the meeting of 15 November, the Italian Commission of the Comintern was represented by Zinoviev, Trotsky, Bukharin, Clara Zetkin, and V. Kuibyshev, the Italian delegation by Gramsci, Bordiga, Edmondo Peluso, Nicola Bombacci, and Angelo Tasca. Tasca's views at this particular moment coincided with those of the Comintern leadership, at least as far as the Italian question was concerned. He argued for the immediate fusion of the Communist Party of Italy with the maximalists, and the formation of a new central committee representing both groups. Bordiga's position was that the Communist Party should try to attract as many disaffected revolutionary members of the Italian Socialist Party as possible, but should not try to win over en bloc any segment of the party leadership as such, all of whom were irremediably reformist. Gramsci agreed essentially with Bordiga. He maintained that the Italian Socialist Party was not really a workers' party, but instead a peasant-based petit-bourgeois party whose leaders, including Serrati, were incapable of grasping the proletarian character of the Russian Revolution, and who had

---

32. Berti 1967, pp. 36–8.

33. For the minutes of this meeting in the only source I know of, see 'La questione italiana al IV Congresso' in *Lo Stato Operaio* (Milanese edition), 13 March 1924, p. 3.

34. Degras (ed.) 1956, p. 455.

a utopian rather than practical and constructive conception of socialism. He branded Serrati as a syndicalist, whose mentality and background, if allowed to penetrate the Communist Party of Italy, would lessen the Party's chances to intensify class-oriented struggle at a time when the Party was in desperate need of an authentic education in revolutionary organisation and strategy. He welcomed the return of the maximalists to the ranks of the International, but took pains to remind the others present at the meeting of the 'pacification pact' between Socialists and Fascists in 1921, which, he said, had blocked the revolutionary thrust of the Italian working masses. He concluded that the main problem of the Italian Communists now was to prevent a return to the ineptitude and sloganeering of the maximalists, a problem which fusion could certainly not solve.

At this point Trotsky intervened, directing his remarks first to the Italian group as a whole. He had been led to believe, he said, that the Italian group had already approved the report on the tactics of the united front given by Zinoviev several days earlier. Had they changed their minds? Was each member of the Italian delegation free to vote as he pleased? If this was the case, then the divergence between the Italian party and the International was on the verge of rupture. He then turned to Gramsci who, Trotsky said, 'seems to want a privilege of intransigence for Italy. On the question of the united front you have lined up with France and Spain'. Other parties, he went on to say, that were originally opposed to the tactics of the united front, had recognised their error, but the Italians had not done so. Trotsky then pointed out that the recent split in the Italian Socialist Party, which had resulted in the expulsion of the reformist Unitarian Socialists, had created an entirely different situation on the Left in Italy which, in combination with the Fascist advent to power, made a closing of ranks by workers' parties an absolute necessity. Adherence to the Communist Party of Italy by individuals was not sufficient.

> I am sure that among the maximalists there are elements opposed to the International, [Trotsky said] elements we'll have to get rid of...But with the system of individual membership you won't succeed in doing that. The best elements are attached to their own party and won't abandon it easily. Individual recruitment would bring to us only the rejects. We propose to you that you accept collective fusion first, then you'll make your individual selections. The Fascists have crushed both sections of the socialist organization. If you don't win the sympathies of the great masses, you will not be able to act illegally. If you want to restrict your base you'll remain without any base at all and you will be considered a sect.

Gramsci was not immediately persuaded by Trotsky's arguments, although he accepted with genuine conviction the principle established by the Charter of the Third International that as sections, and not autonomous units, of a single world Communist Party, each national Communist Party was duty-bound to support, or at the least not to oppose, the majority decisions of the Executive Committee of the Comintern. Thus, without renouncing its views, the majority opposition within the Italian delegation declared that it would follow the will of the Comintern, and remain silent at the forthcoming Plenum.

But misunderstandings and resentments, unresolved procedural issues, personal disputes and ideological conflicts continued to plague relations between the Italian party and the Comintern for a long time after the Fourth World Congress. Gramsci, although increasingly receptive to the line of reasoning developed by Trotsky, was also mindful of the balance of forces within his own party. For about two years, he performed some complicated political acrobatics in his efforts to swing the majority of his party's leadership over to acceptance of the united front and eventual fusion with the maximalists, while at the same time attempting to maintain the unity of his party, which until 1926 was overwhelmingly supportive of Bordiga's hard-line, intransigent rejection of frontism and parliamentarism.

The year 1923 marked a turning point in Gramsci's career. It was during this period from March to September 1923 – which culminated in his letter of 12 September[35] from Moscow to his comrades in Italy outlining an editorial and organisational scheme for a new daily newspaper, for which he proposed the name *L'Unità* – that he achieved full command as a political leader. This process of maturation gave him the confidence he needed to meet the challenge posed by Bordiga's intransigence within his own party, and at the same time to assess from an independent and critical point of view some of the developments taking place in the Communist movement on a world scale.

During these months, and through the period spent in Vienna from December 1923 to May 1924, his indebtedness to Trotsky extended beyond the conceptualisation of united front tactics, whose basic rationale he had accepted and begun to expound in his own party by March 1923.[36] First of all, there is reason to believe that the seed of an idea that was to germinate in Gramsci's mind in 1923 and 1924, and come to full fruition in his reflections in the *Prison Notebooks* – the idea that the conquest of power by the proletariat in the countries of Western Europe would require a strategy significantly different form the one followed by the Russian Bolsheviks – was due not only to the teachings of Lenin, but in some measure also to the various speeches and writings Trotsky devoted to aspects of the Italian situation in 1921 and 1922.

Trotsky was keenly interested in Italian affairs, followed events in Fascist Italy with increasing concern for the fate of the workers' movement there, and looked at the struggle for power in Italy between the forces of revolution and reaction as a kind of test case from which the Communist Parties of other Western countries could learn some valuable lessons.

In a *Report on the Fourth World Congress* delivered on 28 December 1922, Trotsky noted that the Fascist takeover in Italy was 'a lesson of exceptional importance to the European working class which in its top layers is corroded by its traditions, by bourgeois

---

35. This letter shows conclusively that Gramsci had by then fully accepted the policy of a united front with other Italian anti-fascist groups and parties. The full text of this letter was reprinted in the *Rivista Storica del Socialismo*, January–April 1963, pp. 115–16.

36. Somai 1979, pp. 96–100.

democracy, by the deliberate hypnosis of legality'.[37] But it was more Trotsky the ana-
lyst than Trotsky the polemicist who reached Gramsci; more the Trotsky of sweeping
historical imagination than the angry moralist, who at this moment sparked Gramsci's
own powers of reflection and synthesis. Therefore, of more relevance to Gramsci than
the Report of 28 December was Trotsky's earlier *Report on the New Soviet Economic Policy
and the Perspectives of the World Revolution*, delivered at the 14 November 1922 session
of the Fourth World Congress of the Comintern. It was in this speech that one finds the
nucleus of the ideas concerning proletarian hegemony in the West that Gramsci was
to develop fully in the *Prison Notebooks*, and that constitutes one of his most original
contributions to Western Marxism. The subtlety of Gramsci's analysis in the *Notebooks*
surpasses that displayed by Trotsky in the speech of 14 November; his grasp of the intricate cultural, political, and social superstructure of institutions in the West was deeper
and grounded in more concrete experience than Trotsky's. And his sense of revolution
as process rather than as insurrectional event, a distinction on which Trotsky tended
to oscillate a great deal, also clearly sets off Gramsci's thought from that of Trotsky. Yet
the connection is there, and is in fact acknowledged by Gramsci, even if he does so in
the grudging and half-disparaging manner that characterises most of his references to
Trotsky in the *Notebooks*.

One of the several sections in the *Notebooks* that deal with the problem of Communist
strategy in the West, where a highly developed 'civil society' renders the task of winning
power infinitely more difficult than in backward Czarist Russia, and calls for a shift of
tactics away from direct 'frontal assaults' to the notion of a 'war of position', ends with
this paragraph:

> An attempt to begin a revision of tactical methods should have been the one expounded
> by L. Davidovich Bronstein at the Fourth Congress when he made a comparison between
> the Eastern Front and the Western Front, the former fell immediately but was followed
> by tremendous struggles; in the latter the struggles would take place first: It would be a
> question that is of whether the civil society resists before or after the assault, where this
> occurs etc. The question however was posed only in a literarily brilliant manner, but
> without indications of a practical character.[38]

Gramsci was not being entirely fair and objective in this comment. After all, the attempt
at revision, and the ability to assess the development of the world socialist revolution
from a new global perspective, were given a decisive impetus by Trotsky at the Fourth
World Congress. Here, in part, is what Trotsky said on 14 November 1922, at the session
to which Gramsci referred in the passage cited above:

---

37. Trotsky 1972, Vol. II, pp. 220–2.
38. Gramsci 1975, Vol. III, p. 1616.

On 7 November 1917 our party assumed power. As was soon disclosed quite clearly, this did not signify the end of the Civil War. On the contrary, the Civil War actually began to unfold on a large scale in our country only after the October overturn. This is not only a fact of historical interest but also a source of the most important lessons for the Western European proletariat. Why did events follow this course? The explanation must be sought in the cultural and political backwardness of a country that had just cast off Czarist barbarism. The big bourgeoisie and the nobility had gained some political experience, thanks to the municipal Dumas, the *zemstvos*, the state Duma etc. The petit-bourgeoisie had little political experience, and the bulk of the population, the peasantry, still less. Thus the main reserves of the counter-revolution – the well-to-do peasants (kulaks) and, to a degree, also the middle peasants – came precisely from this extremely amorphous milieu. And it was only after the bourgeoisie began to grasp fully what it had lost by losing political power, and only after it had set in motion its counter-revolutionary combat nucleus, that it succeeded in gaining access to the peasant and petit-bourgeois elements and layers; and therewith the bourgeoisie had, of necessity, to yield the leading posts to the most reactionary elements among the ranking officers of noble birth. As a result, the Civil War unfolded fully only after the October overturn. The ease with which we conquered power on 7 November 1917, was paid for by the countless sacrifices of the Civil War. In countries that are older in the capitalist sense, and with a higher culture, the situation will, without doubt, differ profoundly. In these countries the popular masses will enter the revolution far more fully formed in political respects. To be sure, the orientation of individual layers and groups among the proletariat, and all the more so among the petit-bourgeoisie, will still continue to fluctuate violently and change but, nevertheless, these changes will occur far more systematically than in our country; the present will flow much more directly out of the past. The bourgeoisie in the West is preparing its counterblow in advance. We witness this in Germany, we witness this, even if not quite so distinctly, in France; and finally we see it in its most finished form in Italy, where in the wake of the incompleted revolution there came the completed counter-revolution which employed not unsuccessfully some of the practices and methods of the revolution.

What does this mean? This means it will hardly be possible to catch the European bourgeoisie by surprise as we caught the Russian bourgeoisie. The European bourgeoisie is more intelligent, and more farsighted; it is not wasting time. Everything that can be set on foot against us is being mobilized by it right now. The revolutionary proletariat will thus encounter on its road to power not only the combat vanguards of the counter-revolution but also its heaviest reserves. Only by smashing, breaking up and demoralizing these enemy forces will the proletariat be able to seize power. But by way of compensation, after the proletarian overturn the vanquished bourgeoisie will no longer dispose of powerful reserves from which it could draw forces for prolonging the Civil War. In other words, after the conquest of power, the European proletariat will in all likelihood have far more elbow room for its creative work in economy and culture than we had in Russia on the day after the overturn. The more difficult and grueling the struggle for state power, all the less possible will it be to challenge the proletariat's power after the victory.[39]

This passage misses some of the finer points of Gramsci's analysis, but that it helped to stimulate him to rethink the whole question of revolutionary methodology in the West is quite probable. Moreover, Trotsky's use of military analogies to illustrate tactical political problems in this and other speeches, a reflection of his experiences as supreme commander of the Red Army during the Civil War and position as War Commissar in the early 1920s, was a metaphorical device congenial to Gramsci's temperament: the terms 'war of position', 'trench warfare', 'frontal assault', 'pillboxes', and so on recur frequently in his prison notes on Communist tactics in the West.

Another point of contact between Trotsky and Gramsci was their unflinching confrontation of a problem that has been left unresolved by the Communist movement from its inception to the present day, the problem of the relationship between authority and centralisation of power, on the one hand, and the need for open debate and participatory decision-making on the other. Gramsci, like Trotsky, was almost equally sensitive to the claims of both authority and freedom, but the paths of the two men diverged in 1924, because of the different vantage points from which they viewed the nature and function of the Communist Party of the Soviet Union within the total framework of the world Communist movement. Trotsky moved towards a frontal clash with the Russian Bolshevik majority, while Gramsci, although responsive, as we shall see, to Trotsky's arguments, felt that his duty was to uphold the unity and cohesion of the International at all costs.

But despite this divergence, there was substantial agreement between the two men during the first period of serious crisis in the Soviet Union, from mid-October 1923 until the summer of 1924. Many of the criticisms levelled by Trotsky against the bureaucratic degeneration widespread in the Russian Communist Party apparatus, and his passionate appeals for a revival of youthful idealism and an end to what he called 'spineless, servile and career-hunting elements' in the state and Party, are echoed by Gramsci in several of his letters to Italian comrades written from Vienna in the early months of 1924. If we compare Trotsky's open letter on 'The New Course' published in *Pravda* on 8 December 1923, and in *International Press Correspondence* on 15 February 1924,[40] with the general

---

39. Trotsky 1972, Vol. II, pp. 220–2.

40. In his Open Letter of 8 December 1923, one of the first salvoes in his campaign against the Communist Party bureaucracy, Trotsky agreed that the Party could not fulfil its historical mission if it became broken up into fractional groupings. But he pointed out that the only way to prevent the emergence of fractions was to 'develop, confirm, and strengthen the new policy towards workers' democracy'. Suppression of dissent and differences of opinion could only have a polarising effect. In later years, however, Trotsky was to admit the necessity of allowing fractions and currents to form, if necessary, as the only alternative and corrective to an enforced uniformity deadly to socialist democracy.

tenor of Gramsci's attitudes at the same time, we discover a striking similarity between their points of view.

In a letter to Togliatti, Terracini, and other members of the Central Committee of the PCd'I written on 9 February 1924,[41] for example, Gramsci refused to accept the simplistic assumption that Trotskyism was nothing but a petit-bourgeois deviation from Marxism-Leninism. On the contrary, after noting that in the history of the Russian revolutionary movement Trotsky was politically to the left of the Bolsheviks, while in organisational questions he often lined up with the Mensheviks, he proceeded to point out that as far back as 1905 Trotsky had believed in the real possibility in Russia of a thoroughgoing socialist and workers' revolution. The Bolsheviks had, in the main, limited their program to a call for a political dictatorship of the proletariat allied with the peasantry, and had not, prior to 1917, seriously envisioned the advent of a revolution that would strike at the heart of the economic structure of the capitalist system. Lenin and the majority of the party with him had swung over to Trotsky's position in 1917, just as Trotsky had definitively abandoned the Menshevik ranks in 1917 and joined the Bolsheviks. After this brief historical clarification, Gramsci proceeded to consider the recent polemics in Russia, again expressing sympathy for the position taken by Trotsky and the Opposition. What the Opposition wanted, he said, was 'a greater measure of involvement on the part of the workers in the life of the party and a lessening of the powers of the bureaucracy, in order to assure to the revolution its socialist and working-class character'. Then, after a sharp repudiation of the abstentionism and sectarianism of the Bordiga wing of the Italian party, Gramsci pronounced, in somewhat milder form but with crystalline clarity, the same critical judgments of the Italian party that Trotsky had pronounced against the Russian party: passivity of the rank-and-file, a widening gap between the masses of communist and socialist workers and the Party leadership, a conception of the Party as an aggregate of functionaries rather than independent thinkers, and a belief that the Party apparatus in itself would somehow bring about the advent of the revolution. One passage especially in this lengthy letter to his Italian comrades bears the imprint of a Trotskyist influence:

> All participation by the masses in the activity and internal life of the party, unless justi-
> fied by some occasion and authorized by a formal order from the centre, has been seen
> as a danger to unity and centralisation. The party has not been conceived as the result
> of a dialectical process in which there is a convergence between the spontaneous move-
> ment of the masses and the organised will and directives of the centre.[42]

---

41. This important letter has been analysed with admirable subtlety by Simonetta Ortaggi in *Rivista di Storia Contemporanea*, 1974, No. 4, pp. 478–503.

42. Gramsci 1964, Vol. I, pp. 665–7.

Trotsky went further than Gramsci in his criticisms, and he did so in public, not in a private communication to a small group of Party leaders – but the essential link between them at this moment is, I think, reasonably well-established by the letter just cited.

Gramsci's anti-Trotskyism from 1924 to 1926

But the links that connected Gramsci and Trotsky were not strong enough to prevent Gramsci's growing disaffection from Trotskyism after the summer of 1924. The year was an important marker, because it was only when Trotsky's name became an -ism, and was associated with a cluster of political and economic positions in opposition to the prevailing orthodoxy of the Russian Communist Party, that Gramsci began to re-evaluate his attitudes towards Trotsky. Let me try to sketch out in broad strokes why Gramsci became so alienated from the man who, second only to Lenin, had been his mentor in the theory and practice of revolutionary politics.

From August 1924, when he became general secretary of the Communist Party of Italy, to the day of his arrest in Rome on 8 November 1926, Gramsci acted with great self-confidence, unswerving determination to create a disciplined party, and with a degree of personal courage that at times bordered on recklessness. In his relations with the Russian Communist Party and with the leadership of the Comintern, on the other hand, the words that best describe his conduct are prudence, caution, and circumspection. Indeed, Gramsci seems to have been so afraid to become embroiled in the inner-Party struggle in the Soviet Union that in May 1924, according to Victor Serge, he gladly left Vienna for Italy in order to avoid getting caught up in the Russian crisis. 'When the crisis in Russia began to worsen', Serge recalls, 'Gramsci did not want to be broken in the process, so he had himself sent back to Italy by his Party'.[43] We know, of course, that this was not Gramsci's main reason for leaving Vienna, which was to take his seat in the Italian Chamber of Deputies. But Serge's remark cannot be entirely discounted either. It suggests an aspect of Gramsci's attitude towards the Stalin-Trotsky conflict that kept him for a long time in a state of uncertainty. When he finally did pronounce himself definitively on the Russian controversy, he sided with Stalin, even if with doubts and reservations that re-emerged in the letter of 14 October 1926.

Two considerations took precedence in Gramsci's mind during the years 1924 to 1926. The first was the need to create a compactly organised, tightly disciplined, and ideologically unified Communist Party in Italy. The second was his belief that if the dispute in the Soviet Union were to go on without resolution of some sort, it would spell the doom of the entire Third International. Both of these considerations weighed heavily on Gramsci and pushed him towards the labeling of Trotskyism as factious and insubordinate that definitely formed part of his political stance in 1925 and 1926. Issues of principle tended

---

43. Serge 1963, pp. 186–7.

to assume secondary importance in comparison with the immediate problem of survival that faced the communist movement everywhere, in the USSR itself, and above all in countries like Italy, where Fascist reaction threatened to obliterate the advances made by the Italian working-class parties. It is in the context of these two considerations that one must evaluate some of the statements and actions taken by Gramsci against Trotskyism from 1924 to 1926.

But there are other reasons, having to do with Gramsci's analysis of the global balance of forces and with certain features of Trotsky's ideas and political behaviour during this period that also need to be taken into account. From the latter part of 1923, when the failure of the German Revolution punctuated the end of a disastrous period of defeats suffered that year by Communist Parties in Eastern and Western Europe,[44] Gramsci had begun to associate Trotsky's name, together with those of other communists who continued doggedly to apply the methods of October 1917 in situations where they were inappropriate, with an irresponsible 'insurrectionary' approach to revolution; with an anachronistic belief in the efficacy of frontal assaults on the bastions of capitalist power at a time when the diagnosis made by communist theorists in 1917 of the imminent death of capitalism had turned out to be premature. Not only was the patient not dead, but be had shown remarkable recuperative powers that portended a rather long life expectancy.

In blaming Trotsky for the failures and defeats suffered by many of the European Communist Parties, Gramsci was being unfair and indiscriminate. It was Trotsky, with Lenin, who was the chief architect of the united front policy; it was Trotsky who in the early 1920s repeatedly wrote and spoke on the importance of recognising stages and phases in the revolutionary process, and who outlined a program of transitional demands capable of mobilising broad sectors of the working class. Yet Gramsci's concerns on this question were not entirely unfounded. Trotsky did, on occasion, express himself in a manner reminiscent of a conception of revolution that depended on a decisive, climactic event. In the fall of 1923, Trotsky was certainly not alone in his belief that the German proletariat could seize power if it acted resolutely, but he was in the vanguard of those who felt that 'the decisive struggle, the decisive hour' for the German Communist Party had struck. Even more than Gramsci, Trotsky believed in the subjective factor, in the act of will, in the role of leadership and direction such as provided by Lenin and himself in 1917, in the crucial importance of time, of a day, even of an hour, when opportunities could be won or lost. In September 1923, he wrote:

> Revolution possesses a mighty power of improvisation, but it never improvises anything good for fatalists, bystanders, and fools. Victory comes from the correct political evaluation, from correct organization and from the will to deal the decisive blow.[45]

---

44. Agosti 1974, Vol. I, Part 2, pp. 673–97.
45. Trotsky 1972, p. 327.

Correct timing was always central to Trotsky's vision of political struggle, and at certain moments his manner of expressing himself could sound like adventurism, even though the substance of his thought was opposed to such an attitude. Nevertheless, when facing the prospect of prolonged struggle in Italy, and when contemplating the defeats sustained by the Communist Parties and proletariats of so many countries from 1919 to 1923, Gramsci tended to place Trotsky more and more among the reckless insurrectionists, when what was needed was organisation, clandestine cohesion, education of cadres, defensive systems, well dug and fortified 'trenches' from which to carry on a successful 'war of position'.

Moreover, Trotsky's temporary withdrawal from active political life in 1925 tended to strengthen Gramsci's opposition to Trotskyism. In that year there was a lull on the Russian front, and Trotsky himself seemed to have repudiated fractionalism, or at the very least to have accepted party discipline, although without renouncing his personal convictions. In May 1925, Gramsci published an article entitled 'The Moral of Trotsky's Return',[46] in which he observed that

> as expected, as a seasoned militant, a disciplined soldier of the revolution, Trotsky has returned to the ranks. Having accepted the judgment of the majority that his political conceptions were mistaken, Trotsky has submitted to party discipline.

What could be learned from this, Gramsci asked. We learn 'that individuals, no matter how great their value and merits, are always subordinate to the party, the party is never subordinated to individuals, even if they are exceptional like Trotsky'. The concluding paragraphs of this article show to what extent Gramsci had been influenced by the increasingly authoritarian attitudes and methods of the Stalinist era, which can be said to have begun in 1925.

An important personal experience lay behind the article just cited: Gramsci's attendance, together with Mauro Scoccimarro and several other Italian Communists, at the sessions of the Fifth Enlarged Executive of the Comintern that took place in Moscow from 21 March to 6 April 1925. At these meetings, Gramsci became more integrated than ever in the administrative and political apparatus of the Comintern; at the opening session of 21 March, he was elected to membership in the political commission, the commission on trade union unity, the Czechoslovakian commission, and the Yugoslav commission.[47] During the three weeks he spent in Moscow, he met Stalin and spoke at some length with him, since Stalin, having moved effectively towards consolidating his authority as secretary of the Russian Communist Party, had now for the first time begun to take an active interest in the affairs of the International.[48]

---

46. Gramsci 1974, pp. 307–9.
47. *International Press Correspondence*, Vol. 5, No. 26, 4 April 1925, p. 350.
48. Berti 1967, pp. 218–19.

Giuseppe Berti attributes Stalin's new involvement in the work of the Comintern to his realisation that he could not achieve complete victory over Trotsky in the Soviet Union unless he also undermined his adversary's international prestige. This is a plausible thesis. Trotsky had become Stalin's principal opponent concerning key issues on which Stalin had staked his personal fortunes and those of the Soviet Union as a whole: the 'building of socialism in one country', the restrictive interpretation of democratic centralism and the equating of differences of opinion with 'fractionism', and the continued pursuit of the New Economic Policy inaugurated by Lenin, which favoured liberal concessions to the small landowning farmers. In order to gain support for these policies at home, Stalin felt that he needed the backing of the leadership of the major Communist Parties abroad. For this reason, the two main subjects discussed at the Fifth Enlarged Executive were the Bolshevisation of the world Communist movement, and the struggle against Trotskyism. Bolshevisation now meant the line that led from Lenin to Stalin, entirely excluding Trotsky and his followers. In his conversations with the members of the Italian delegation, Stalin specifically requested that they speak out against Trotskyism. There is no record of Gramsci's having done so, but Gramsci's comrade Mauro Scoccimarro did deliver an address on the question, on 3 April 1925, which ended with the unequivocal judgment – probably then shared by Gramsci – that one of the Italian party's immediate aims was 'the elimination of Trotskyism from its ranks'.[49]

Some of what is said above is conjectural. What is not conjectural is that after his return to Italy, and during the entire period just before and after the Italian party's Third Congress in January 1926 in Lyons, Gramsci adhered closely to the directives emanating from Moscow. Segments of his *Report on the Third Italian Communist Party Congress*, presented in February 1926, have an unmistakably Stalinist ring to them. In saying this, I have no intention of denying the significant contributions of the Lyons Theses to our understanding of the material bases of Fascism and of class relations in Italy. But the subject of this inquiry is the Gramsci-Trotsky question, and in this sense, there can be little doubt that by February 1926 Gramsci had moved decisively away from Trotsky and felt himself to be in close association with Stalin. In the above-mentioned *Report*, Gramsci asserted that

> the loyalty of all elements of the Party towards the Central Committee must become not only a purely organisational and disciplinary fact, but a genuine principle of revolutionary ethics ... It is necessary to infuse into the masses of the Party a deeply-rooted conviction concerning the necessity that fractionist initiatives and every attempt in general to unsettle the compactness of the Party must find at the base a spontaneous and immediate reaction that suffocates it at its very inception. The authority of the Central Committee between one congress and another must never be placed under discussion, and the Party must become a homogeneous bloc. *Only* under such conditions will the

---

49. Scoccimarro 1925, pp. 3–4.

> Party be able to triumph over its class enemies...The Party does not intend to allow
> any further indulgent play with fractionism and lack of discipline; the Party wants to
> achieve a maximum of collective leadership and will not allow any individual, whatever
> his personal value, to oppose himself to the Party.[50]

At this time, in fact since the summer of 1925, the only person in the Italian party's
Central Committee who had spoken out vigorously in defense of Trotsky was Amadeo
Bordiga. Even though Gramsci was aware of the differences in ideology between Trotsky
and Bordiga, he probably feared that a confluence of the two currents in a renewed Left
alliance would pose a direct threat to the 'Leninist stabilisation' he believed the Party
had achieved under his own leadership.

In the final analysis, however, I think it must be granted that in his personal conduct
and relations with his opponents in the Communist Party of Italy, Gramsci was different from the Stalinists in Russia and elsewhere.[51] He was against drastic disciplinary
measures, against expulsions and excommunications, against personalising what were,
in essence, political and ideological differences, against abandoning friends and longtime
comrades because their ideas diverged from his, against abusive harangues and slander.
He continued to acknowledge the enormous contributions made by both Trotsky and
Bordiga to the cause of the world socialist revolution. No doubt, he found repugnant in
the extreme the falsification of the past to fit the contingencies of the present, and the
cynical manipulation and exaggeration of temporary differences between Party leaders
that normally occur in the course of daily struggle, that had by 1926 become standard
procedure in the ruling circles of the Party and state in Soviet Russia. It seems to me
that the letter of early October 1926 illustrates this essential difference between Gramsci
and the Stalinists, even at a time when his language and posture displayed the contours
of the Stalinist mould.

The period of the *Prison Notebooks*

One other phase in the story of the Gramsci-Trotsky question calls for some comment,
the period of the *Prison Notebooks*, specifically the years from 1929 to 1932 when, as
a prisoner in Turi di Bari, Gramsci devoted some of his reflections to Trotsky and to
Trotskyism.

Current and former Italian Trotskyists[52] have argued, convincingly I think, that
although it is impossible to document a direct Trotskyist influence on Gramsci during

---

50. Gramsci 1974, pp. 105–30.
51. On this aspect of Gramsci's personality and way of dealing with Party members, see Quercioli (ed.) 1977.
52. Notably Alfonso Leonetti, among the long-time members of the Fourth International. Gramsci's biographer, Giuseppe Fiori, believes that if Gramsci had stated his views in the early 1930s
publicly, he would have been expelled from the Party.

his years in prison, the political positions taken by the two men in response to the Left-sectarian turn taken by the Comintern after the Sixth World Congress reveal many common features. Both rejected the labelling of social democrats as social-fascists, for the simple reason that in a time of extreme danger, when the forces of the Left were faced with ever more menacing threats from an organised and powerful coalition on the Right, Communist parties needed to expand their contacts with other working-class parties and movements, not restrict them; to seek possible areas of joint defence and collaboration, and not isolate themselves from their potential allies if a showdown of force became necessary. Both men urged the promulgation of a transitional program of demands, embracing the concept of a Constituent Assembly in countries dominated by rightist dictatorships, which could mobilise broad working-class and anti-fascist support for the struggle against reaction. For both Gramsci and Trotsky, to label social democracy as a particular form of fascism lacking only the trappings and slogans conceived by Mussolini and Hitler, was to take a giant step towards self-liquidation. The evidence corroborating their substantial agreement on most of the immediate political choices facing the Communist movement in the late 1920s and early 1930s is abundant and persuasive, and may signify that their interaction when the policy of the united front was being formulated a decade earlier was still present in Gramsci's mind.

As far as his opinion of Trotsky the man is concerned, if we can believe the testimony of Angelo Scucchia, a fellow communist inmate at Turi, Gramsci did not give any credence to the Stalinist slander of Trotsky as a bandit, a renegade, a loose gun of Fascist reaction, a sort of superhuman demon who somehow managed to be everywhere at once, whenever anything opposed to Soviet interests happened to occur. Scucchia relates that in 1930–1, an Italian translation of Trotsky's *Autobiography* was circulating in the Turi prison. In reaction to this book, one day Gramsci said of Trotsky: 'A great historian, a great revolutionary, but he is an egotist, he sees himself at the centre of all events, he has no sense of the Party'.[53]

This was a very similar appraisal of Trotsky's personality to the one made by Lenin in 1922, and in any event had nothing in common with the insinuations, accusations, and degrading diatribes that sullied Communist Party polemics in those years. Moreover, Gramsci maintained a lively interest in Trotsky's writings after the latter's deportation from the Soviet Union in January 1928. In order to obtain three of Trotsky's works – the autobiography, in Italian translation, and French translations of two works, *Vers le capitalisme ou vers le socialisme* (*Towards Capitalism or Towards Socialism*) and *La révolution défigurée* (*The Revolution Betrayed-What is the Soviet Union and Where is it Going?* – Gramsci stubbornly persisted and finally succeeded in overcoming the regulations in Fascist Italy that usually disallowed such reading by political prisoners, especially Communist prisoners.

---

53. Quercioli (ed.) 1977, pp. 215–26.

In the *Notebooks*, Gramsci makes the following assertions concerning Trotsky and Trotskyism: 1) Trotsky had become the major theorist of a strategy based on the concept of a 'frontal assault' by revolutionary forces against the capitalist order, at a time when such a strategy could only lead to defeat. Unlike Lenin, who understood that while a war of movement had been victorious in Russia in 1917, a war of position was the only practicable strategy in the West, Trotsky had clung obdurately to the former; 2) Trotsky's theory of permanent revolution was, in all likelihood, merely the political expression of his theory of a war of movement, of decisive assault, which was inapplicable except in countries such as Russia where 'the framework of national life is embryonic and amorphous and cannot become 'a trench or fortress'; 3) Trotsky's repudiation of the possibility of building socialism in one country during a period of retreat and retrenchment on the Left, and his insistence on pursuing the revolution uninterruptedly on an international scale, revealed that he was a typical 'cosmopolitan' intellectual with little understanding, therefore, of the all-important national characteristics and problems that all Communist Parties must take into account in order eventually to integrate their national movements into the international framework of struggle. Using Trotsky's real family name, Bronstein, Gramsci said that 'Bronstein, who gave the impression that he was Western in his culture and general political outlook, was instead a cosmopolitan, and only superficially Western and European. Ilich (Lenin) on the other hand was profoundly national and profoundly European'.[54]

What this last assertion amounts to is the claim that Trotsky did not grasp what Gramsci regarded as a key requirement of successful revolutionary movements in the West, that they be 'national-popular', that they avoid abstract and utopian idealism, that they root themselves in the concrete living experience of the peoples in whose name they were fighting, and become part of a widespread consensual trend without which the ultimate hegemony of the working class would be unrealisable. I shall return to this point in a moment. Let us look briefly first at Gramsci's other opinions of Trotsky's methods and ideology.

We have already seen that, with respect to the theory and practice of revolutionary politics, a certain divergence did take place between Gramsci and Trotsky, insofar as the latter remained convinced that in the West a situation requiring prompt and decisive revolutionary intervention by the Communist-led working class could arise at any time, even quite unexpectedly, whereas the former grew more and more attached to the idea of a prolonged 'war of position' in which no decisive thrust for power was likely. Gramsci saw a gradual building of socialist hegemony through penetration of all the pores and interstices of bourgeois society and institutions as a much more likely and reasonable course to follow. But Gramsci did not absolutely exclude the possibility of a decisive clash between bourgeoisie and proletariat for the conquest of state power, and Trotsky was always mindful of the need to adapt tactics to the objective situation at any given

---

54. Gramsci 1975, Vol. II, pp. 865–6.

moment in time. Trotsky certainly believed that revolutionary opportunities could be missed, but he also saw that the surest way to condemn a revolutionary movement to failure was to choose the wrong time to attempt a seizure of power, and to close off other transitional avenues of action. In short, the difference between the two men on this question is not, in my view, an essential one, but rather one of emphasis deriving from their diverse experiences. Let it not be forgotten that it was Trotsky who taught Gramsci something of what he knew about revolutionary tactics, and about the general conditions governing political struggle in the West as opposed to the East.

As for the comments in the *Notebooks* on Trotsky's theory of permanent revolution, it is necessary to remember that during the years 1923 and 1924, Gramsci himself used this expression in what would appear to be a Trotskyist sense on several occasions. He did not use it consistently or coherently, however, so that it is safe to conclude that this central component of Trotsky's political thought was not an integral part of Gramsci's vision of things. Another point to be made here is this: in the *Notebooks*, Gramsci says that 'it remains to be seen whether the famous theory of Bronstein on the *permanence* of the movement is the political reflection of the theory of a war of movement...'[55] Gramsci leaves the question hanging, even as he suggests the probability that a link between the two ideas exists. The distinction is not trivial, for it indicates a degree of uncertainty about Trotsky's theory which is psychologically and politically germane to what I said at the outset of this essay concerning the ambivalences, the contradictoriness, the shifts and changes in interpretation that one finds in Gramsci's whole interaction with Trotsky. I would add here also that, if Gramsci's observations on Trotsky's theory of permanent revolution had not been expressed in a hypothetical manner, then Livio Maitan would be right in saying that Gramsci's interpretation of this aspect of Trotsky's thought is tantamount to a 'vulgar caricature'.[56] Here is the way Trotsky himself summarised the three main features of his theory:

> The theory of the permanent revolution, which originated in 1905,...pointed out that the democratic tasks of the backward bourgeois nations lead directly, in our epoch, to the dictatorship of the proletariat and that the dictatorship of the proletariat puts socialist tasks on the order of the day. Therein lay the central idea of the theory. While the traditional view was that the road to the dictatorship of the proletariat led through a long period of democracy, the theory of the permanent revolution established the fact that for backward countries the road to democracy passed through the dictatorship of the proletariat. Thus democracy is not a régime that remains self-sufficient for decades, but is only a direct prelude to the socialist revolution. Thus there is established between the democratic revolution and the socialist reconstruction of society a permanent state of revolutionary development.

---

55. Ibid.
56. Maitan 1958, pp. 579–84.

The second aspect of the 'permanent' theory has to do with the socialist revolution as such. For an indefinitely long time and in constant internal struggle, all social relations undergo transformation. Society keeps on changing its skin. Each stage of transformation stems directly from the preceding one. This process necessarily retains a political character, that is, it develops through collisions between various groups in the society which is in transformation. Outbreaks of civil war and foreign wars alternate with periods of 'peaceful' reform. Revolutions in economy, technique, science, the family, morals, and everyday life develop in complex reciprocal action and do not allow society to achieve equilibrium. Therein lies the permanent character of the socialist revolution as such.

The international character of the socialist revolution, which constitutes the third aspect of the theory of the permanent revolution, flows from the present state of economy and the social structure of humanity. Internationalism is no abstract principle but a theoretical and political reflection of the character of world economy, of the world development of productive forces and the world scale of the class struggle. The socialist revolution begins on national foundations – but it cannot be completed on these foundations. The maintenance of the proletarian revolution within a national framework can only be a provisional state of affairs, even though, as the experience of the Soviet Union shows, one of long duration. In an isolated proletarian dictatorship, the internal and external contradictions grow inevitably along with the successes achieved. If it remains isolated, the proletarian state must finally fall victim to these contradictions. The way out for it lies only in the victory of the proletariat of the advanced countries. Viewed from this standpoint, a national revolution is not a self-contained whole; it is only a link in the international chain. The international revolution constitutes a permanent process, despite temporary declines and ebbs.[57]

What this passage suggests to me is that the divergence of views between Trotsky and Gramsci lay in their understanding of how the national and the international dimensions of the socialist revolution should be understood. This brings us back to Gramsci's opinion that Trotsky, because of his 'cosmopolitanism' and 'superficial' view of both the national and the international aspects of the socialist revolution, did not have a firm grasp of national particularities, that he was too grand and sweeping in his vision to see the unique features of each national landscape, too fond of his vast universal design to fasten on to the *verità effettuale*, the effective truth, to use a famous Machiavellian phrase, of political struggle as waged by each party against the background of customs, traditions, modes of thought, institutional forms rooted sometimes, as in the case of Italy, in centuries of historical experience. In effect, Trotsky's internationalism, and his theory of permanent revolution, seemed too abstract, too purely ideological for Gramsci's taste. In this context, perhaps it was not entirely by chance that in the passage cited by Gramsci

---

57. Trotsky 1969, pp. 132–3. The passage was written in 1933.

on Trotsky's 'cosmopolitanism', he called Trotsky by his real family name, Bronstein. It may be that one of the aspects of their personalities and experience as revolutionaries that tended to separate them was what Isaac Deutscher has called an element of 'non-Jewish Jewishness' in Trotsky's conception of life.[58] In any event, I offer the following two passages, the one by Valentino Gerratana concerning Gramsci, the other by Isaac Deutscher concerning Trotsky and the Left Opposition in Russia, as one among several possible stimulating points of departure for further thought and research on the relationship between Gramsci and Trotsky as individuals, and between the currents of Marxist praxis that they represent:

Here is Gerratana on Gramsci:

> For [Antonio] Labriola, as for Lenin at around the same time and later for Gramsci, Marxism becomes a truly living force in the consciousness of a country and can produce in each country all of its effects only when the general principles of the doctrine assume a particular national form, tied to a tradition and open to an independent development.[59]

Deutscher on Trotsky:

> Jews were, in fact, conspicuous among the Opposition although they were there together with the flower of the non-Jewish intelligentsia and workers. Trotsky, Zinoviev, Kamenev, Sokolinikov, Radek, were all Jews (There were, on the other hand, very few Jews among the Stalinists, and fewer still among the Bukharinists.) Thoroughly 'assimilated' and Russified though they were, and hostile to the Mosaic as to any other religion and to Zionism, they were still marked by that 'Jewishness' which is the quintessence of the urban way of life in all its modernity, progressiveness, restlessness, and one-sidedness. To be sure, the allegations that they were politically hostile to the mushik were false and, in Stalin's mouth, though perhaps not in Bukharin's, insincere. But the Bolsheviks of Jewish origin were least of all inclined to idealize rural Russia in her primitivism and barbarity and to drag along at a 'snail's pace' the native peasant cart. They were in a sense the 'rootless cosmopolitans' on whom Stalin was to turn his wrath openly in his old age. Not for them was the ideal of socialism in a single country. As a rule the progressive or revolutionary Jew, brought up on the border lines of various religions and national cultures, whether Spinoza or Marx, Heine or Freud, Rosa Luxemburg or Trotsky, was particularly apt to transcend in his mind religious and national limitations and to identify himself with a universal view of mankind.[60]

Because of fundamental differences in their backgrounds, personalities and ways of dealing with comrades and adversaries, Gramsci and Trotsky could not possibly see

58. Deutscher 1968.
59. Gerratana 1954, p. 750.
60. Deutscher 1965, Vol. I, pp. 258–9.

eye-to-eye on many issues. Yet despite these differences, it is remarkable how much they did have in common. Both men were above petty intrigues, both had contempt for the type of compromises that sacrifice principle for expediency, and both placed great emphasis on the lesson for revolutionaries contained in Marx's Third Thesis on Feurbach: if historical circumstances shape human beings, it is also true that human beings create history; if objective economic systems and predominant modes of production determine the consciousness of individuals, one must also remember that it is through the subjective apprehension of these systems and modes that consciousness can, in turn, become an active propulsive force in history.

For Gramsci and Trotsky, the cultural life of society was never merely a problem of organisation, of technological efficiency, of methods and systems. Culture had to do with values, and values were the achievement of lived experience, of trial and error, of struggle and conflict between diverse trends and schools of thought They believed that if culture was to be authentic and original, not passively received and imitative, it had to be nourished by a process of dynamic interaction between creative personalities and the masses.

No doubt Gramsci was more willing than Trotsky to accept and to live with the bureaucratised structures created by the Soviet leaders in the fields of economic planning and political organisation. He was less visionary and less prone to bursts of revolutionary enthusiasm than Trotsky, less given to rhapsodic flights of idealism such as one finds in the concluding paragraph of Trotsky's *Literature and Revolution.* Gramsci was shrewder, more cautious and tactful in his relationship to power, more attuned to the daily routine of Party work than Trotsky, who always craved a vast field of operation, preferably of international dimensions, for his exuberant energies and capacities.

As communist intellectuals, Gramsci and Trotsky elaborated their own ideas on politics and culture and their own methods of applying Marxism to the new tasks and perspectives facing the world socialist community after the victorious Bolshevik Revolution. By remaining faithful to themselves, they were able to envisage forms of collective economic and social life that were not ends but means for liberating the latent creative powers that exist in all human beings. Both men were defeated, as far as the immediate outcome of their struggles was concerned. Yet each in his own way set an example, both before but especially after his personal defeat, of endurance in the face of acute suffering, and of intellectual vitality in conditions that would have destroyed lesser men. And the name of each is today associated with a philosophy of Marxist praxis – to use Gramsci's term – that, in some fundamental respects, provides alternatives to the Stalinist model that dominated large sectors of the Communist world for close to six decades. This, I think, is another reason why the relationship between Gramsci and Trotsky is not only an intriguing historical problem, but one that is currently relevant to everyone concerned with the cause and future direction of socialism in the world.

The fact that Gramsci's name became associated with the accommodating parliamentary gradualism and consensual politics of the Italian and Spanish Communist Parties, known as Eurocommunism, while that of Trotsky is linked with the more stringent revolutionary politics of the Fourth International, ought not to obscure another fact: that in some basic areas of socialist thought and practice, and at important moments of political crisis in the 1920s and 1930s, the two men came to similar conclusions. We should not seek for an impossible reconciliation between all facets of their lives as Marxist revolutionaries; but neither should we prevent ourselves from seeing points of convergence, from which new lines of thought and new courses of action might emerge.

Chapter Two
Antonio Gramsci and the Italian Communist Press in the Fascist Era

Gramsci and *L'Ordine Nuovo*

The first issue of *L'Ordine Nuovo*, subtitled a 'weekly review of socialist culture', appeared in Turin on 1 May 1919. The review was launched by four dedicated left-wing Socialists who, in January 1921, were among the founders of the Communist Party of Italy: Antonio Gramsci, Palmiro Togliatti, Angelo Tasca, and Umberto Terracini.

Gramsci was the leader of the quadrumvirate. He was a small, hunchbacked man, but his lucid intelligence and tenacious will compensated for his physical disabilities. He had left his native Sardinia in 1911 to pursue a course of literary and philological studies at the University of Turin. During World War I, he resumed his early interests in politics and economics, and by the beginning of 1917 he was named secretary of the Turinese section of the Italian Socialist Party. From that point on he devoted himself to the task of building a militant socialist movement in Italy.

The weekly *L'Ordine Nuovo* of the years 1919 and 1920 reflected the experiences and thought of those Italian socialists who, like Gramsci and his friends, were dissatisfied with what they regarded as the excessively cautious and opportunistic policies of their party's leadership and who aspired to place the Italian Socialist Party at the vanguard of a revolutionary movement capable of rebuilding Italian society on new foundations. The review spurred on the Turin workers in their struggles against the city's managerial and industrial class. To this end, its editors elaborated a programme for the creation of workers' councils that were, in fact, successfully if only temporarily established in many of the factories of Turin. Gramsci's speaking voice was thin and reedy, yet he was able through sheer force of personality and focused intelligence to hold the attention of workers on the shop floor. Among other qualities, he was a gifted speaker and teacher.

In January 1921, coincident with the founding of the Communist Party of Italy, which became a member organisation of the recently founded Communist International, *L'Ordine Nuovo* was transformed from a weekly into a daily newspaper whose motto, borrowed from the Swiss socialist and friend of Karl Marx, Ferdinand Lassalle, read 'to tell the truth is revolutionary'. But Lenin, not Lassalle, was the real driving force behind the new communist daily. Nearly all of Gramsci's writings in *L'Ordine Nuovo*, although bearing the imprint of an independent and creative mind, were inspired by the teachings of Lenin.

The most painful 'truth' to be told, according to Gramsci, was that in Russia a workers' state had been founded on the principle of the dictatorship of the proletariat, while in Italy the Italian Socialist Party, despite its mass following and many opportunities for revolutionary action, had indulged in futile sloganeering and had allowed itself to be overwhelmed by the assaults and raids of Fascist militiamen. In this situation, Gramsci concluded, it had become clear that only a genuinely revolutionary Communist Party, functioning within the framework of the Third International, could mobilise the energies of the working class in its struggle to overthrow the capitalist system.[1] Gramsci did not deviate from this position in the next few years. As Fascist violence increased and as it became evident that the National Fascist Party would probably seize power in Italy, his point of view appealed to those Italians who looked to the young Soviet Union as a model of revolutionary politics.

Throughout the year 1921, Gramsci grappled with the phenomenon of Italian Fascism, which he thought reflected the ideology of a disaffected petty bourgeoisie. This was the segment of Italian society that was providing the men and ideas for the Fascist movement; they were the organisers of the 'punitive expeditions' against socialist and labour organisations; they supplied the Fascists with the peculiar mix of nationalism and authoritarianism that was emanating increasingly from the mouth of their leader Benito Mussolini.

But Gramsci went to considerable pains to point out as well that the petty bourgeois ideologues who formed the shock troops of the Fascist movement were in the final analysis instruments in the hands of Italian capitalists, who through Fascism were attempting to resolve the problem of capitalist production and trade resulting from the recent war through the establishment of a dictatorship of the Right able to safeguard their economic interests.[2] But like Lenin in *Imperialism: The Highest Stage of Capitalism*,

---

1. Gramsci 1964, Vol. I, pp. 547–50. The article appeared in *L'Ordine Nuovo*, 1 January 1921.
2. Gramsci 1964, Vol. I, pp. 547–50.

Gramsci also saw the crisis of Italian society as part of the general crisis of international finance capital.

As for Mussolini, Gramsci regarded him as the embodiment of the worst Italian petty bourgeois traits. The Fascist leader was 'a subversive reactionary, an illogical, inflated, grotesque, superficial' man who sooner or later would bring catastrophic ruin upon the Italian people.[3]

In June 1922, Gramsci left Italy, and for the next two years he worked first in Moscow and then in Vienna for the Third International. In Vienna, he was responsible for coordinating the work of the PCd'I with other European Communist Parties. He returned to Italy a few weeks before the assassination of the Socialist leader Giacomo Matteotti on 10 June 1924 in order to take up his duties as a newly elected Communist deputy to the Italian Chamber of Deputies.

On 1 March 1924, *L'Ordine Nuovo* had been refounded as a bi-monthly review in which Gramsci sought to outline new proposals and goals for the Communist Party of Italy, of which he was now general secretary. As of late October 1922, Fascism was in power, and the Italian working class was demoralised and lacking a sense of direction. His proposals were bold and decisive, if unrealistic, given the political realities of the moment. He called for the independent political action of the working class and the mobilisation of small, disciplined groups of Communist labour organisers, advocated a strengthening of ties with the Third International, and proposed the formation of special cells and schools to train Party propagandists.[4] His program reflected the imminent need for the kind of clandestine, conspiratorial apparatus that the Italian Communists did in fact create in the next several years.

Because of Fascist raids, censorship and other harassments, only six issues of *L'Ordine Nuovo* appeared in 1924 and only two in 1925. Yet had it not been for the example set by Gramsci and his fellow editors, it's likely that the Italian Communists would not have been able to function as effectively as they did during the next 18 years and to play a central role in the Resistance movement in Italy from 1943 to 1945. Gramsci himself did not live to see the end of Mussolini's régime. He died in a Rome clinic, under police guard, on 27 April 1937, after serving nine years of a sentence imposed on him in 1928 by the Fascist Special Tribunal. Of his three comrades, Terracini was also imprisoned and served his sentence until 1943, while Togliatti escaped to Moscow and Tasca to France.

Gramsci's contribution to the Italian Communist movement was not limited to his activities as a political strategist and journalist. If, as noted by Aldo Garosci, the Communist Party of Italy 'was born through the direct intervention of the Comintern', it was also true that the party 'had native roots' and was from its inception an authentic

---

3. Gramsci 1964, Vol. I, pp. 592–4. Originally in *L'Ordine Nuovo*, 22 June 1921.
4. Gramsci 1964, Vol. I, pp. 720–5.

'representative of certain historical traditions of the Italian working class'.[5] Gramsci was largely responsible for imparting this 'national' character to Italian communism. One of his concerns was 'to translate the Mazzinian tradition into socialist terms'.[6]

In both his early writings and in the *Prison Notebooks*, Gramsci expounded his belief that a thoroughgoing socialist revolution in Italy was the only way to fulfil the promises and struggles of the nineteenth-century Risorgimento. His analysis of the economic and social problems that plagued the Southern Italian peasantry, whom he saw as the main potential ally of the country's industrial proletariat, also 'imparted a national character to the projected socialist revolution in Italy, since only this kind of revolution could complete the unification of the country by ending the 'colonial' subjection of the South'.[7]

Another strongly Italian aspect of Gramsci's intellectual formation was his lifelong indebtedness to the neo-idealist philosopher Benedetto Croce, whose influence at the University of Turin was spread, during the years Gramsci studied there, through the appointment in 1913 of Croce's disciple Umberto Cosmo as professor of Italian literature. From his study of Croce, Gramsci developed a strongly voluntaristic approach to life that, at least in his early years, led him to repudiate any and all forms of historical determinism.

L'Ordine Nuovo was not the only Communist periodical that challenged the rule and the ideology of Fascism. There were quite a few newspapers produced clandestinely by workers and journalists, such as *Battaglie Sindacali* which, from 1927 to the late 1930s, waged a continuous campaign in defence of independent unionism and working-class solidarity as the organ of the anti-fascist segment of the General Confederation of Labour. Other clandestine newspapers that were either completely or in large part the result of initiatives taken by Communists included *La Riscossa* and *ll Giovane Operaio* in Trieste, *Bandiera Rossa* in Turin, *La Fiaccola* in Genoa, and *La Scintilla* in Milan.

L'Unità and *Lo Stato Operaio*

Particular attention must be given to the Communist Party's official organ *L'Unità*, a name that Gramsci himself proposed in order to highlight the policy of a 'united front' between Communists and other radical and leftwing labour groups that had been advocated by both Lenin and Trotsky beginning in 1921. Gramsci had initially resisted the idea of a united front, but came around to accepting it when other lines of attack were ruled out as impractical. The newspaper is important because during the Fascist era it confronted many of the national and international issues that were later to re-emerge during World War II.

---

5. Garosci 1951, p. 159.
6. Gramsci used this expression in a short treatise written in 1917 called *La città futura* ['The city of the future']. See Cammett 1967, p. 43.
7. Cammett 1967, p. 177.

The first issue of *L'Unità* appeared on 12 February 1924, and for the next two years, despite threats, censorship, and other forms of repression imposed on the Communist Party by the new Fascist régime, managed to appear fairly regularly in the major Italian cities. When the Special Laws in Defence of the State of November 1926 effectively ended independent journalism in Italy, and the subsequent trials and imprisonment of Gramsci and many of his comrades forced the Party to go underground, a group of Party propagandists and functionaries who had avoided arrest began to prepare the first entirely clandestine issue of *L'Unità*, which was dated 1 January 1927.[8]

During the first seven months of 1927, the newspaper's beleaguered staff, headed by Camilla Ravera, Alfonso Leonetti, and Felice Platone, worked in rapidly improvised headquarters in a house on the outskirts of Genoa. In August of that year, the house in Genoa was abandoned in favour of safer headquarters in Lugano, in the prevalently Italian-language region of Switzerland.

The first 'Genoese' issues dated 1 January, 21 January and 5 February 1927 set the tone and policy that remained characteristic of the newspaper up to the outbreak of World War II in 1939. Its message was directed to the working class, which was told that Fascism represented the interests of Italian industrialists and large landowners in league with the tycoons of international finance capital; that Fascism would inevitably plunge the Italian people into war; that only through strikes, protests, demonstrations and eventual armed struggle could the Italian working class hope to regain its autonomy and ability to bring about the end of Mussolini's régime.

The clandestine *L'Unità* fulfilled the important function of providing its scattered and intrepid readers with reports and analyses of events in Italy and in the world at large that the Fascist press either ignored entirely or interpreted in accordance with the directives promulgated by the Ministry of the Press and Propaganda in Rome. The officially approved press told its readers that the Italian Fascist state was invulnerable to the economic chaos afflicting the capitalist countries in 1929 and 1930, while *L'Unità* spoke of the millions of unemployed in Italy, and of a workforce reduced to hunger and sickness by pay scales that were below those of the rest of Europe. In 1933, the year that Hitler took power in Germany, *L'Unità* warned its readers of the reactionary and aggressive nature of the Nazi movement. In 1936 and 1937, while the Italian people was being told of Italy's 'civilising mission' in Africa and Italian industry was supplying Franco's insurgents with planes, tanks, guns and 'volunteers', *L'Unità* called the invasion of Ethiopia an imperialist adventure and, in 1936, began raising funds to support an Italian contingent of volunteers to help defend the Spanish Republic. This became the Garibaldi Brigade, led for several years in Spain by the Communist Luigi Longo.

---

8. According to Cesare Rossi, four-fifths of the 5,072 sentences imposed by the Special Tribunal on political enemies of the régime were against Italian Communists. See Rossi 1952 and Pajetta 1962. The correspondence of imprisoned anti-fascists during the 1920s and 1930s contains a high percentage of letters written by both leading and rank-and-file Italian Communists.

The policy supporting a 'Popular Front', based on an inter-class alliance that included 'bourgeois liberal' parties, was approved by the Seventh World Congress of the Comintern in the summer of 1935. It promoted contacts among Italian anti-fascists that had been severed in the preceding seven to eight years. Thus, in 1936 and 1937, instead of denouncing liberals and social democrats as traitors to the cause of working-class solidarity, *L'Unità* now acknowledged that Fascism was a threat to the democratic nations of the world. In an undated article of 1937, the newspaper made the following appraisal of events in Spain, not long after the Falangist uprising:

> Each passing day allows the Italian people to understand more and more clearly that its own cause is identical to the cause for which the Spanish Republicans are fighting and dying... It is necessary that every militant opponent of the Fascist régime, every anti-Fascist, every worker and citizen who is dissatisfied with the present situation realise that the victory of the Spanish Republic will make possible an uprising of the Italian people against the régime that has oppressed our country for fourteen years and that the Republic's defeat will plunge Italy into a new bloodbath... Therefore just as there exists a close tie between the Fascist oppressors of our country and the criminal Generals Franco, Mola, and Queipo de Llano, in the same way there must be a close solidarity between the Spanish and Italian peoples.[9]

The Italian Communists were again forced to make a major readjustment in their attitude toward non-communist anti-fascists in the wake of the Nazi-Soviet non-aggression pact of 23 August 1939. Palmiro Togliatti, the general secretary of the Party from 1927 to his death in 1964, made various attempts in the postwar years to discredit 'the ridiculous calumny that we were against the war of Hitler and Mussolini only in the interests of the Soviet Union and after the USSR was attacked [on June 22, 1941]'.[10] However, there is evidence showing that the pact threw the PCd'I into a state of utter confusion. At least two prominent Italian Communists, Leo Valiani and Romano Cocchi, the latter general secretary of the Italian People's Union, resigned from the Party. The historian Aldo Garosci notes that 'young Party militants like Lombardo-Radice, Natoli, Buffalini, as well as old-timers like Umberto Terracini and Girolamo Li Causi, took positions at this time that carried them nearly outside the Party'. But he adds that 'once the critical moment had been surmounted, they were taken back into the fold'.[11] It was a moment of crisis whose effects lasted well beyond World War II in the form of unresolved internal ideological differences that proved to be permanently divisive.

The task of justifying the non-aggression pact fell temporarily to the monthly journal *Lo Stato Operaio*, whose very title evoked the idea of the Soviet Union as a model 'workers' state' to be emulated by all loyal Communist Parties. The journal moved its

---

9. *L'Unità*, No. 3, 1937, p. 1. Available at the Centro Gobetti in Turin.
10. Togliatti 1958, p. 92.
11. Garosci 1951, p. 176.

headquarters and publishing activities to New York City in 1940 and remained in the United States until 1943. This move was necessitated by the French government's closing of the Paris branches of the French and Italian Communist parties in September 1939, shortly after the pact was announced to a startled world. Suddenly the premises of the Popular Front fell to pieces, to be replaced by the idea that there was no fundamental difference between the Fascist powers and the bourgeois-liberal countries. In an editorial of 15 March 1940, *Lo Stato Operaio* argued that

> The longer the war goes on the more the people are aware that phrases about 'the repa-ration of suffered injustices' or 'living space' (in Germany), like phrases about 'the war for freedom, against Hitlerism' (in France and England) are lies to push the people to massacre each other for imperialistic interests, by exploiting – in Germany – the feel-ing of nationalism and – in France and England – the anti-fascist sentiments of the masses.[12]

The notion of 'the people' and of 'the masses' had been a part of the Party's lexicon for several decades. Gramsci used them frequently for the purpose of highlighting the authenticity and spontaneity of ordinary working people as opposed to the lock-step automated masses who marched to the Fascist drumbeat. But during the period when the pact was in force, this important distinction fell by the wayside, the victim of opportunism and obfuscation.

The Nazi invasion of the Soviet Union on 22 June 1941 required a return to the Popular Front as articulated back in 1935. After June 1941, *Lo Stato Operaio* resumed its appeals for democratic solidarity against the Axis powers. *L'Unità*, too, again took up its struggle in the name of a united democratic front against Hitlerism and Fascism and, in fact, was destined to become one of the most important and widely diffused underground news-papers of the Italian Resistance from 1943 to 1945.

As already indicated, from 1927 to 1939, the main theoretical organ of the PCd'I was the monthly journal *Lo Stato Operaio*, whose first issue appeared in Paris in March 1927. Its managing editor was Palmiro Togliatti, one of the few prominent Italian Communists who managed to stay out of prison. He took over the reins of the Party after Gramsci's arrest. From 1927 to the mid-1930s, he travelled back and forth between Paris and Mos-cow as the leading Italian delegate to the Communist International. From 1936 to 1939, he worked in Spain as a tactician and propagandist for the Spanish Communist Party. He devoted himself to organisational activities in France and Belgium in 1939 and 1940, when he emigrated to the Soviet Union. He remained in the Soviet Union until late March 1944, when he returned to Italy to help direct the Communist Party's participation in the Resistance movement.

---

12. *Lo Stato Operaio* 15 March 1940, p. 3. The quoted paragraph is taken from an article headed 'Let's struggle for Peace! Italy should stay out of the war!'

In several of his articles in *Lo Stato Operaio*, Togliatti continued Gramsci's effort in *L'Ordine Nuovo* to define and interpret the Fascist phenomenon. His emphasis fell on economic considerations, but he failed, as did most other analysts of the time, to understand that Fascism was also a mass phenomenon that had won a kind of ideological war against both democratic and communist conceptions of the state's role in promoting the interests of the masses.

One of his writings on this question appeared in the first issue of the new journal, in March 1927. Entitled 'The Workers' state',[13] it began by belittling the campaign of the Aventine secessionists of 1924 and 1925. An 'insurrection' of public opinion and a 'moral revolt' would never topple a régime based on force, he said. The overthrow of Fascism would be accomplished only with guns and tanks, and insofar as the Aventine had limited itself to peaceful tactics it had become counter-revolutionary.

Following this opening barrage against the Aventine, Togliatti proceded to examine the origin and nature of Fascism. It was, he said, the force that had 'saved the capitalistic régime in Italy from the insurrection of the working masses, of the proletariat and the peasants'. It had 'furnished the Italian industrial and agrarian bourgeoisie with the means to attempt a stabilization of capitalism in Italy'. No accurate historical analysis of Fascism, he asserted, could ever be made unless Fascism and capitalism were understood to be inextricably interrelated phenomena.

Togliatti was willing to concede that the economic and political system created by Fascism was not 'a normal capitalistic régime' and that the type of person whom Fascism had raised to the pinnacle of power was exceptionally rapacious and exploitative. This fact, however, did not disprove the equally obvious truth that 'what Fascism today embodies and defends is Italian capitalism in the form that it has had, fundamentally, in all the periods of its development since the formation of the unified Italian state'.

Thus, Togliatti based his analysis of Fascism on a more primary view of the development of Italian capitalism from the post-Risorgimento era to the end of World War I: Italian capitalism had always been reactionary, it had always relied on the state for economic and political support, it had always sought to suppress the struggles of the Italian working class. The crisis of the war had compelled Italian capitalism to ally itself with the Fascists in 1922 and 1923, for without such a régime in power there would have been 'a new, more vast and more decisive uprising of the masses than had taken place immediately after the end of the war'.

Togliatti concluded from this argument that there was 'a need for the hegemony of the proletariat in order to liberate Italy from Fascist tyranny'. Fascism could be overthrown only by the working class, which alone was capable of leading other strata of the population in a revolt against the régime. 'The struggle to overthrow Fascism and to eliminate it entirely from Italian political life', he said, 'coincides with the struggle for the establishment of a workers' state in Italy'.

---

13. *Lo Stato Operaio*, March 1927, pp. 1–9. For the term 'Aventine', see note 16 of Chapter Six.

In 1928, Togliatti demonstrated a more subtle and precise understanding of Fascism than in the article just cited. In his 'Observations on the policy of our Party',[14] published in June 1928, Togliatti criticised many of his comrades for having failed, in 1922, to see that capitalism was not always synonymous with Fascism. The PCd'I, he said, had grossly underestimated the impact that Fascism had on the political institutions of the nation and on matters affecting the working class. The reasons for this error lay in assumptions hastily made about the equivalency between Fascism and big business. It was necessary, Togliatti said, to examine the concrete situation that had allowed Fascist reaction to take root in various sectors of the population. This required the kind of analysis that he and Gramsci had made of the 'relations of force' in Italy in their jointly written speech at the Third Party Congress in February 1926.

The process of rethinking the Fascist phenomenon became evident in August 1928 when Togliatti spoke of Fascism as it had manifested itself specifically in Italy. He was now operating on the assumption that Fascism was a particular form of reaction that demanded close attention to the Italian class structure and to the mindset that had welcomed relief, from whatever source, from the anxieties and uncertainties prevalent in postwar Italy. Moreover, the formula expounded by the Italian Communists in the early 1920s that 'Fascism was purely and simply capitalist reaction' had turned out to be grossly inadequate. The appeal of Fascism hinged on other things as well, such as its ability to attract disaffected members of the rural petit-bourgeois class and even of disaffected artisans and agricultural workers. Fascism was not purely and simply an urban and a capitalist movement. It had gone beyond these limits to create a paramilitary organisation that was largely independent of traditional bourgeois-liberal restraints and that won the loyalty of thousands of declassed, embittered individuals who lacked a secure political identity. Fascism gave these people a new lease on life, a new sense of being recognised above and beyond their strictly class affiliations. The intensely 'nationalistic' nature of Fascist ideology also had a strong hold on the minds of war veterans who were alienated from leftwing political parties because of their insistence on internationalism and class struggle rather than on patriotism and national cohesion. Indeed, Mussolini's first rejection of his socialist affiliations during World War I was based on his perception that socialist propaganda had neglected the appeal of nationalism to ordinary Italians, especially those who had spent several years engaged in trench warfare.

Togliatti continued to see the capitalist system itself as organically related to the rise and success of Fascism as a mass movement. But class alone and economic interests were no longer of sufficient explanatory power to rule out many other points of entry into the task of understanding this arrogant new upstart on the Italian political scene. Later in the 1930s, when the Nazis and the Falangists expanded the Fascist sphere of influence in Europe, the need for further analysis and study became of paramount importance to Togliatti and to the Communist movement in general.

---

14. This article has been reprinted in Alatri (ed.) 1973, Vol. II, pp. 83–4.

Hitler had not spoken idly when he credited Mussolini with showing him how a movement bent on assuming total power could be successful in a liberal-democratic country. This admiration was one of the factors that induced Italy and Germany to enter into a series of pacts and alliances in the 1930s that foreclosed any opportunity Italy might have had either to return to its liberal origins or to acquire a new identity as a nation led by the Left.

Chapter Three

The Contemporary Relevance of Gramsci's Views on the Italian 'Southern Question'

Antonio Gramsci's writings from 1916 to the 1930s on Italy's 'Southern question' remain relevant in the twenty-first century not only to the relations of force in postwar and contemporary Italy, but also to a larger set of issues having to do with the history of colonialism and postcolonialism.

Gramsci's writings on the Southern question from 1916 to 1924

When addressing themselves to Italy's 'Southern question', Italian politicians and demographers often speak of 'the Italian South and the islands' as a way of acknowledging the particular history and economy of Sicily and Sardinia while at the same time insinuating the notion that the two islands are part of a wider Southern Italian backwardness. The inferior political status of Sardinia in the minds of self-satisfied 'continentals' was an attitude that the young Gramsci bitterly resented.[1] In his teenage years he became an ardent Sardinian patriot[2] with a mission to struggle for the autonomy – even for the complete independence, if necessary – of his native island. He reacted indignantly to

---

1. In an autobiographical note of 1933, Gramsci spoke of his 'continuous attempt to go beyond a backward way of living and thinking typical of a Sardinian at the beginning of the century who wanted to appropriate a way of living and thinking no longer regional and village-like but national', to which he added that 'if it is true that one of the most prominent needs of Italian culture was to deprovincialise itself even in the most advanced and modern urban centers, this process should appear all the more evident as experienced by a triple or quadruple provincial such as a young Sardinian certainly was at the beginning of the century.' Gramsci 1975, Vol. III, p. 1776.

2. Gramsci 1990, p. xi.

theories of genetically transmitted racial and ethnic traits that were rife in Europe at the turn of the century and that still have many adepts today. By the time he began his university studies in Turin in 1911, he was aware, as Mary Gibson has pointed out, that by the 1890s racialist theories had ceased being exclusively based on biology and skin colour and had slipped over into the realm of social class, with especially dire implications for how the Italian peasantry was perceived in polite society and by many members of the intelligentsia. 'Race', Gibson explains, 'was used in Italy...to explain persistent differences within the nation, especially divergences between North and South'.[3] Indeed, it is precisely this notion that implicitly underlies the politics of the Northern League today, with its regionally based network of groups claiming identification with the civilisation of 'Padania', (an allusion to the relatively prosperous regions of the Po Valley, *la valle padana*), which obviously draws a prejudicial dividing line between North and South.

In an article of 1 April 1916, entitled 'The South and the War', Gramsci emphasised an historical perspective on the Southern question that he had first evinced in a school essay of 1910 or 1911, entitled 'Oppressed and Oppressors'.[4] Specifically, he pointed up what he regarded as the fatal tendency of Italy's conservative politicians in the 1860s and 1870s to conceive of national unification as possible only under 'a single centralised régime', which for the South had had disastrous consequences. Instead of recognising and validating the particular needs and problems of the South, the new Italian ruling class, in slavish imitation of the French model of state formation, had moved immediately to centralise all major state functions, and by so doing, ironically, had created a new united Italy that was in reality more divided than ever into two trunks, Southern and Northern, 'in absolutely antithetical conditions'.

Gramsci was not only concerned about the political inequities built into the North-South relationship. He spoke also of the economic imbalances resulting from the huge flow of liquid capital from the South to the North, which reflected government policy that encouraged wealthy landowning Southerners to invest their capital in Northern industries rather than in initiatives designed to improve Southern agriculture and give a boost to nascent industries in the South. These investment practices, Gramsci argued, went hand in hand with a recalcitrant industrial protectionism, which was not counterbalanced by an agricultural protectionism that would have benefited the producing class in the South. Furthermore, such policies had negated the otherwise beneficial effects of emigration. It made no sense, Gramsci continued, to blame Southern miseries on a Southern lack of initiative. The fact was that capital would always seek its most profitable outlets and means of employment, unless those responsible for guiding social and

---

3. Gibson in Schneider (ed.) 1998, p. 100. This aspect of Italian social history has been exhaustively studied by Moe 2006.
4. Gramsci 1990, pp. 3–6.

economic policy made a concerted effort to bring the profiteering of private capitalist interests under democratic control.

Three years later, in a seminal essay entitled 'Workers and Peasants', Gramsci confronted the Southern question in its connections with the World War and with the new possibilities opened up to the proletariat and to the peasantry by the Russian Revolution. Here, we see plainly evident the enormous strides in confidence and conviction that he had made since his first somewhat tentative exploration of economic and social injustices in 'Oppressed and Oppressors'. No longer was he tempted even fleetingly to see suffering and inequality as ineluctable facts of the human condition. Now, with the support of his fellow editors, he felt ready and able to denounce the war as a horrific sacrifice of millions of lives that had 'equalised' only one thing: the deprivations and death experienced by the proletarian masses. But he glimpsed some positive outgrowths of the war, mainly one thing: that four years of trench warfare had strengthened ties of solidarity among men who had shed their blood together, a majority of whom were of peasant origin. This sense of solidarity, he observed, was one of the essential conditions of revolution.

The tone of Gramsci's writing in this article of 2 August 1919 is one of urgent immediacy that demanded an effort by his readers to envision something in Italy analogous to what had transpired in Russia. Perhaps for the first time with such vehemence, he made the following assertion:

> Factory workers and poor peasants are the two driving forces of the proletarian revolution.... They represent the backbone of the revolution, the iron battalions of the advancing proletarian army, which overturns obstacles by its sheer weight or lays siege to them with its human tides that demolish and corrode, through patient work and tireless sacrifice. For them, communism represents civilization: it stands for the system of historical conditions in which they will acquire a personality, a dignity, a culture, and through which they will become a spirit creating progress and beauty.[5]

People who know Gramsci only through the *Prison Notebooks* could be excused for having difficulty in recognising him as the author of such incandescent prose and the bearer of such fervent political enthusiasm. It's important to remember that the Gramsci who penned this article of 1919 was in a very different state of mind than that of the man who toiled away in prison ten years later on thoughts written *für ewig*, for posterity. Yet this difference is something that we need to think about. Is it so essential as to allow us to say that the author of 'Workers and Peasants' and the writer of the *Prison Notebooks* were virtually two different individuals, unrecognisable to each other and to us? Another way of putting this question is: does the political background against which Gramsci wrote this article of 1919, involving as it does events, ideas, and personalities that many

---

5. Gramsci 1990, Vol. I, p. 86.

feel have been thoroughly discredited in recent decades, mean that what Gramsci did and thought in response to them has lost all of its relevance to contemporary political debates and struggles? I think not, because Gramsci conducted his analysis of politics and culture in the notebooks in relation to what he had learned in the earlier years, which was that even defeat can serve the cause of revolutionary struggle, provided that the proper theoretical conclusions were drawn from it.

One of Gramsci's writings of 1923 on the Southern question calls for comment. It is a letter of 12 September that he sent from Vienna to his comrades in Rome explaining why he had chosen the name *L'Unità* for the new Communist Party of Italy newspaper.

The political orientation underlying the letter on *L'Unità* was somewhat different from the one that he had expounded from 1919 to 1922, inasmuch as the Italian Communists, after a fairly long period of dissent from the 'united front' policy pursued since 1921 by the Soviet Communist Party, had in 1923 come around to accepting the broader definition of unity given by the Comintern, which now favoured parliamentary and extra-parliamentary collaboration with non-communist labour and social-democratic groups.

With regard to the Party's policies concerning the future direction of Italian society, Gramsci made two proposals. One was to follow the decision made by the Enlarged Executive of the Comintern, on which he had served while in the Soviet Union in 1922 and 1923, to move resolutely toward 'a workers' and peasants' government, and to give a special importance to the Southern question'. This involved seeing the relations between workers and peasants in Italy not only as 'a problem of class relations, but also and especially as a territorial problem, that is, as one of the aspects of the national question'. His other proposal called for a workers' and peasants' government that in Italy would embrace the slogan of a 'federal republic of workers and peasants'.[6]

In using the term 'republic', Gramsci and his party were signalling their repudiation of the Italian monarchy, which had lent its support or acquiescence to the dictates of the Fascist régime, in power since October 1922. The word 'federal' in the Italian context meant looking at the relations among various regions and territories in terms of their relative autonomy within a unitary but decentralised state. This is why Gramsci spoke of the southern question here as a 'territorial' problem forming part of the Italian 'national question'. This historical framework is what gave Gramsci's proposals at this point their relevance not only to the immediate outcome of events in the 1920s and 1930s but also to the form and substance of the Italian Republic that was to emerge from World War II and the anti-fascist Resistance. In effect, Gramsci was talking implicitly about the need for a fundamental constitutional reform in Italy within the revolutionary framework of a struggle for socialism and democracy.

---

6. Gramsci 1978, Vol. II, pp. 161–3.

Gramsci on the 'Southern question' in 1926 and in the *Prison Notebooks*

Gramsci's speech[7] at the Third PCd'I congress in Lyons, France, in February 1926, written jointly with Palmiro Togliatti, was a kind of summing up of his own and his Party's positions since its founding in 1921, and an attempt to trace certain currents in Italian political history that had foreshadowed a radicalising turn in Italian politics after World War I. Speaking now as the Communist Party's general secretary, and doing so in an increasingly repressive and threatening atmosphere, he also tried to take the measure of other left-wing and anti-fascist parties, especially the Italian Socialist Party, whose deficiencies he subjected to close scrutiny. A noteworthy feature of the speech was Gramsci and Togliatti's assessment of the 'Italian social structure', in the course of which they carried out an acute class analysis designed to show how politics and class were enmeshed with each other in a now Fascist-dominated country.

In several sections of his address, Gramsci returned to the 'territorial' as well as class character of relations between industry and agriculture in Italy. It was in this context that he gave voice to his penchant for seeing a close analogy between the way colonial powers dominated their colonies and the kind of relationship that existed within certain nation-states, notably Italy, between ruling and subordinate classes and social groups. This is an important issue in the twenty-first century that lies at the centre of controversies where the conventional categories of relations between states have been applied to oppression based on racial, class, and gender differences. This theme comes up three times, in explicit terms, in the 1926 address.

Gramsci wanted to highlight what he called the 'semi-colonial relationship between Northern and Southern Italy'. In economic terms, he said, the South was a captive market and a source of cheap labour. Lenin's considerations in his *Theses on the National and Colonial Questions*, of 5 June 1920, and other writings on the same subject probably formed the theoretical substratum of some of what Gramsci had to say in his speech. Lenin had spoken of oppressed groups within countries, such as black people in the United States, as 'colonialised' peoples. The Russian leader had urged his fellow communists to reject 'bourgeois abstract and formal principles' and to make 'a precise appraisal of the specific historical situation, and primarily of economic conditions'.[8] Lenin had also stressed the political importance of 'backward states and nations characterised by feudal or patriarchal and patriarchal-peasant relations', of which Italy and Russia were prime examples. Lenin's analysis was in all likelihood present in Gramsci's mind when he, Gramsci, spoke of 'the toiling masses of the South' as being

---

7. Gramsci 1978, Vol. II, pp. 340–75.
8. Lenin 1975, p. 620.

in a position analogous to that of a colonial population. The big industry of the North fulfills the function vis-à-vis them of the capitalist metropoles. The big landowners and even the middle bourgeoisie of the South, for their part, take on the role of those categories in the colonies which ally themselves to the metropoles in order to keep the mass of working people subjugated. Economic exploitation and political oppression thus unite to make of the working people of the South a force continuously mobilised against the State.[9]

The work that is generally regarded as Gramsci's most significant analysis of the Italian southern question is an unfinished essay he wrote in October–November 1926, only a few weeks or possibly even a few days before his arrest and imprisonment on 8 November of that year. Entitled *Some Aspects of the Southern Question*, the essay was published in 1930 in the Paris-based Communist Party of Italy journal *Lo Stato Operaio*, so that its impact was much more direct on Italian anti-fascist organisations abroad than on the scattered anti-fascist forces in Italy.

The language Gramsci employed in this essay in recalling the work of the *L'Ordine Nuovo* group in 1919 and 1920, is more nuanced than that of the Party speech he made eight months earlier:

> [In 1919 and 1920] the Turin communists posed concretely the question of the 'hegemony of the proletariat': i.e. of the social basis of the proletarian dictatorship and of the workers' State. The proletariat can become the leading and the ruling class to the extent that it succeeds in creating a system of class alliances which allow it to mobilise the majority of the working population against capitalism and the bourgeois State. In Italy, in the real class relations which exist there, this means to the extent that it succeeds in gaining the consent of the broad peasant masses. But the peasant question is historically determined in Italy; it is not the 'peasant and agrarian question in general'. In Italy the peasant question, through the specific Italian tradition, and the specific development of Italian history, has taken two typical and particular forms – the Southern Question and that of the Vatican. Winning the majority of the peasant masses thus means, for the Italian proletariat, making these questions its own from the social point of view; understanding the class demands which they represent; incorporating these demands into its revolutionary transitional program; placing these demands among the objectives for which it struggles.[10]

This passage has a much stronger affinity with the dominant themes of the *Prison Notebooks* than do the other passages I cited above. In one of the few such instances in his pre-prison writings, Gramsci uses the word 'hegemony' not only to designate rule based on superior material and armed power but also in the sense of rule that wins

---

9. Gramsci 1978, p. 345.
10. Gramsci 1978, p. 443.

over the ideological consent of the ruled. Gramsci speaks here of the proletariat as 'the leading and ruling class' whose aim is to 'mobilise the majority of the working population against capitalism and the bourgeois state'. The distinctions made between 'leading' and 'ruling' in this sentence are the ones we associate with Gramsci's approach to politics in countries where groups struggling to change society in fundamental ways must win a 'leading' role before they can begin to envision themselves as potentially a 'ruling' class.

This dyadic conception rests on a foundation of sociologically complex concepts that are largely absent elsewhere from Gramsci's writings of these years. Also significant is his use of the phrase 'the majority of the working population', a more comprehensive formulation than 'the majority of the working class'. The words 'working population' refer to a far broader category of people than 'working class'. It embraces virtually all wage-earners, not just industrial and agricultural workers. Moreover, the class alliance of which Gramsci speaks would have to 'gain the consent of the broad peasant masses'. The conventional term 'consent' acquires a denser specific gravity here within the context of Gramscian social theory. Beyond all of this, we also see in the above-quoted passage the kind of historical consciousness that prefigures the many brilliant pages on Italian history in the notebooks. In sum, we begin to see in this passage the emergence of a strain of thought that will form the core of Gramsci's writing on cultural politics in the *Prison Notebooks*.

Some Aspects of the Southern Question is noteworthy in at least two ways. One is its historical perspective, which allowed Gramsci to place the strategy of his own Party in relation to that of other Italian groups and parties against a background of widely known events and personalities. He touches on the progressive proposals of Gaetano Salvemini, on the struggles of the Sardinian Action Party, and, in a surprisingly heartfelt tribute to the dynamic liberalism of Piero Gobetti, whom Gramsci had come to know in Turin in the early 1920s. Gramsci was able to recognise the contribution Gobetti had made to narrowing the ideological gap between left-wing and liberal intellectuals. He had done so, Gramsci believed, by putting his own intellectual powers and that of his collaborators at the disposal of the working class; not only in his writings for *La Rivoluzione Liberale* but concretely in regular exchanges of ideas and in shared struggles.

Gramsci's judgment of Gobetti was memorable because it was at once severely critical of a certain mindset prevalent among 'syndicalist' intellectuals and deeply appreciative of Gobetti's unique brand of liberal activism. The following passage illustrates these two sides of his remarks on Gobetti: What consequence did these contacts with the proletarian world have for Gobetti, Gramsci asked. His answer was that

> They were the source and stimulus for a conception which we have no wish to discuss or develop: a conception which is to a great extent related to syndicalism and the way of thinking of the intellectual syndicalists. In it, the principles of liberalism are projected from the level of individual phenomena to that of mass phenomena. The qualities of excellence and prestige in the lives of individuals are carried over into classes, conceived

almost as collective individualities. This contemplation and the noting down of merits and demerits, amounting to an odious and foolish position, as referees of contests or bestowers of prizes and punishments. In practice, Gobetti escaped this fate. He revealed himself to be an organiser of culture of extraordinary talents, and during this last period had a function which must be neither neglected nor underestimated by the workers. He dug a trench beyond which those groups of honourable, sincere intellectuals who in 1919–1920–1921 felt that the proletariat would be superior as a ruling class to the bourgeoisie did not retreat.[11]

The distinguishing trait of Gramsci's notes on the Southern question in the *Prison Notebooks* is that they are even more grounded in history than in *Some Aspects of the Southern Question*. Whatever Gramsci had to say in the notebooks about politics and society in connection with the Southern question was placed firmly in an historical context, in a much more pointed manner than in his pre-prison writings.

One example of this appears in Notebook 19, written in 1934–5, devoted to the Risorgimento. In these notes, we see that the many decades of debate in Italy around the presumed inferiority of Southerners compared with Northerners is not treated by Gramsci as merely a manifestation of racial or 'semi-colonial' prejudice, but rather is described as a phenomenon with precise political and economic causes and implications within the overall history of the Risorgimento. His aim in the notebooks was to point out how the Southern question formed part of a precise political strategy on the part of the government of Francesco Crispi, Italian prime minister during the 1880s and generally regarded as a man sincerely committed to democratic reformism. But Gramsci looked at the policies of the Crispi era with unblinkered eyes. For Gramsci, Crispi was the product of a mentality 'obsessed' by the idea of unity and prepared to sacrifice the particular needs of agriculture in the Italian South. Such an attitude, Gramsci believed, was

> Another element that serves to assess the real implications of the obsessively unitary policy of Crispi . . . The 'poverty' and backwardness of the South was historically 'inexplicable' to the popular masses of the North; they did not understand that Italian unification had not taken place on the basis of equality, but rather as the hegemony of the North over the South in the territorial relationship between town and country, that is, that the North was concretely a leech-like 'octopus' that enriched itself at the expense of the South and that its increasing economic-industrial strength was to be seen in direct relation to the impoverishment of the southern economy and agriculture.[12]

It is fair to say that Gramsci deepened the historical dimensions of his analysis in the notebooks, even in comparison with the essay *Some Aspects of the Southern Question*. The difference lies, I think, in the fact that in these notes, far from the din of daily political strife, and determined to expound ideas and insights that might stand the test of time in

---

11. Gramsci 1978, Vol. II, pp. 460–1.
12. Gramsci 1975, Vol. III, pp. 2021–2.

a way that his journalistic pieces and official writings could not, Gramsci was not aiming so much to clarify as to complicate the problems of interest to him. His writing in the notebooks – in a special way when dealing with Italian history – has something of the 'thickness' of which Clifford Geertz speaks in his discussion of the methods available to cultural anthropologists.

Gramsci and postcolonialism

Postcolonialism, as one offshoot of postmodernism, is a body of thought and practice that in the domains of social, cultural and literary theory has placed concepts such as hybridity, indeterminateness, and unpredictability at the forefront of its investigations. Underlying this turn away from traditional norms and certainties is a deep-seated belief that there can be no cohesive and secure correspondence between language and the realities that language seeks to describe or evoke. But the term postcolonialism also refers to the anti-imperialist cultural criticism produced by writers such as C.L.R. James, Edward Said, Gayatri Spivak, Sylvia Wynter, and Stuart Hall. None of these figures is an orthodox Marxist – far from it. Yet I would argue that they have all contributed decisively to the kind of social and cultural analysis that should inform a Marxist analysis of bourgeois society.

The theoretical and methodological innovations associated with postcolonial theory have been critically examined in brilliant fashion by E. San Juan, Jr.[13] But I want to raise a question about one aspect of San Juan's arguments, where he claims that the anti-Marxism of postcolonial theory ought to be attributed partly to Edward Said's eclecticism and his belief that American Left criticism was marginal, and his distorted if not wholly false understanding of Marxism based on doctrinaire anti-communism and the model of 'actually existing socialism' during the Cold War.

San Juan's critique of Said is the reverse side of his appreciation of Gramsci, whom he considers one of the foremost Marxist thinkers of the twentieth century who never yielded to the anti-materialist blandishments that seduced Said. In San Juan's view, Gramsci becomes almost an anti-Said, a corrective to Said's uncritical idealism, rather than a valuable source of some of Said's insights.

But if we look carefully at how Said uses Gramsci, it is clear, it seems to me, that he valorises several of Gramsci's key concepts, one especially, that 'ideas, cultures, and histories cannot seriously be understood or studied without their force, or more precisely their configurations of power, also being studied'.[14] What Said has to say in *Culture and Imperialism* about Gramsci's essay *Some Aspects of the Southern Question* gives no hint of diverging from a fundamentally historical-materialist reading of that work, provided that

---

13. See especially San Juan Jr. 1998.
14. Said 1979, p. 5.

we understand materialism in the way the mature Gramsci understood it, as referring not only to the processes of material production underlying the economic system of any society, but also to ideas, attitudes, beliefs, and in general the domains of discourse and subjectivity, which he regarded as constitutive facets of social life, not 'as some mere epiphenomenon of the economic infrastructure'.[15]

In sum, I would argue that Said's critique of bourgeois culture is rooted in a historical-materialist approach to literary and cultural studies that owes a great deal to Gramsci. For this reason, and if Said's *Orientalism* is one of the foundational texts of postcolonialism, then it is not unreasonable to conclude that Gramsci helped open the way for the most far-reaching and dynamic aspects of postcolonial thought.

---

15. Crehan 2002, p. 34.

Part Two

Gramsci's Prison Experience

Chapter Four
Antonio Gramsci's Letters from Prison

Gramsci's letters from prison were mainly a correspondence with two families, one in Sardinia, where he was born and grew up, the other in the Soviet Union, where his wife Julca Schucht, whom he had met in Moscow in 1922, his two sons, Delio and Giuliano, and other members of the Schucht family were living. His main correspondent was his sister-in-law, Tatiana (Tania) Schucht, who had been living in Rome since 1908 and remained in Italy throughout the years of his imprisonment in order to minister to his needs.[1]

Gramsci's dependence on Tania was not merely of a material nature. It was deeply emotional as well, in that she was his principal link to the outside world, and everything she said or did on his behalf, whether in direct written or spoken communication with him, or in interpreting his wishes on intellectual, familial, and legal matters, had an immediate impact on him. It was this necessary dependence on her, combined with the doubts and uncertainties that often afflicted him concerning his relationship with his wife Julca, that generated many of his reflections on the prison experience, some facets of which I explore in the first section of this essay.

The second section attempts to elucidate aspects of Gramsci's conception of life that emerge more strikingly from the letters than from anything else he wrote. I focus mainly on how he saw problems of education and religion, which he spoke about frequently in his correspondence with

---

1. At the time I wrote this essay in the 1980s, my main source for the letters was Caprioglio and Fubini 1965. Their work was superseded by my edition, Gramsci 1994, and by that of Santucci, Gramsci 1996. Quoted passages in this essay are taken from the 1994 English-language translation done by Raymond Rosenthal.

various family members and as part of his effort in prison to assess the experiences and relationships that had exerted a shaping influence on his life.

Gramsci's ordeal

Gramsci was arrested in Rome on 8 November 1926, during the climactic phase of Fascist government repression that deprived him and other anti-fascist deputies of their parliamentary mandate. After sixteen days in Regina Coeli prison in Rome and two months of police confinement on the island of Ustica, he was transferred to San Vittore prison in Milan. On 28 May 1928 he and a group of his Communist co-militants were tried by the Special Tribunal, which sentenced him on 4 June to twenty years, four months and five days in prison. Because of his medical problems, the most serious of which was chronic uremia, he was assigned to a prison for the physically infirm in Turi di Bari, in the Southern region of Puglia on the Adriatic coast.

As a result of repeated efforts by Tania and his friend Piero Sraffa, Gramsci was released from Turi on 19 November 1933, and transferred to a prison in Civitavecchia, then to a clinic in Formia, where he received medical attention but was kept under strict police surveillance. In October 1934, he was granted 'conditional freedom', but poor health prevented him from taking advantage of his new legal status. In August 1935, still under police surveillance, he was again transferred, this time to the Quisisana clinic in Rome, where he died of a cerebral haemorrhage on 27 April 1937.

The subject matter of Gramsci's prison letters was determined in some measure, of course, by the identity of his correspondents. When writing to his mother, for example, he was explicit about how he understood the events that led to his arrest and about the political and moral significance that he attributed to his status as a prisoner. Although highly intelligent and resourceful, his mother was not a politically sophisticated person; indeed, she apparently found it difficult to conceive of prison as anything but a terrible misfortune, a place of degradation where people were punished for sinful and unlawful acts. She never forgot her husband's imprisonment[2] and the mark of dishonour it had brought to her and to her family, and she knew very little about the struggles that, since 1912, had determined the character and purpose of Gramsci's life.

In his letters to Tania and to his wife, on the other hand, Gramsci had no need to explain the causes of his imprisonment. Julca and Tania were raised in a communist family, and were fully aware of the reasons why Gramsci was in prison. Their confidence in the justness of his political conduct was never at issue. Gramsci's feelings in relation to his wife and to a lesser extent his sister-in-law were extremely complex and personal in

---

2. In 1897, Gramsci's father Francesco was arrested and sentenced to five years, eight months and twenty-two days for 'embezzlement'. Giuseppe Fiori suggests that the charge and sentence were motivated by small-town political rivalries and that Francesco was guilty, if at all, of a minor administrative infraction. See Fiori 1977, pp. 13–16.

nature. Unlike his letters to his mother and siblings, his letters to his wife and to Tania are characterised by pangs of regret, by accusations and apologies, and above all by a haunting uncertainty, which generated the type of metaphorical language that he often used when he spoke to them of his 'imprisonment'.

The contrast between the two sets of letters is striking. In the eleventh month of his pretrial detention at San Vittore prison in Milan, he assured his mother that his life had always been 'ruled and directed by my convictions', and that because of this 'prison, too, was a possibility to be faced, if not as a light diversion, certainly as a de facto necessity that did not frighten me as an hypothesis and does not depress me as a real state of affairs'.[3] To his sister Teresina, he frankly asserted that his mother's attitude regarding his imprisonment worried him: 'There is a whole area of emotion and ways of thinking that forms a kind of abyss between us', he wrote in February 1928.

> For her my incarceration is a dreadful misfortune, somewhat mysterious in its concatenation of causes and effects; for me it is an episode in the political struggle that was being fought and will continue to be fought not only in Italy but throughout the world, and for who knows how much longer. I have been caught in it, just as during the war one could become a prisoner, knowing that this could happen and that even worse could happen.[4]

On one occasion, Gramsci drew from folklore (one of his mother's passions) to convey his message that being in prison had nothing to do with his 'rectitude' or 'conscience', with his innocence or guilt, but was simply a matter of political enmity. In a letter written to his mother but doubtless intended for everyone dear to him in his hometown of Ghilarza, he recalled the way children who wet their beds were cured of their habit in certain rural areas of Italy. Evidently, the prison censor did not grasp the connection he was trying to make, since he left these words as written:

> You know what is done to little children who pee in their beds, don't you? They are threatened that they will be burned with hemp flaming at the end of a pitchfork. Well: just imagine that in Italy there is a very big child who continually threatens to pee in the bed of this grand genetrix of oats and heroes; and I and a few others are the flaming hemp (or rag) that is waved about to threaten the impertinent one and prevent him from soiling the snow-white sheets. Since this is how things are, one must be neither alarmed nor harbor illusions; one must just wait with great patience and endurance.[5]

The misunderstandings that prevented Gramsci and his wife from achieving a genuine 'correspondence' in their letters, as he himself observed, was due to a fundamental incompatibility of temperament, which neither the fervent romantic passion of their

---

3. Gramsci 1994, Vol. I, p. 158.
4. Gramsci 1994, Vol. I, p. 177.
5. Gramsci 1994, Vol. I, pp. 102–3.

first years together, nor their two children, nor their common political ideals, nor Julca's love for Italy and good command of the Italian language could overcome. This difference of temperament, combined with Gramsci's growing sense of isolation in prison and Julca's attacks of depression and persistent fear of being overwhelmed by the burdens of work and motherhood, were among the elements of a psychological morass from which Gramsci strove in vain to free himself. As his physical condition deteriorated and Julca's emotional problems required frequent periods of rest and therapy, each frequently felt neglected and abandoned by the other. Tania tried, without much success, to mediate their differences and to interpret the feelings of each to the other.

Of the people who belonged to Gramsci's intimate world, Julca was among the least able to satisfy the demands of his personality and conception of life, at least during the years of his imprisonment. Perhaps the best word to describe the tone of her letters, not only those written to Gramsci in prison but others written many years earlier, when she was a teenager in Italy and was studying music, specialising in the violin, at the Accademia di Santa Cecilia in Rome, is 'crepuscular', because of its association with a group of Italian lyrical poets who, in the early twentieth century, wrote self-effacing, fragmentary, allusive poems that literally vibrated with the rhetoric of the anti-rhetorical. Gramsci craved concrete, detailed, discursive letters filled with narrative description and preferably accompanied by photographs of his children and other family members that would bring him into touch with their personalities as they changed through time. What he received from Julca, instead, with a few exceptions, were rather short letters characterised by ellipsis marks between each sentence, and brief, fragmentary, vague evocations of her feelings, vexations, problems in coping with daily life that could not help but leave him in a state of acute frustration. The infrequency of her letters also galled him. When she stopped writing regularly, he reacted at first with some anger, then with concern and fear mixed with 'uncertainty' that plagued him like a festering wound.

Those of Julca's letters that have been made available reveal a person of exquisite sensitivity who had strong feelings of love for her husband and children, and an ability to express her emotions, but not in ways that could satisfy Gramsci. She was a romantic soul, a dreamer and lover of nature in its soft and idyllic aspects, a tender and passionate woman whose formative years in Italy had been devoted to music and poetry but who in Russia, apart from her work as a violin teacher, was compelled to take on other types of jobs, such as office work, not at all suitable to her temperament. She lacked self-confidence, and was forever berating herself for real or imaginary deficiencies. Because of her feelings of inadequacy, she entrusted the job of daily care for her sons to her older sister Eugenia, whose dominating tendencies made her feel small and incompetent. In any case, her problems could not be solved by the type of approach suggested by Gramsci, which required disciplined self-analysis followed by a concerted plan of action, concrete goals, organised budgeting of time, and so forth. Moreover, although he did, before his imprisonment, express intimate feelings to Julca in a direct and uninhibited way, after he entered prison, because of a natural restraint induced by awareness that censors read every word he wrote, he almost never responded to her expressions of warmth and affection with words that could provide her with the gratification she needed.

If the following section of a letter from Julca, written on 26 December 1927 is typical of her communications, one can agree with Gramsci that they were vague and allusive, but certainly not that they were lacking in affection and a sense of closeness:

> Dear,
>
> Again I have let a lot of time go by without writing you ... An anxious period ... The little one has been very sick and the doctors thought that he was sicker than he was ... They supposed that he had diphtheria. Afterwards they denied it; it seems he had a so-called pseudo-croup (does such a word exist?)
>
> You won't think that I want to excuse myself for not having written to you? In this moment I feel more strongly the lack of a continuous contact ... I am unable to say what seems most important to me, what keeps my life in suspense ... Still, I don't feel further away from you as a result of these years of separation ... I always feel like your little girl.... Although you are changed, although I am changed.... Although you are disoriented/ Is that really true? Doesn't it seem to you that it would be enough to pass your hand over my forehead for us to really feel together? We have so many ties/Do you remember? You once said that it was important to create so many of them/ created by life itself that makes us dear to each other, that makes us secure, strong through each other.[6]

A hint of Julca's tendency to withdraw from the workaday world into the security and comfort of a rest home, a tendency that Gramsci deplored and never fully understood because it was the principal cause of his own pain, appears in two brief letters she sent to Tania, the first in August 1931, the second in August 1934. Both were written from a sanatorium in the Crimea. Her sensitivity to natural beauty, the joy she experienced in simple things, the note of self-effacement (which Gramsci thought masked an aggressive, angry side of her nature), her fondness for diminutives, in short, the 'crepuscular' tone typical of her writing from adolescence on, are all present in these short letters:

> Soci, August 1931
>
> Tanicinka,
>
> I write to you seated in front of the window, down below I see some flower-beds, the flower gardens, the sweet-smelling pea and the reseda; I also see some pine trees, an ash tree and some weeping willows. After finishing this letter I'll go for a stroll. A kiss to my dearest sister. Julca

---

6. These two letters and the two that follow below, together with some others written by Julca in her teenage years, are collected in Cambria 1976.

Soci, 18 August 1934

Tanichinka,

It's possible that I may not succeed in doing it too well, still I absolutely want to express today a few words of affection and intimacy to Tatiancinka and to the Daddy of our little Delio.

Dearest, in a few days I'll see our children and I want to transmit to them, as best I can, all your tenderness and your presents. I am sure of their joy. A hug and many kisses. Julca

During the first three to three and a half years of his imprisonment, in Milan and then in Turi, from 1927 to 1930, Gramsci tried to look upon prison as a laboratory that offered him a unique learning experience, provided that he maintained a certain 'ironic humour' and detachment from his surroundings, and an ability to observe himself and others in a variety of situations. Yet even during these years, there were moments of dismay, of isolation, of apathy, of fear that he was losing his grip on reality and being victimised by what he called 'the monstrous machine' of prison routines that destroyed all initiative and individuality. He relied more and more on his wife and Tania to keep him in touch with the outside world. To Julca he complained, as early as November 1928, that her allusive, fragmentary letters prevented him from grasping the concrete particularities of things, without which, he said, 'one cannot understand what is being generalised and universalised'.[7] His letters to Julca continued, however, to be extremely rich in intellectual content, full of vitality and humour, with only occasional lapses into pessimism and sadness, until May 1930, when for the first time he expressed a feeling that had evidently been gnawing at him for some time: the feeling that his wife was unwittingly increasing the sense of powerlessness that the Fascist Special Tribunal had originally imposed on him by sentencing him to twenty years of imprisonment. Gradually, as the months and years passed, and as his tolerance for frustration decreased, Gramsci began to think of his wife as virtually an unconscious accomplice of the state that was oppressing him. The Fascist state's aim was to isolate him, to render him impotent, to cut him off from society. Psychologically and spiritually, he felt that she was accomplishing the same end by not writing to him, by not keeping him regularly informed about her health and about his children, so that prison had become much more than a limitation on his physical freedom. In truth, he said, there were two prisons, the one that the state had erected in stone to segregate its undesirables from the rest of society, the other consisting of spiritual isolation imposed by the very people on whom he was most dependent for his sense of personal, intimate freedom.

Gramsci quickly learned that not knowing, that suspicion without proof, that uncertainty and a feeling of victimisation are inherent in the condition of the prisoner, and he blamed his wife for making this aspect of his incarceration much more painful and constant than was necessary. Moreover, he accused her of worsening his lot in prison by

---

7. Gramsci 1994, Vol. I, p. 233.

giving him the impression that she did not understand how really 'squalid and empty' his existence was, that somehow she had formed a false 'idyllic' picture of prison life, which hurt him more than the actuality of daily regimentation. Gramsci's feeling that his wife (and, in her own way, Tania, too) had caused him to be 'doubly imprisoned' became a persistent obsession. So deeply embedded in his psyche was his feeling that Julca and others who were equally 'well-intentioned' in his regard had contributed to his victimisation that as late as 16 June 1936, writing from the Quisisana clinic in Rome, almost three years after his release from Turi, he bluntly summed up all of the associations that had taken shape in his mind in the preceding six years.

The reason for his return to this theme did not hinge entirely on illusory fears. It had a realistic basis to it as well, now as in the past. In this particular moment, Julca's inability to decide to come to Italy and the vagueness of her letters had not only kept him in a state of anguished suspense but had also again made him feel the crushing weight of his segregation from the normal world of human intercourse:

> I don't want to write to you about myself; I think I'm suspended in midair and so any judgment of mine can only be false. My life does not rest in my hands; it rests in the hands of the police authorities first of all and then depends on many other circumstances. I would now like to tell you about a train of thought that used to come to me when I was in prison: I would try to answer the question: 'Who has sentenced me to prison, that is, to lead this particular life in this particular way'? The answer wasn't easy because, in reality, besides the principal force that determines the act in its complexity, there exist many other forces that consciously or unconsciously have a share in the concrete determination of one circumstance or another and that are at times felt more forcefully than the main act itself. In sum, I am trying to tell you that your uncertainty determines my uncertainty and that you must be strong and courageous to give me all the help you can, just as I would like to do for you and unfortunately cannot. I embrace you. Antonio.[8]

Gramsci wrote many letters to Tania on the subject of prison and the various levels and dimensions of meaning it had for him. His 231 letters to Tania constitute a graphic record of the physical and psychic pain he endured as a prisoner. All of the horrible details he spared his wife and others were poured into his letters to her. In them, we witness the drama of his tenacious effort to live against the onslaught of chronic uremia, which twice kept him bedridden for several months; two episodes of internal bleeding caused by tubercular lesions in the upper lobe of his right lung; Pott's disease; circulatory problems and hypertension; pyorrhea, which resulted in the loss of almost all of his teeth; disturbances in his digestive system and nausea that made food, or even the thought of food of any kind, distasteful; unexplained fever, which he charted with typical thoroughness, and reported to Tania; and, in the last phase of his imprisonment, culminating in the

---

8. Gramsci 1994, Vol. II, pp. 357–8.

atrocious suffering of 1933, fainting spells, chest pains, dizziness, and finally hallucinations that he also recorded afterwards on the basis of what the doctors and his prison-mates told him that he had said.

There were times when he would get some relief from one ailment, only to be afflicted by another. The only symptom that never seems to have left him in peace and that was aggravated by the prison guards at Turi, was insomnia. At night, the guards habitually pounded their truncheons on the cell doors, which resulted in acute sleep deprivation. There were nights when he never closed his eyes; two to three hours of sleep a night was the most he could expect, even with the help of sedatives that Tania sent to him.

He depended heavily on Tania to supplement the diet and medicines available to him in prison. Her affectionate and lively letters and occasional visits were welcome relief from the numbness and torpor induced by a regimented existence, every moment of which was governed by a code of regulations he placed in the same category as the Catholic catechism and the corporal's manual. But Tania's visits could also cause him discomfort, since she looked so much like Julca and, he suspected (again like Julca), tended to conceal from him everything she regarded as unpleasant and that might upset him. He did not want to be consoled, pitied or indulged, so her kindness sometimes left him more aggrieved and embittered than ever.

His successful efforts to obtain a cell for himself, to receive books, magazines, and newspapers, and, after February 1929, to write in his cell, were crucial to his survival in prison, but month after month of solitary intellectual activity sometimes made him feel detached from reality, irrelevant, alone on an island of pure ideas unrelated to the objective world. The censorship of his letters was a constant torment, to which he never accustomed himself. Rumours about amnesties and other legal matters affecting the lives of prisoners served to remind him of his dependence on the will of individuals for whom he was merely a pawn in an elaborate political strategy designed to consolidate the power of a hated régime. His relations with many of his fellow prisoners,[9] including those who shared his communist ideals, were often severely strained. The memoirs and letters of men who were with him at Turi for various periods of time speak of him admiringly, as a natural guide and teacher, but also describe political differences that made Gramsci decide finally to cut off all conversations with his comrades and seek the company of two or three men who leaned more to anarchist than to communist ideas.

There can be little doubt that it was to this break in communication with some of his fellow communist prisoners at Turi, and not only to problems in his relationship with his wife and loved ones, that Gramsci was alluding when, in a letter to Tania of 3 August 1931, he explained his state of mind as one of 'isolation' different in character from the isolation he himself had wanted and accepted in previous periods of his life. Now, he said, the isolation was occurring not, as before, because *he* had 'shifted his ground' in

---

9. See the relevant pages on Gramsci's troubled relations with his fellow prisoners in Fiori 1973 and in Quercioli (ed.) 1977.

any fundamental sense, but instead because others who supposedly shared his ideas had moved away from him, causing what appeared to be a permanent 'breaking of threads' linking him to his past life. In this same letter, he also spoke in a resigned manner of his sense that the 'world' of his emotional relationships had become used to the idea that he was in prison.[10]

These feelings and problems had at their core Gramsci's conviction that the only thing left to him after years of imprisonment was his 'will', and that even this precious component of his self was either being disregarded or completely forgotten by everyone who claimed to be acting on his behalf. Two months after arriving at Turi, he wrote the first in a series of angry letters to Tania that blamed her for making him feel 'doubly imprisoned'. By taking initiatives that affected his life, but without obtaining his explicit approval, she had unwittingly aligned herself with the prison authorities in that 'you too are beginning not to acknowledge that I have any will, to order my life however you see fit, without listening to my opinion, and I'm the one in prison, I know what it is, I have its painful marks on my skin'.[11]

What Gramsci thought was Tania's disrespect for his will and the resulting sense of powerlessness that this engendered in him was one aspect of that 'other prison' to which he referred in several letters. It hinged on the failures and lapses in communication with his wife, but it was mainly to Tania that he expressed his fears. The powerlessness of his condition as a prisoner was intensified by his suspicion that many important facets of the lives of those who were dearest to him were being kept from him. His suspicions were not entirely unfounded, although he himself was partially responsible for not understanding how sick his wife was. Despairingly, he asked Tania how he could be of some help if the silence of those on whom he relied for information kept him unaware, cut off, deprived of the power to act. On 19 May 1930, he wrote the following to Tania:

> I think that you have not given sufficient thought to my case and are unable to break it down into its various elements. I'm subject to various prison régimes: there is the prison régime constituted by the four walls, the bars on the window, the spy hole on the door etc. etc.; this had already been taken into account by me and as a subordinate probability, because the primary probability from 1921 to November 1926 was not prison but losing my life. What had not been included in my evaluation was the other prison, which is added to the first and is constituted by being cut off not only from social life but also from family life etc. etc.
>
> I could estimate the blows of my adversaries whom I was fighting, I could not foresee that blows would also come at me from other sides, from where I would least suspect them (metaphorical blows, of course), but the code also divides crimes into acts and omissions; that is, omissions too are faults or blows.[12]

---

10. Gramsci 1994, Vol. II, pp. 50–1.
11. Gramsci 1994, Vol. I, p. 221.
12. Gramsci 1994, Vol. I, p. 331.

Tania was sensitive to Gramsci's complaints, and did her best to consult him whenever possible on even minor matters that affected him. Nevertheless, she did on several occasions make important decisions without his approval if she felt that his life or Julca's peace of mind was at stake. For example, she agreed with his family in Sardinia not to tell him about his mother's death in late December 1932, fearing that the news would have a detrimental effect on his health. Eventually he probably found out about her death, but a letter that Gramsci wrote on 8 March 1934 was addressed to his mother.[13]

In May 1933, Tania also took it upon herself to set in motion procedures required to have Gramsci examined by a competent physician, which resulted in his transfer in November of that year from Turi to a clinic in Formia and, two years later, to Rome.

Another aspect of Gramsci's life in which Tania acted independently concerned his relationship with Julca. It was as a loving sister more than as a devoted helper to Gramsci that Tania wrote the following letter to him, on 18 January 1930, shortly after receiving from him a request that she tell Julca how abandoned and betrayed he felt by her long silences:

Dear,

You must not believe that I was unable to understand your state of mind, but since this is a matter of a really monstrous attitude on your part towards Julca, I did not think it at all opportune even to allude to this morbid state of yours, which is very understandable given the appearance of things, but which does not correspond to the reality of the facts because calculations of time that passes between the beginning of one of your letters to Julca and her answers, although possibly correct in a material sense, do not correspond to the time that has really elapsed between your missive and her answer. I would like you to reread that letter of hers in which she refers to the comfort she felt in having received a few lines from you that spoke of the children. This feeling of hers is sufficient to make her state of mind clear to you. If you are literally segregated from the world, Julca has been violently and pitilessly cut off from you completely. With respect to the kind of human ties that have been maintained since your imprisonment, her situation is infinitely worse than yours. You, dear, have your mother, your brother, me; she doesn't have anyone who can communicate the real sense of your existence to her, who can convey to her the meaning of your intimate link to each other, so that even a single allusion by you to the children you have borne was enough to give her a profound sense of comfort, the sensation of the reality of your bond, of your love.... Perhaps, it never occurred to you that spiritually Julca is without doubt in a situation of greater detachment from you than you are from her, in view of the fact that we can communicate with you while you are very limited in this sense.[14]

---

13. Gramsci 1994, Vol. II, pp. 343–4.
14. Gramsci 1994, Vol. I, p. 308. This and other letters that I cite from Tania and Julca to Gramsci were made available to me by Elsa Fubini.

Gramsci was often critical of Tania's and his wife's impulsiveness and emotionality, which he attributed to the excessively 'Genevan' or 'Rousseauian' education the Schuchts had given to their children. Yet Tania sometimes found it necessary to 'discipline' what she considered to be disordered and impulsive tendencies in Gramsci. There is no doubt that because of his physical suffering in Turi, from the summer of 1932 to his release from that prison in November 1933, he was not always capable of thinking rationally. No sooner had he lashed out at Tania or at one of his siblings than in the next letter he was apologising for his erratic and unfounded accusations. The physical pain he endured was too great, the effects of chronic insomnia too debilitating for him to be able to maintain his customary self-control. Something he said, an idea he proposed, might seem momentarily reasonable to him, but to Tania's educated sensibilities appeared self-destructive and fruitless.

The most dramatic clash between them during this period concerned Gramsci's wish that he expressed in a letter of 14 November 1932,[15] to give his wife freedom to dissolve their marriage. He told Tania that he had been thinking about it for a long time, and had come to the conclusion that the only fair thing to do in the circumstances was for Tania to act as an intermediary between husband and wife, and to interpret his wishes to Julca in such a way as to make the decision to end their marriage a mutual one. Gramsci did not want the decision to dissolve their marriage to be unilateral, and he hoped that Tania would find a way to introduce the idea to her sister in an acceptable manner. But Tania's will and intent in this matter were opposed to his. In categorically rejecting his request that she make his wishes known to Julca, she threw back to him the very words he had used in another letter, in which he had said that in reaching decisions that affect not only oneself but also someone else, especially someone dear, one must first carefully weigh all the implications and ramifications of that decision. She answered Gramsci's letter of 14 November on 11 December. After explaining that she had delayed responding to his 'infamous letter in question', out of fear that she might express herself with too much anger and vehemence, she said:

> And now I want to respond immediately to your explicit question as expressed in yours of 14 November, namely your request that I answer yes or no. Naturally, you have already understood that my answer can only be a 'No' of the most definitive kind. And I don't wish to accompany this 'No' of mine with anything except the last sentence of your letter sent on the 5th of this month: 'Good and affectionate intentions are not enough, much more is required before making a decision that doesn't only concern oneself: what is needed first of all is the explicit consent (and in the specific case I would say, the aspiration, the need, the necessity and similar impulses) of the interested party on whom will fall the *disastrous consequences that one cannot always foresee.*[16]

---

15. Gramsci 1994, Vol. II, pp. 228–30.
16. Gramsci 1994, Vol. II, p. 230.

The words between parentheses in this passage and the emphasis on the words 'disas-trous...foresee' were added by Tania.

Physical suffering, obsessive fears and insecurities, moments of alienation from friends, family, and comrades, were part of Gramsci's prison experience. Yet that experience can also be looked upon as a victorious struggle to maintain his integrity. No one was more important to him in the unfolding of this process than Tania Schucht. She was the crucial interlocutor who always listened sympathetically but critically to what Gramsci had to say, and whose dialogue with him contributed in so small measure to the subtlety and vitality of his letters from prison.

Prison reflections on family life, education, and religion

Many of the themes and lines of intellectual inquiry pursued by Gramsci in his prison letters intersect and overlap with those of the *Prison Notebooks*. But in the latter, Gramsci almost always developed his ideas in a predominantly objective manner; he avoids inter-posing personal experiences into his ruminations on education, philosophy, religion, politics, and history. The letters, on the other hand, are an important source for under-standing Gramsci ideas and feelings as they were shaped in the crucible of experience, of hard struggle, of complex interaction with family, friends, and comrades. In short, a salient feature of the letters is that they expound Gramsci's ideas in the context of sig-nificant personal experiences and relationships.

Gramsci was thirty-five years old when he entered prison, and as he looked back to pick up the threads of his life he frequently returned to his early years in Sardinia. One of his earliest memories was his brush with death at the age of four.

> The doctor had given me up for dead and until about 1914 my mother kept the small coffin and the special little outfit in which I was supposed to be buried; one of my aunts insisted that I had come back to life after she anointed my little feet with oil from a lamp dedicated to the Madonna and therefore whenever I refused to perform the religious observances she would reproach me bitterly, reminding me that I owed my life to the Madonna, something that didn't impress me much, to tell the truth.[17]

Gramsci's portrait of himself as a boy emphasises the adventurous and imaginative sides of his personality. Not at all discouraged by his diminutive size, he seized every chance he had not only to learn from reading, a passion which he shared with his sister Teresina, and later with his older brother Gennaro, but from direct contact with objects and ani-mals, with other children, and with the forces of nature. He assured Julca that as a boy he was not especially zealous in his studies, and from age seven to about twelve or thir-teen he was primarily 'an intrepid pioneer and explorer, a builder of boats and wagons',

---

17. Gramsci 1994, Vol. II, p. 65.

who knew naval terminology and dreamed of sailing the high seas but who was 'always prepared for being stranded on a desert island'.[18] He enjoyed running in the open fields, throwing stones into a nearby pond, or ruminating in his beloved Valle del Tirso, where he spent hours watching the fish jump out of a small lake formed by a partially dammed-up stream that flowed by the village church.

Notwithstanding his denials that he had early scholarly tendencies, it is evident that Gramsci was intellectually precocious. His readings included *Robinson Crusoe, Treasure Island*, Grimm's fairy tales, *Pinocchio*, and the adventure stories of Emilio Salgari, all of which stimulated his lifelong interest in literature for children of all ages. He speaks of his strong early bent for natural sciences and mathematics, and for classical languages, history and poetry. But many of his remembrances of school days are distinctly unpleasant. He was rebellious from the start of his career in formal education, and had little respect for most of his grammar school teachers, whom he found pompous and interested in teaching students how to memorise, not to think.

Among the most vibrant pages in the letters from prison are those in which Gramsci recalls his boyhood love for animal and plant life. At the age of six, he already displayed a talent for raising and training animals of all kinds. Not that he was motivated only by Franciscan sympathy for all creatures when he was a boy; lizards, eels and snakes were the victims of his hunting forays. But his more enduring enthusiasm was for animal pedagogy. In one letter to his elder son Delio, who at the time, in 1932, was busy in a science programme experimenting with the feeding of finches and various types of fish, Gramsci, after explaining how to seize a finch if it escapes from its cage, went on to tell his son that when he was a boy, he raised and trained all sorts of animals, among which were hawks, white owls, parrots, cuckoos, magpies, crows, cardinals, canaries, finches, larks, snakes, weasels, turtles, groundhogs and dogs. His favourite pet, he confessed in a deliciously funny letter, was an incorrigible mongrel dog: no matter how many times he scolded the mutt, it would turn over on its back and urinate on its belly, requiring endless washings.

Animal imagery enlivens many of his letters, and shows how closely connected Gramsci felt to the creaturely world. In this sense, the child was truly the father not only of the man but of the prose stylist. Like the Sicilian novelist Giovanni Verga, he made excellent use of the animal world for symbolic and psychological purposes. Animals figure prominently in almost all of the stories he enjoyed telling his children, many of which were based on real experiences, such as his story of an encounter with hares that 'danced' in the moonlight and a group of hedgehogs gathering apples. They are an indispensable part of Gramsci's way of depicting states of mind, relationships, moods and attitudes.

But there was also a deeply unhappy side to Gramsci's early years in Sardinia, which emerges just as vibrantly from his pen as does the expansive, adventurous part of his experience. From many of the letters that describe the bitterness and hardships of his

---

18. Gramsci 1994, Vol. I, p. 276.

boyhood, one can understand why he became a Sardinian 'nationalist' and 'autonomist', then a socialist and finally a Marxist revolutionary and founding member of the Communist Party of Italy. His resentments ran deep, his anger never entirely left him as a consequence of what he saw, felt, and experienced growing up on his native island. In part because of his physical deformity and natural desire to prove himself, but mainly because of the precipitous decline in his family's fortunes after his father's imprisonment, Gramsci began to work when he was still very young. At the age of 11, he began to contribute to his family's income. For ten hours a day, he moved huge bookkeeping registers from office to office, and went home at night 'to cry in secret' because of the pain he felt after each day's labour. This was one of the experiences that caused him to observe to Tania that 'I have almost always known the most brutal aspects of life and I've always more or less gotten by'.[19]

One senses from Gramsci's letters that, at bottom, it was the situation within his own family that most deeply offended his sense of justice, and that impelled him to search for the reasons underlying the common fate of so many other depressed and oppressed people. To his sister Grazietta he wrote, concerning his mother, that 'one of the bitterest things in my life, that has had such a profound effect in forming my character, was seeing how her existence never found a moment of respite, how her life was devoid of satisfactions and enduring peace'.[20] In this same letter, he wondered whether he or any of his siblings would have been strong enough to do what his mother had somehow succeeded in doing when they were young: 'to be alone, against a terrible storm and save seven children'. Certainly, he told Grazietta, 'her life has been exemplary to us in that she overcame difficulties that seemed insurmountable even to men of great fibre'.

Gramsci admired and strongly identified with his mother. Yet there were periods when the Gramsci home was permeated by an atmosphere of religiosity and superstition which, when combined with a lack of candour concerning his father's imprisonment and other matters that were considered taboo by his mother and adult relatives, stirred feelings of resentment and rebelliousness in him.

Gramsci describes himself in the letters as a person who struggled to reconcile two different sides of his worldview, which he synthesises metaphorically in the terms Renaissance and Reformation. The Renaissance stood for culture in its aesthetic and scientific manifestations, while the Reformation embodied the ineradicable moral content of human society. An excess of Renaissance culture could lead to various forms of corrupt and self-serving individualism, while moral rigour unaccompanied by the control of intellect and artistic refinement could engender fanaticism.

It is possible, on the basis of the letters alone, to grasp the nature of Gramsci's indebtedness to Karl Marx. He believed that Marx, more than any other European thinker, gave his disciples the tools with which to achieve a full integration of what was best in

---

19. Gramsci 1994, Vol. II, p. 215.
20. Gramsci 1994, Vol. II, p. 219.

Renaissance culture, with its stress on the development of man's aesthetic sensibilities and scientific proclivities, and in the Reformation, with its call for moral rigour and the primacy of individual conscience and consciousness. For Gramsci, Marxism established a proper relationship between subjective and objective factors in the historical process, factors that were interdependent and indissolubly connected to each other. Marxism, thought Gramsci, gave full value to the spiritual aspirations that in earlier times had been expressed primarily in religious and supernatural forms.

Gramsci's letters on Benedetto Croce[21] and on neo-Hegelian idealism in general reproduce in more synthetic form what he has to say on the subject in the *Prison Notebooks*. In the letters (as in the notebooks), Gramsci does not place himself in a purely oppositional stance towards Croce. He credits Croce with having 'surpassed metaphysics', with having, that is, overcome the transcendental, supernatural categories of thought characteristic of idealist philosophy up to and including Hegel. It was precisely this aspect of Croce's philosophy that Gramsci considered Italy's major contribution to modern secular humanism. He made this observation while recalling his literary studies at the University of Turin under the tutelage of his mentor, and then personal friend, Professor Umberto Cosmo. In 1912, when he took Cosmo's seminar on Italian literature, Gramsci felt that he shared with his teacher, as with many other contemporary Italian intellectuals, the conviction that

> we were participating wholly or in part in the movement of moral and intellectual reform initiated in Italy by Benedetto Croce, whose first point was this, that modern man can and must live without religion and that means without religion [whether] revealed or positive or mythological religion or whatever else you want to call it. This point seems to me even today the major contribution to world culture made by modern Italian intellectuals, I regard it as a civil achievement that must not be lost and so that somewhat apologetic tone displeased me and gave rise to that doubt.[22]

Gramsci had recently read several works by Cosmo that seemed to backtrack on the religious question, and to suggest that his former teacher had re-embraced the Catholic faith. He did not doubt the sincerity of Cosmo's beliefs, but he was 'displeased' by the possibility that he might have moved away from the rigorous historicism that Crocean philosophy had sought to inculcate into the modern generation of Italian intellectuals.

Having grown up in a milieu pervaded by religious sentiment and ritual, one of Gramsci's first intellectual struggles involved the need to come to terms with the religious question. He seems to have done so quite early, and definitively, even before adolescence. He never denied others the right to believe; he was not fanatical in reverse, against rather than in favour of religious faith. Yet on a conceptual level, as an exponent

---

21. Gramsci's most important letters on Croce and historical materialism span the months from March to June 1932.
22. Gramsci 1994, Vol. II, p. 56.

of Marxism and integral humanism, he insisted on the importance of interpreting the traditional categories of religious thought in realistic, materialist terms. He treated the subject gingerly, with affectionate respect, when writing to his mother, who was a believer throughout her life. But even in these letters he was explicit about his own view of supernaturalism. In an especially tender moment, he communicated the following thought to his mother, in recalling her 'beneficent' presence in the Gramsci home:

> If you think about it carefully all questions of the soul and of the immortality of the soul and of paradise and hell are basically only a way of seeing this simple fact: that each of our actions is transmitted to others in accordance with its value, both for good and for evil, it passes from father to son, from one generation to another in a perpetual movement. Since all the memories we have of you are of goodness and strength and you have given your strength to raise us, this means that since those early years you have already been in the only paradise that exists, which for a mother is, I think, the hearts of her own children.[23]

This passage expresses a conception of human interaction and responsibility that is more rigorous in its demands on the individual than the traditional Catholic view, in that Gramsci's morality does not seem to allow for the possibility of correcting past errors through repentance and forgiveness. Once an action is taken, once a relationship is made or broken, it has its impact on others directly or indirectly affected, and cannot be undone by rituals of confession and purification. His strictly human ethics and human morality places a heavier burden on the individual than the theocentric, transcendental religion of his mother. In a remarkable letter to Tania in July 1933, a week or so after he had recovered partially from the combined effects of insomnia, high fever and circulatory disturbances, Gramsci explained that his physical deterioration had affected his psychic state, and that he viewed his situation as precarious. He then went on to report that at the critical point of his illness, according to some people who were near him, 'in moments of delirium there was a certain lucidity in my rambling and disconnected thoughts':

> The lucidity consisted in this: that I was convinced I was dying and I tried to demonstrate the uselessness of religion and its inanity and that I was worried that, taking advantage of my weakness, the priest might make me perform or perform for me ceremonies that I found repugnant and from which I was unable to defend myself. It seems that throughout one whole night I spoke about the immortality of the soul in a realistic and historicist sense, that is, as a necessary survival of our useful and necessary actions and their becoming incorporated, beyond our will, with the universal historical process etc. There was a worker from Grosseto who listened to me, although he was dead tired, and who I think believed I was going mad, which was also the opinion of

---

23. Gramsci 1994, Vol. II, p. 40.

the prison guard on duty. However, the worker remembered all the main points of my tirade, points that I kept on repeating. Dearest, as you can see, the very fact that I have written you these things proves that I do feel a little better.[24]

In this letter, Gramsci applied his conception of human interaction not only to interpersonal relations but to a universal historical process that unfolds independently of the individual's will. Yet the idea of accountability is still very much present in this as in the other passage cited above. Gramsci was a moralist who believed that each individual must take full responsibility for his actions, and accept their consequences. It was this belief in individual responsibility towards oneself and others, and his feeling for the interplay of ideas and influences that forms part of all human intercourse that gave him his lifelong interest in education.

Problems of education were among the topics on which Gramsci's creative imagination was most constantly at work in prison. There were practical as well as general philosophical reasons for this. His two sons in the Soviet Union, and several nieces and nephews in Sardinia, were in elementary and grammar school during the years he was in prison, and thus Gramsci had a paternal and avuncular interest in what was happening in the classrooms of Soviet Russia and Fascist Italy. He recognised from the outset of his experience as a prisoner that prison itself could be transformed into a 'university' of sorts, provided that conditions were such as to allow convicts to read and study in their cells and to allow for some conversation among convicts with common intellectual and political interests. Whenever possible, Gramsci took part in educational enterprises in prison, first on the island of Ustica, then for a short while in Milan, and at brief intervals in Turi. But even without these practical motives, Gramsci would probably have devoted some of his letters to education, since it was a subject for which his background, training and temperament suited him.

The point of departure for considering one important facet of his philosophy of education is the third of Marx's Theses on Feuerbach, which points out the one-sidedness of a materialist doctrine that treats human beings as the products of circumstances and upbringing, and forgets in doing so that it is human beings who change circumstances and that the educator himself needs education. Marx believed that the only way to reconcile the notion of changing circumstances with an active, creative view of human history was to be found in the concept of 'revolutionising practice'. Gramsci seems to have integrated both aspects of the third Thesis into his own conception of the educational process as it takes place inside and outside the schoolroom. He felt in general that parents and school administrators of the previous two generations had relied much too heavily on the notion of 'instinctive' drives and 'natural' processes and that the basic function of the educator, which is to form and guide the growing person, had been all but forgotten. Growing up was not merely a matter of adapting to one's environment,

---

24. Gramsci 1994, Vol. II, p. 314.

but also of 'dominating and controlling it'. This control could not be left to mechanical or 'haphazard' influences. It could only be the outcome of a governing intelligence.

Gramsci regarded the pre-adolescent years as the most formative period in the moral and intellectual life of all human beings. It was during the years from age three or four to the onset of puberty that the fundamental work of education had to take place. The adolescent, if not 'formed' beforehand, would see all outside intervention, all shaping influences, no matter how well-intentioned, as 'hateful and tyrannical'. Adolescence was characteristically a time of rebellion, of alternating dependence on and rejection of authority, of complicated psychological and biological processes which could easily run riot unless constrained and channeled to constructive ends by habits of self-discipline inculcated in the pre-adolescent years. He felt that his brother Carlo and sister Teresina, who were in charge of the education of his niece Edmea, had not intervened actively enough in the formation of her character and had concentrated their attention instead on her acquisition of skills. Certainly, he said, Edmea was intelligent, quick-witted and 'naturally good', but he was more interested in her strength of will, love of discipline, capacity for sustained effort and constancy of purpose. But even her basic skills would suffer unless her teachers and other adults responsible for her development took care to be critical of written work and other types of assignments that were done in a routine, conventional fashion. One of Edmea's compositions had struck Gramsci as rather conventional, and he urged Carlo and Teresina to be persistent in encouraging the girl to strive for greater clarity of expression and a more distinctive style. In this instance, as in all other aspects of her education, Gramsci reminded Carlo and Teresina that 'it is the educator who needs to be educated'.

The Marxist origins of Gramsci's ideas on education are evident in his letters to his wife about their two sons. Unfortunately we do not have any of Julca's letters that deal in detail with her sons' education, so what Gramsci says to her in this regard must be taken as his interpretation of her thoughts, based on fragmentary impressions. His complaints were twofold. First, he felt that while in Soviet Russia, although theoretically convinced that in a new socialist society undergoing rapid change in many areas of life, parents and teachers were acting in their private spheres of activity as representatives of a vast collective enterprise, in practice Julca was still tied to what he called 'traditional habits of mind' rooted in 'spontaneist' and 'libertarian' conceptions of education. Intellectually, she knew that she had the duty to play a shaping role in her sons' lives, but in her daily conduct she continued to act as if no 'coercion' were necessary, that a permissive attitude was acceptable, that somehow the 'natural potential' of the boys' personalities would emerge without strong direction from her.

Gramsci's other objection to Julca's approach to education placed him in a critical position concerning what he judged to be a dominant practice in Soviet schools, a practice that Julca seemed to accept. On the one hand, he saw the Soviet state from an Aristotelian point of view, as a kind of educative agency, and as a Marxist, in that this socialist state – directed by the guiding intelligence of the Communist Party – was engaged in a collective effort to remake human society, to humanise humanity fully by ending the exploitative relations typical of capitalism and replacing them with associative relations. But when he began to look as closely as his few documentary sources and Julca's letters would allow at what was happening in Soviet education, he noted with some concern that in their zeal to turn all Soviet citizens into useful members of society, educators in the Soviet Union had ended up by 'accelerating artificially the professional orientation of young people and falsifying the inclinations of the children'.[25] Soviet youngsters, Gramsci thought, were being made into specialists much too early in their lives, with the result that they were losing sight of the purpose of school to the age of fourteen or fifteen, which was 'to lead children to a harmonious development of all their faculties, up to the point that the formed personality reveals its deepest and most permanent inclinations'. Here, Gramsci wrote as an Italian humanist as much as a Marxist. Indeed, he expressed the hope to Julca that the Soviet Union would one day be able to produce some Leonardo da Vincis.[26]

Another of Gramsci's concerns about his sons' education stemmed from his own experience as a boy with the forces of nature. Sometimes he got the impression from Julca's letters, and from his sons' short notes written in the 1930s, that they were being overprotected, not exposed enough to the earth, prevented from testing their powers in an uninhibited way. He was unhappy about a report he had read in an English magazine to the effect that Russian children were too 'clean'. He was relieved to hear from Julca that his sons enjoyed catching frogs, a skill in which he was an expert. He wanted to feel sure that they read exciting adventure stories, but even more importantly, that they were learning how to scale stones, build kites, catch lizards and frogs, identify wild flowers, seize birds, breed and train various animals, fashion useful objects from materials available in their immediate environment, and excel in at least several sports. He studied the photographs of his two sons that Julca and other members of his family sent to him from time to time with an eye to precisely this aspect of their personalities. Were they sensitive and alert to the world around them? Did they feel comfortable with themselves as physical beings? Did their faces reveal an expansive, optimistic outlook on life, or were they inclined to introversion and sullenness? These were the questions he repeatedly asked his wife, and tried to probe in his often hyper-critical letters to his sons. Inevitably, he was disappointed when the evidence he had turned out to be inadequate. He was equally curious about what was happening in educational theory and practice in Fascist Italy, and urged his relatives in Sardinia to send him information on curricula, programmes, legislation, anything that might help him understand what the new régime was trying to accomplish in its schools.

---

25. Some of what Gramsci said in his letters to Julca anticipates radical-Left criticism decades later of the constricting methods and technocratic emphasis of Soviet education.

26. Gramsci 1994. Vol. II, p. 195.

At the core of Gramsci's interest in education was his view of the dialectical nature of reality in all its aspects and manifestations. Just as the human race transforms itself in the process of transforming nature for human ends, so the individual child undergoes fundamental changes not only in his or her self-image but in his or her relationships to objects and to the world at large as a result of the educational process. In fact, he thought that if such changes did not occur, if new methods of teaching and learning did not result in arousing in young people a new way of conceiving nature and life, one could not speak of an authentically new mode of education, however ingenious the toys, games and pedagogical devices available in schools might be.

Gramsci's letters to his wife and to Tania, and several of Tania's letters to him, touch now and then on his attitude toward women. The fact that Gramsci was at times extremely harsh and judgmental in his letters to Tania, and sharply critical of his wife's lack of resoluteness, is not in itself, as some people have alleged, a sign of male pretentiousness. He was entitled, after all, to express disapproval of their behaviour if he was convinced that they were causing unnecessary difficulties either for themselves or for him.

But it is not the specifics of his complaints that is at issue, but rather his assumptions about what constituted worthy conduct and about the traits of character he deemed to be desirable in men, which he then automatically applied to women as well. His standards and criteria of judgment were conditioned by a male-oriented value system and by a male-dominated society. Only his mother seems to have lived up to his ideal of strength and resolute energy in her role as head of family. He was attracted to women such as Julca and Tania, who were more delicate in their sensibilities and more cultivated than his mother intellectually and aesthetically, and dreamier, more contemplative, more prone to introspection. But they were also inclined to procrastinate, and lacked what he regarded as true constancy of purpose. Their failure to live up to his expectations often made him furious.

On one occasion, he told Tania in a half serious manner that she seemed unable to envision his situation in prison. He did not expect her to grasp totally new things, he said, but rather that she build on what she already knew of prison in order to form a more or less realistic picture of his existence. But he found her inadequate on this score.

> You, like all women in general, have plenty of imagination and little fantasy, and what's more in you (as in women in general) imagination operates in only one direction, in the direction that I would say characterises (I can see you jump) ... that of societies for animal protection, vegetarians, nurses: women are lyrical (just to raise the tone) but they are not dramatic. They imagine the life of others (of their children too) only from the point of view of animal suffering, but they don't know how to recreate with their fantasy all of another person's life, as a whole, in all its aspects (mind you, I am observing, not judging, nor dare I draw consequences for the future; I describe what exists today.[27]

27. Gramsci 1994, Vol. I, p. 105.

A telling example of Gramsci's view of women occurs in his exchange of letters concerning their elder son's pleasure while looking at his image in the mirror. Julca tended to see this behaviour as childish narcissism, while Gramsci viewed it as an expression of a child's natural desire to know himself, to acquire a sense of his own being and identity as an autonomous person in his own right. Gramsci called his wife's attitude 'naïvely womanish, the quintessence of femininity'.

Whether Gramsci or Julca had the right interpretation of their son's behaviour is not the main point, here, but rather that Gramsci associated certain undesirable traits and tendencies with women, while particular virtues and strengths, even if possessed by some women, were essentially masculine. Tania's defence against Gramsci's reproaches and carping criticisms was either to ignore them or, if she felt personally offended, to acknowledge that she had her shortcomings, attributable to her upbringing and family background, but that these shortcomings had little if anything to do with what Gramsci assumed about her or Julca's motives and behaviour.

Tania was not a feminist in the contemporary sense of that term. She willingly conceded differences between the sexes, and tended to see her own personality as irrevocably shaped by forces over which she could not exert any effective control. But essentially she saw herself as an individual very different in many respects from Gramsci. What he was prone to dismiss as superfluous, she considered essential, what he regarded as a 'luxury', she regarded as a 'primordial necessity', as she said in one memorable letter. In sum, she felt that they had two entirely different ways of viewing the world. For Tania, it was not a question of right or wrong, but simply of different temperaments and different ways of responding to life. She was not at all convinced by Gramsci's doctrine of the ruling power of will and intellect. For both men and women, she believed, it was not thought, but feeling, that determines behaviour.

In her rather humble and self-effacing way, Tania stood her ground in her disputes with Gramsci. She reminded him that the role traditionally assigned to women, that of organising domestic life and attending to the basic needs of the family, was not of marginal importance to the destiny of the human race. Her own assistance to him, she implied, was of a type that women performed better than men because they were not so puffed up with their own importance as to believe that the satisfaction of creaturely needs was a function unworthy of serious and constant attention. She did not, however, pass beyond this line of defence to positions that would satisfy contemporary feminists. Her own self-definition was too restrictive for such leaps into the realm of unfettered liberty and equality. She saw herself, despite her own intellectual and professional accomplishments (she held a doctorate in natural science from the University of Rome) as primarily someone who ministered to the needs of others. In this sense, one can speak with justification of Tania as a woman cast in the classic sacrificial mold.

Gramsci understood the importance of women's struggle for liberation. He was one of the few Italian theatre critics to appreciate the significance of Nora's decision to leave her husband and children in Ibsen's *The Doll's House*. That he did not think as creatively on women's issues as he did in other areas of politics and culture is obvious. However, his failure to break away from the sexist prejudices of his time and place in history does not negate the exceptional political, moral, and philosophical value of his prison letters. They are testimony to the same qualities of thought and perception that make the *Prison Notebooks* a seminal work in the history of the revolutionary Marxism of the twentieth century.

Some comments on two foreign-language editions of the prison letters

The first Italian-language edition of Gramsci's prison letters appeared in 1947, an 'expurgated' version edited by two veteran Italian Communist leaders, Felice Platone and the then general secretary of the Party, Palmiro Togliatti. Their politically motivated editorial interventions, which included the deletion of sentences and even whole passages deemed likely to spoil the image of Gramsci as an unblemished paladin of Italian Communism, were later corrected when the more liberal and tolerant political atmosphere of the 1960s and 1970s made this first edition something of an embarrassment for the PCI. The 1965 volume *Lettere dal carcere* edited by Sergio Caprioglio and Elsa Fubini was the first Italian version free of censorship, and was notable for its philologically rigorous method.

As for the foreign-language editions, let me cite just two of the more than twenty that provide important insights into Gramsci's legacy. They are Gregorio Bermann's prologue to the Spanish translation (in Argentina) published in 1950, and Gerhard Roth's German edition of 1972.

Bermann's prologue to the Argentinian edition includes a shrewd judgment of Gramsci's complex personality. Of Gramsci the man as reflected in his letters, Bermann observed that 'this cold rationalist, this practical and concrete mind, this dispassionate observer, was at the same time endowed with a touching tenderness and delicacy of feeling'. Bermann was perceptive in his assessment of Gramsci's epistolary style. After noting Gramsci's avoidance of all 'intentional' pathos and heroic posturing, Bermann compared Gramsci's 'terse, sober, elegant' Italian with the occasionally 'lachrymose' prison letters written by Silvio Pellico in the 1820s, and, in a twentieth-century setting, with those of Lenin, Karl Liebknecht and Rosa Luxemburg. Bermann thought that the letters from prison written during World War I by Liebknecht and Luxemburg differed from those of Gramsci in that they were 'passionate, romantic, stirred by a vision of imminent freedom and of a vast field for action'.[28] After he was sentenced to twenty years, four months and five days of incarceration in June 1928, Gramsci had no such vision, and his reaction to prison censorship as well as his own instinctive restraint blocked whatever tendency he might have had to adopt an emotive, declamatory or 'passionately' romantic mode of expression. Bermann appreciated Gramsci's talent for narrative and for concise depiction

---

28. Bermann 1950, p. 11.

of character, as evidenced especially in the letters written during the early years of his imprisonment, when he was in relatively good health and still in a cheerful mood.

Translators who published their versions of Gramsci's letters after 1965 enjoyed the advantage of having at their disposal the 1965 Einaudi volume and of working in a political climate no longer as dominated by Stalinist rigidity on the one hand, and anti-communist hysteria on the other, as had been the period from the late 1940s to the mid-1960s. Gerhard Roth, the translator of the 1972 German edition, explained that the purpose of his translation of the letters was

> to awaken interest in the personality and work of the man who, next to Georgy Lukács, was the most important Marxist philosopher of the period between the two World Wars and who, at the same time, even if posthumously, had a decisive role in the process of liberating Marxism from the rigid forms of Stalinist orthodoxy.[29]

But, Roth quickly added, sympathy for the man Gramsci and admiration for his intellectual accomplishments did not justify a devotional attitude. After noting that, as seen in some of his letters, Gramsci could be insulting and unjust, hypercritical, and extremely demanding, Roth told his readers that 'with this selection of the letters from prison nothing is further from our purpose than that devotional legend of the inflexible martyr, firm Marxist-Leninist and faithful and concerned father, which up to now has been the most effective means of preventing a critical understanding of Gramsci'. Citing Giuseppe Tamburrano, in reference to some Gramsci studies in Italy, he said something that Gramsci himself would have applauded: 'The worst fate that a thinker can suffer is not to fall into oblivion. Worse than being forgotten is hagiography'.[30]

Roth recognised the value of Gramsci's letters as a 'gripping document' on a strictly personal and psychological level, but he also stressed his belief that for the uninitiated reader the letters constituted a more accessible introduction than the *Prison Notebooks* to certain aspects of Gramsci's philosophy and to some of the technical and intellectual problems connected with it. His selection thus favoured those of the letters which were most important for understanding Gramsci's philosophy, especially those which refer to his studies on history and the function of intellectuals and to his relationship with his most formidable intellectual adversary, Benedetto Croce.

Editors and translators such as Bermann and Roth played an indispensable part in making Gramsci known to critically minded people who had no need for hagiographical versions of his life and work, and who could recognise the unvarnished merits of a man who had given his life to the cause to which he was committed.

---

29. Roth 1972, p. 5.
30. Roth 1972, p. 6.

Chapter Five
Gramsci's Analysis of Canto X of Dante's *Inferno*

It was never Gramsci's intention to work out a theory of literary criticism, but he did on occasion have things to say about various literary texts that have important theoretical implications. One such occasion was his analysis of Canto X of Dante's *Inferno*.[1]

Gramsci's interest in Canto X spans a period of more than twenty years, from his student days at the University of Turin on the eve of World War I to the early 1930s, when he occupied a cell in the prison for the infirm and disabled in Turi di Bari and was composing the 2,848 manuscript pages that eventually comprised the *Prison Notebooks*.

Personal experiences, historical judgments, and a critical methodology based in large measure on Marxist premises flowed together in Gramsci's interpretation of Canto X. It hinged on the 'little discovery' to which he referred in a letter he sent from prison to his sister-in-law Tania Schucht on 26 August 1929,[2] where he spoke of an intimate, dialectical relationship between the doctrinal content and the poetic force of Canto X. As I will argue in the concluding section of this essay, what Gramsci had to say in this letter and in other scattered remarks can be read profitably in the larger context of his debate with the philosophy and aesthetics of Benedetto Croce and, more generally, with Italian idealist thought.

Gramsci's study of Dante exemplified his belief that it is necessary to situate literary works within the always complex and contradictory nature of historical reality. But for Gramsci

---

1. My references to the pages in the *Prison Notebooks* devoted to Canto X are taken from the section entitled 'Canto 10 of the Inferno' in Gramsci 1996. Vol. II, pp. 246–58.

2. Gramsci 1994, Vol. I, pp. 282–5.

the effort to understand an author and his work in historical perspective was not an exact science, a way of avoiding value judgments by taking refuge in the realm of positive data. Exactitude was the point of departure, not the point of arrival, of literary criticism, as far as Gramsci was concerned. He was convinced that critical readers needed all of their emotional resources as well as intellectual powers to deal adequately with dense, multi-dimensional works such as the *Divine Comedy*, which lived insofar as the reader was able to penetrate and to interact with the creative energy present in them. His models for criticism, in the Italian tradition at least, were Francesco De Sanctis and Renato Serra, who based their approach to literary materials on an all-important spontaneous and intuitive moment in the reading process. Gramsci followed their example. Erudition and 'science' were not enough. In reaction against what he felt to be the dry-as-dust academicism of much Dante scholarship, which made the *Divine Comedy* into 'a tower that was impenetrable to the uninitiated',[3] he tried to combine philological rigour and historical research with an emotional openness to the reading experience.

Gramsci as a reader of the *Divine Comedy* before his imprisonment

In his student days, Gramsci was an assiduous and responsive reader of the *Divine Comedy*, which he studied under the tutelage of Professor Umberto Cosmo at the University of Turin. During the period from World War I to his stay in the Soviet Union in 1922–3, he sometimes turned to the verses of Dante's epic poem for both enlightenment and consolation.

In a theatre review written in 1917, for example, Gramsci noted that meditation upon the love between Paolo and Francesca as depicted in Canto V of the *Inferno* could have a beneficial influence on modern readers and theatregoers assaulted by degraded forms of sexuality that 'completely ignored the spiritual force present in love in its highest form'.[4] On another equally grave matter involving the idea of 'faith', the young Gramsci also appears to have looked to Dante for guidance. One day several of his socialist comrades were struggling to formulate a definition of the word when Gramsci interrupted them by quoting from *Paradiso*, Canto XXIV: 'Faith is the foundation of things hoped for, and the evidence of things unseen; this to me is its essence'. This was a concept first enunciated by Saint Paul. But if translated into secular terms, it can also be read as a concise conceptualisation of the kind of faith that constituted the foundation, the 'essence', of Gramsci's political commitment to building a socialist society of the future.[5]

Young Gramsci found correspondences between his own feelings and ideas and those of Dante. Such a correspondence occurred during the early tempestuous phase of his

---

3. Gramsci 1980, p. 24.
4. Gramsci 1966, pp. 272–3.
5. The episode referred to here is recounted by Carlo Boccardo in Quercioli (ed.) 1977, pp. 39–40.

romance with the Russian woman who was to become his wife and the mother of his two sons, Julca Schucht. Two letters he wrote to Julca, one from Moscow in early 1923, the other from Rome on 6 October 1924, reveal that the famous verse in Canto V of *Inferno*, where Francesca da Rimini recalls her doomed love affair with Paolo Malatesta da Rimini, 'Love, which absolves/None who are loved from loving',[6] had formed the substance of long impassioned talks with Julca and that it had in some way helped him to cope with his lifelong fear that 'there was an absolute impossibility, almost a fatal impossibility, that I could be loved'.[7]

Hints of Gramsci's early interest in Canto X of the *Inferno* suggest that it stimulated him not only to ruminate on personal and philosophical matters but to undertake the first steps of what turned out to be a persistent search for insight into a key aspect of Dante's art. It is noteworthy also that, as in the case of *Inferno* V and *Paradiso* XXIV, Gramsci probed the psychological subtleties of *Inferno* X with someone who was close to him, a friend named Ezio Bartalini.

In 1916, while on leave in Turin from military duties, Ezio was introduced to Gramsci, and the two men immediately plunged into a discussion of Ezio's doctoral thesis, which concerned in part the character of Farinata degli Uberti in Canto X. Ezio's daughter Isa recalled that Gramsci and her father were both fascinated by the depiction of another character in Canto X, Cavalcante de' Cavalcanti, which they commented on many times together.[8] Cavalcante was important because of what and how he asked about his son Guido in Canto X. The poet Guido Cavalcanti was Dante's closest friend, and was still alive at the time Dante chose to set his poem, which was Easter of the year 1300.

Evidently, the talks with Bartalini stimulated Gramsci to look more deeply than he had thus far into the intricate interweaving of psychological and spiritual questions present in Canto X. In fact, it was during the years 1916–17 that Gramsci found the piece of evidence which, he believed, clinched the case for his contention that in Dante's art, doctrine was not at all extrinsic to poetry, but intimately and indissolubly bound up with it.[9] The piece of evidence in question was the precise date of Guido Cavalcanti's death, which he came across while reading Isidoro Del Lungo's study of Dino Compagni's early fourteenth-century work *Cronica fiorentina*. Gramsci did not at that time pursue all of the implications of this discovery, which I shall explain further on. He instead turned his attention to another aspect of the Canto in an article entitled 'The Blind Tiresias', which appeared in the column 'Under the great tower' (a reference to the Mole Antonelliana in Turin), in the Turin edition of *Avanti!* on 18 April 1918.[10]

But it was not until the prison years that he put the several pieces of his interpretation together into a relatively coherent form. I am going to argue later that this amalgamation

---

6. Alighieri 1954, p. 51.
7. Gramsci 1964, Vol. II, p. 23.
8. Ormea 1975, pp. 36–7.
9. Gramsci 1994, Vol. II, p. 140.
10. Gramsci 1960, pp. 392–3.

took place as a result, at least in part, of the conditions that Gramsci had to deal with in prison, which paralleled in a striking manner those depicted by Dante. What needs to be noted, here, is that Gramsci had a strong tendency to recall passages and episodes in literature that corresponded to or dramatised his own real life experiences. This tendency – as we shall see in the interpretation of Canto X that he developed while in prison – could also result in a counter movement from the lived experience to the literary work. Art could illuminate life, but experience could in its turn illuminate levels of meaning in art that study alone was unlikely to reveal.

Before proceeding to a summary of the points made by Gramsci in 'The Blind Tiresias', a brief synopsis of Canto X is in order. The scene is the sixth circle, the first of four that comprise the city of Dis in lower Hell. In this circle the founders and followers of heretical beliefs are punished; the heretics who occupy the centre of Dante's attention are the Epicureans, those 'who make the soul die with the body'. They, like all other heretics, are buried in open fiery tombs. As Dante passes by with his guide Virgil, one of the damned, Farinata degli Uberti, a leader of the Tuscan Ghibellines, calls out to him.

To Dante, the majesty of Farinata's bearing and his defiance of Hell are almost overpowering in their perverse integrity. After recognising each other as members of opposed factions, Farinata and Dante begin to discuss politics, but are interrupted by another shade, who rises from the same tomb. It is Cavalcante de' Cavalcanti, father of Guido, Dante's closest friend and fellow poet. Cavalcante inquires about his son, asking why, if poetic genius accounts for Dante's great journey, his son is not with him. Cavalcante mistakenly infers from Dante's momentary hesitation that Guido is dead, and falls back in despair into the flames. Farinata then resumes the speech he had begun before Cavalcante's appearance, and prophesies Dante's banishment from Florence. In answer to a question from Dante, he explains how it is that the damned can foresee the future but have no knowledge of the present. He also names others who share his fate in Hell. Dante takes his leave with a sense of respect for his proud enemy, pausing only long enough to ask Farinata to tell Cavalcante that his son is still alive.

In 'The Blind Tiresias', Gramsci attributes the popularity of Canto X, especially the part of the Canto that concerns the prescience of the damned coupled with their ignorance of the present, to the fact that it belonged to an 'enormous' historical experience according to which individuals endowed with exceptional powers, in particular the gift of prophecy, must be punished in various ways; often by blindness, as in the case of Tiresias, but also in other ways: by grievous loss of something or someone treasured, or by not being believed, like Cassandra. Whether consciously or not, Gramsci thought, Dante made use of this popular tradition, but he did not do so in the obvious manner, by imposing a literal blindness on his heretics of the sixth circle, but instead by depriving them of all knowledge of present occurrences on Earth. Just as in two recent episodes reported by Italian newspapers, in which children who predicted the end of the World War were said to have been immediately struck by blindness (episodes that Gramsci cites as examples of the way in which ordinary people perpetuate the great archetypal themes of popular poetry), so in the same way, but in a learned and highly refined form, 'Farinata and Cavalcante are punished for having wanted to see too far into the future, and thus, because they have moved outside the bounds of Catholic doctrine, they are punished by being deprived of all knowledge of the present. Gramsci then very briefly summarises a central point of the interpretation that he will later develop in prison, namely that Cavalcante, and not Farinata (who had previously customarily received the lion's share of the attention of critics and readers of Dante) is the character through whom Dante truly dramatises the plight and the suffering of the damned in the sixth circle. He alludes to the momentary agony of doubt, of uncertainty, through which the father Cavalcante must pass when he mistakenly thinks that his son Guido is dead.

Gramsci oscillates at this point of his analysis between intense emotion and critical detachment as he contemplates the 'atrocious destiny' of all those who must pay 'the ineluctable compensation that nature demands from its exceptions'. Cavalcante, says Gramsci,

> sees the future and in the future his son is dead; but in the present? Tormenting doubt, dreadful punishment in this doubt, an extremely profound drama that is concluded in a few words. But a *difficult* drama, a complicated one, that to be understood requires reflection and reasoning; one that is horrifying in its rapidity and intensity, but that emerges only after critical scrutiny. (Gramsci's emphasis)

Whether Gramsci was correct in attributing the punishment of Farinata and Cavalcante to their 'having wanted to see too far into the world beyond' is open to question. More plausible explanations for the heretics' prescience have been offered by various scholars. Sapegno proposes two possibilities:

> the condition that Farinata describes, of a knowledge limited to future things and incapable of perceiving them when they approach and become present, is, according to some scholars, shared by all the damned; according to others, it is characteristic of the Epicureans alone, with respect to whom it would acquire a more evident function of *contrappasso* (retaliation commensurate with the sin being punished), striking them in the essence of their sin, which was precisely to believe only in the present and to reject the sense of the eternal.[11]

The fact remains, however, that the relationship between knowledge of the future and ignorance of the present is of more crucial importance in Canto X than in any other Canto, so that, despite his probably erroneous explanation of why the heretics are punished in this manner, Gramsci's grasp of the intellectual and dramatic significance of Dante's art was sound.

---

11. Alighieri 1978, p. 118.

The article 'The Blind Tiresias' is noteworthy in three respects. It places Cavalcante de' Cavalcanti, and not Farinata degli Uberti, at the centre of the Canto's dramatic interest; it establishes a nexus between popular and learned poetry; and finally, the article affirms the importance of approaching literature through a process of reflection and analysis, and implies that Dante's work owes much of its poetic impact and beauty to a carefully wrought 'structure' of ideas and relationships that must be intellectually grasped in order for the full aesthetic value of the Canto to penetrate the reader.

Gramsci's interpretation of Canto X after his imprisonment

Gramsci resumed his study of Canto X in the latter part of 1928, at the prison of Turi di Bari, where he arrived on 19 July 1928 after a horrendous twelve-day train ride from Rome. But we should first note a passage in one of his letters from San Vittore prison in Milan written in February 1927, which again illustrates his tendency to move back and forth between life and literature in moments of especially intense experience, and also reveals the hold that Canto X had on his imagination.

In this letter, he described to his wife and to Tania two chance encounters he had had with a prisoner named Arturo, who was serving a life term for an undisclosed crime. Their first meeting took place in Naples, when Gramsci was struck by the man's fine elegant features and by his way of speaking precisely and clearly, with impressive self-confidence. The second took place when Gramsci caught a glimpse of Arturo in the prisoner registration room of the Ancona prison, and waved hello to him. He noted that Arturo was handcuffed, even though the path to his cell led through a protected internal courtyard. At this moment, the figure of Farinata flashed through Gramsci's mind, and he wrote the following:

> He was a different man from the one I had seen in Naples. Truly he made me think of Farinata: the hard, angular face, the sharp, cold eyes, his chest thrust forward, his whole body taut as a spring ready to uncoil. He shook his head two or three times, then disappeared, swallowed up by the prison walls.[12]

Gramsci had begun his own journey through the hell of prison life, and, like Dante, he could not help but engage in significant, even if brief, exchanges with some of the people that he met along the way.

In the Turi prison, Gramsci obtained permission to read and write in his cell in January 1929, and on 8 February of that year he began his first Notebook by listing sixteen subjects he intended to study in the coming years of imprisonment. The fifth of these sixteen subjects is entitled 'Cavalcante Cavalcanti: his position in the structure and in the art of the *Divine Comedy*'. Between February and August 1929, Gramsci must have com-

---

12. Gramsci 1973, p. 71.

pleted the process of combining into a relatively coherent whole the various fragments of his interpretation of the tenth Canto, but it is doubtful that he had yet put down any of his thoughts in his notebook. In any event, on 26 August 1929, in a letter to Tania,[13] after reminding her of his previous request that she send him a book on Canto X by Vincenzo Morello, he informed her that he had made 'a little discovery' that he believed was interesting and that 'would help to correct in part a thesis expressed in too absolute a fashion by Croce on the *Divine Comedy*'. He speaks in this letter of his intention to examine what other critics and scholars had had to say about Canto X, and then to put down his own little 'Dante comment' and perhaps send it to Tania. He did, in fact, send it to her, but not until two years later, on 20 September 1931, in a letter[14] that was actually written to his former professor, Umberto Cosmo, to whom Tania forwarded it with the request that he send her his opinion of Gramsci's interpretation as soon as possible. Cosmo sent his answer[15] instead to Gramsci's good friend, the economist Piero Sraffa, who sent it on to Tania. Gramsci finally received Cosmo's answer from Tania between late February and mid-March of 1932. Although Cosmo did not think that Gramsci had proven the inadequacy of Croce's thesis concerning the poetry and structure of the *Divine Comedy*, he did acknowledge the originality and acuity of Gramsci's interpretation, and praised especially his former student's interdisciplinary approach to literary texts.

Gramsci describes his 'little discovery' as one that 'strikes a vital blow at Croce's thesis on the poetry and the structure of the *Divine Comedy*'.[16] It hinged, he said, on two crucial elements: the exact determination by Isidoro Del Lungo of the date of Guido Cavalcanti's death, 29 August 1300, and the consequent illumination of Guido's father's plight in Hell (which is first depicted dramatically by Dante, in action, as Gramsci points out repeatedly) contained in Farinata's answer to Dante's request for clarification concerning the apparent future knowledge of the damned (as already demonstrated by the shade of Ciacco in Canto VI and by Farinata himself when he predicts Dante's exile) and their ignorance of events on earth 'when things draw near, or happen'.

Since the action of the *Divine Comedy* takes place in the early spring of 1300, Guido's death in late August of that year would lie within the span of time of events that 'draw near', and therefore his father Cavalcante is in that state of anguished uncertainty, of tormenting doubt, that, in Gramsci's interpretation, constitutes the dramatic lynchpin of the entire Canto, and exemplifies even more poignantly than the situation of Farinata the punishment inflicted on heretics in the sixth circle; through the figure of Cavalcante, Gramsci argues, we see this punishment experienced 'in an immediate and personal way'. Whereas Croce had completely missed this connection, and had read Farinata's 'doctrinal' speech as a 'break in coherence' and as incongruous for a character who first

---

13. Gramsci 1994, Vol. I, p. 284.

14. Gramsci 1994, Vol. II, pp. 73–7.

15. The complete text of Cosmo's letter is in Gramsci 1965, pp. 593–4, n. 1. On the relationship between Gramsci and Cosmo, see Gramsci 1965, pp. 411–14, 465–8, and 482.

16. Gramsci 1994, Vol. II, p. 75.

appears in the Canto as a proud, disdainful, formidable individual completely absorbed in his 'patriotic and political' thoughts',[17] Gramsci maintained that Farinata's explanation was not only an indispensable passage that allows the reader to grasp and to relive Cavalcante's torment, but was also the expression of a personal human exchange with Dante; for Dante, says Gramsci, does not ask Farinata to enlighten him only to gain doctrinal knowledge for its own sake. He does so because he has been moved and disoriented by Cavalcante's sudden disappearance, by the pain that he had seen on the man's face as he inquired about his son.

Gramsci concludes from the judgments and relationships just summarised that 'if one does not keep in mind the drama of Cavalcante in this circle, one cannot see the torment of the damned in action' [*in atto*]:

> the structure ought to have led to a more exact aesthetic evaluation of the canto ... The structural passage is not only structure, therefore, it is poetry, it is a necessary element of the drama that has unfolded. ... Without the structure there would be no poetry and therefore the structure too has poetic value.[18]

But Gramsci stood in opposition to Croce not only in his insistence on the interdependence and mutual reinforcement of the lyrical and conceptual components of Dante's poetry, but was anti-Crocean also in his determination to 'articulate the relationship between the artistic fact as such and the larger social and historical reality to which it corresponds', and 'to enlarge his critical focus' without, however, losing sight of the intrinsic and irreducible elements of poetry as an art form with its own inner laws and reason for being.[19]

The pages he devoted elsewhere in the notebooks to Dante the political thinker are illustrative of his dual commitment to historical contextualisation on the one hand, and on the other hand to analysis of the process through which historical reality is assimilated and transmuted by the poet's imagination. The pages on Dante the political thinker end, significantly, with an acute observation about Dante the poet.

As a political thinker and actor during one of the most tumultuous periods in Italian history, Dante appeared to Gramsci as 'truly a transitional figure', in that he stood at the forefront of a great movement of secular reform, but drew intellectual and moral sustenance from a system of belief that was expressed in a thoroughly 'medieval language:' On the one hand, Gramsci believed, Dante represented a current of thought that aimed to place severe limits on the power and authority of the Catholic Church, a current of thought that was to culminate in the anti-clerical political theory of Machiavelli. On the other hand, Dante's solution to the problem of relations between state and Church was cosmopolitan, universalistic, and 'utopian' and therefore out of touch with the deeper

17. Croce 1940, p. 66.
18. Gramsci 1996, Vol. II, p. 599.
19. Jameson 1971, pp. 331–2.

tendencies of political and social life in the fourteenth century, which were moving in the direction of the nation-state, not towards a resurrection of a new supra-national imperial order. Thus his political ideas, although inspired by lofty principles, had no 'subsequent development', at least in the world of practical political action.

In taking cognisance of these 'transitional' dilemmas and contradictory aspects of Dante's thought, Gramsci was characteristically sensitive to the way in which the Florentine poet's Ghibellinism was at once the product of his personal defeat after being caught up in his city's civil strife, and the creative force behind the new vision that, after his exile, was to become embodied in the verses of the *Divine Comedy*. It was at that crucial moment after exile, notes Gramsci, that Dante's 'political doctrine' assumed its 'utopian' aspect, which in turn was transformed into an incipient poetic and imaginative conception that will achieve its completion in the *Divine Comedy*, both in the structure – as a continuation of the attempt (now in verse) to organise his feelings into a doctrine – and in poetry as passionate invective and a living drama.

Thus in his notes on Dante the political thinker, Gramsci was able to extract from the crucible of the poet's lived experience some important insights into the origins and character of the *Divine Comedy*. He was able to see that the ideas which turned out to be unfruitful in a 'historical-cultural' sense could generate powerful emotions of the kind that, when combined with a personality and genius such as Dante possessed, produces great poetry. There is a subtle and barely perceptible movement in Gramsci's analysis of Dante the political thinker from history to thought to poetry, from experience to idea to creative expression.

A distinctive feature of the critical methodology Gramsci employed in his analysis of Canto X are the analogies he makes with three other art forms: drama, painting, and music. The main burden of his argument falls on the frequent analogies he makes between the poetry of Canto X and the techniques used by playwrights. For example, he compares the so-called 'doctrinal explanation' provided by Farinata with the stage directions given by playwrights whose purpose is to safeguard their own aims by controlling the tendency of both directors and actors to become 'arbitrary' in their interpretations of the playwright's work. The assumption underlying this analogy is that to a poet like Dante, whose intention was often 'dramatic' and not at all exclusively 'lyrical', doctrinal and structural features of his work were as important and integral to his total poetic conception as were stage directions to a playwright who has something definite to communicate to his audience and who strives to impose limits on those who are bringing his work to life on the stage.

Throughout the pages devoted to Canto X in the notebooks, and in the letter of 20 September 1931 to Tania, the word 'drama' and other theatrical terms are used over and over again to characterise Dante's art. When referring to Cavalcante's three anguished questions addressed to Dante, Gramsci calls them *battute* (the Italian word for the lines delivered by an actor). And when speaking of Dante's urgent plea to Farinata to tell

Cavalcante that his son is still alive, Gramsci calls this a kind of 'catharsis', thus appropriating a term traditionally applied to tragic theatre.

Gramsci's experience as theatre critic for the newspaper *Avanti!* from 1916 to 1920, and his enduring enthusiasm for stagecraft in all its forms and on all levels, is strongly in evidence in his reading of Canto X. Two of the judgments he expressed as drama critic in 1916, both of which concern Shakespeare, prefigure the reasons that stimulated his sustained interest in Canto X of the *Inferno*.

Speaking of *Hamlet*, Gramsci observed that this tragedy was a theatrical masterpiece because in it 'every word, every act, every character of the drama is saturated with poetry; there is nothing useless, nothing that can be disregarded, every small reference or hint, contributes to the catastrophe and is indispensable in order to justify it'.[20]

The same point of view, but expressed with a different emphasis, guided Gramsci in his review of Ruggero Ruggeri's portrayal of Macbeth, which Gramsci found far inferior to the character created by Shakespeare. In *Macbeth*, he noted, 'every word has a reason, every physical and spiritual attitude stems necessarily from a personality that has been conceived in that particular way and in no other'.[21] One might easily differ with Gramsci on the necessary fixity and definiteness of theatrical characters, but this possible weakness of his argument in 1916 is not important, here. What matters for our concerns is that Gramsci drew upon his felt experience as a theatre-goer and drama critic in order to identify features of Canto X that nobody before him had seen so clearly. As in *Hamlet* and *Macbeth*, so, too, in Canto X, no word, no action, no character is useless, no detail can be omitted, every physical and spiritual gesture has its importance in the overall economy of the work. Perhaps it was this aspect of Dante's achievement that made Gramsci think also of the creative process involved in musical composition, when he noted that the three gestures of negation that Farinata made in response to Dante interact contrapuntally with the three rapid phases of Cavalcante's torment: the look of horror on his face, the collapse of his body, and his disappearance into the tomb.

The analogy that Gramsci tries to establish with painting is linked to the way in which Dante represented the suffering of Cavalcante, which Luigi Russo called 'indirect representation', a phrase borrowed by Gramsci in his own analysis. Like Russo, Gramsci did not think that Dante 'renounced' anything, and that if he chose not to depict an emotion directly he did so not because he lacked the words for the depiction, but rather because he was convinced that the suggestion or indirect evocation of that emotion was more powerful than a direct representation of it. Thus, instead of describing in detail all the grimaces of Cavalcante's face as he misinterprets Dante's hesitation in answering his question about Guido, he has Cavalcante fall back into the tomb, never to be seen again.

---

20. Gramsci 1966, p. 231. The review is dated 20 February 1916.
21. Gramsci 1966, p. 244. The two reviews of *Macbeth* are dated 23 and 25 May 1916.

Drawing on various readings and memories of lectures in art history at the University of Turin, Gramsci mentions the often cited case of the painter Timanthes[22] who, according to Pliny, after demonstrating his ability to express human suffering in the faces of all the people who were about to witness the sacrifice of Iphigenia, chose to cover the face of Iphigenia's father Agamemnon with a cloak, since such elemental and unspeakable pain was better left hidden. Gramsci correctly cites the fresco at Pompeii, presumably derived from the original by Timanthes, that shows Agamemnon with his face covered moments before the sacrifice is consummated. But it is curious, and perhaps psychologically significant, that Gramsci cites another analogy with veiled suffering in painting that turns out to be incorrect: on four occasions in the text of his analysis he mentions the Pompeii fresco of Medea 'whose face is veiled as she kills the children she has had with Jason'. But the frescoes at Pompeii do not show Medea in the act of killing her children. In one, she is seated in a somber contemplative mood as she appears to lament her destiny as a mother; in another, she is standing near her children, with a rather vacant, expressionless stare. In neither of these frescoes is her face veiled.[23] Thus, although Gramsci characterises a mother's grief at the death of her children as 'pain in its most elementary and profound form', the example he gives in classical painting of a father's pain is the one that is historically accurate. This fact is one of several intriguing hints of an intermingling of life experience and critical-historical judgments in Gramsci's interpretation of Canto X.

Several aspects of Gramsci's public and private life are mirrored in the characters, situations and problems of Canto X. The plight of the damned in Canto X was Gramsci's own plight. Although his political experience, knowledge of history, and Marxist education gave him the ability to project a vision of the ideal 'city of the future', in the present, as a prisoner whose contacts with the outside world were extremely limited, he was powerless to act, shut off from knowledge that was crucial to understanding immediate reality. Moreover, like the fictional and historical characters recalled by Gramsci in his various writings on Canto X, his exceptional intellectual powers were enclosed in an infirm, misshapen body. It could be said that Nature had taken its revenge on Gramsci. In return for bestowing certain gifts on him in a lavish manner, he had to pay dearly with physical disability and with the loss of his freedom; still worse, with the loss of direct contact with those who were dearest to him, his wife and two sons. It does not seem unreasonable to suggest that Gramsci's focus on the centrality of Cavalcante, although already manifest in his reading of Canto X years earlier, was considerably sharpened by his prison experience.

---

22. Gramsci studied the history of medieval and modern art in 1912 under Professor Pietro Toesca at the University of Turin.

23. In the entry 'Medea' of the *Enciclopedia dell'arte antica*, pp. 950–7, it is said: 'In the mural painting of Pompeii, Medea is never depicted in the act itself of killing but rather in the spiritual struggle that precedes the crime'. The *Enciclopedia* has photos of the two frescoes to which I refer.

In two paragraphs of his reflections on Canto X, Gramsci is at pains to distinguish his own interpretation of Cavalcante's sorrow from the ones offered by Italian scholars who had insisted on the 'rational' and the 'political' motivations of Guido's father. Nothing of the kind, argued Gramsci. On the contrary, his suffering was solely that of an aggrieved and heart stricken father.

Three Gramsci scholars, Giansiro Ferrata, Sebastiano Aglianò, and Carlo Muscetta, have taken note of the parallels between Gramsci's personality and situation in prison, and the leading motifs of Canto X.[24] Alluding to the plight of Cavalcante and Farinata, who see the future but not the present, Ferrata observes that this unhappy condition might easily be applied to Gramsci, who was 'blamed' by some people for 'having been able to foretell at a distance the threat of a Fascist (or Fascist-like) régime in Italy, but for having failed to give sufficient credit to this threat when it was very close'. Aglianò and Muscetta also identified a basic aspect of the parallel when they conjectured that Gramsci's interpretation of Canto X may well have been 'connected from the very beginning with personal and psychological elements'.

Gramsci was a man of action whose career was at its apex at the moment of his arrest, 8 November 1926. At that time he was general secretary of the Communist Party of Italy, and a prominent, respected figure in the world Communist movement. To be deprived suddenly of the ability to intervene in political life and to have some influence over the course of events was, therefore, a harsh aspect of his existence as a prisoner, which troubled him more and more as the years passed and as he felt the ties that connected him to the practical world loosen and then fall away altogether.

Yet it would not be correct, in my opinion, to say that Gramsci's deepest suffering in prison was caused by his inability to be politically active. He was sustained by considerable confidence in the ultimate victory of the cause to which he had dedicated his life, and by a conviction that he had taken the only road open to him in view of his responsibilities as a Communist Party leader. His attitude towards his imprisonment was always one of stoical acceptance combined with proud, steadfast defiance of all the inducements periodically offered to him to curry favour with the Fascist government. He was a jealous guardian of his personal dignity and honour, and he felt only contempt for political prisoners who threw themselves at the mercy of the régimes that oppressed them. There was pain associated with his loss of political freedom, of course, but not torment, not the same kind of emotional turmoil and sense of powerlessness he experienced almost uninterruptedly as a result of his loss of regular contact with his loved ones. It was in this personal, this private realm of existence that Gramsci's ordeal reached its most excruciating levels of intensity. He made this clear to Tania in a letter of 25 January 1932 (which I also cite in Chapter Six):

---

24. Ferrata in Gramsci 1964, Vol. I, p. 104; Aglianò in his work of 1953, p. 9; and Muscetta in his work of 1953, pp. 109–19, especially pp. 115–16.

You still haven't well understood what the real psychology of an imprisoned person is. What causes one to suffer the most is the state of uncertainty, the indeterminateness of what is going to happen due to persons who are not prison guards, because this is added (but with a much different effect) to the condition of uncertainty and indeterminacy that is inherent in one's being incarcerated. After much suffering and many efforts at restraint, one becomes used to being an object without will and without subjectivity vis-à-vis the administrative machine that at any moment can ship you off in any direction, force you to change ingrained habits, etc. etc.; if to this machine and its irrational stops and starts you also add the irrational and chaotic activities of one's own relatives, the incarcerated man feels crushed and pulverised.[25]

It is difficult to say whether Gramsci suffered more in prison as a husband or as a father. In relation to both Julca and to his two sons, his anguish increased with the passing of the years. Yet with Julca he had memories and associations to hold on to, shared commitments, and a common desire to restore the bonds that had once linked their lives so closely. The pain of separation from his sons, on the other hand, was unrelieved by any feeling that he had given them something of himself, beyond the all too few months he had spent with his firstborn infant son Delio in 1924 and 1926. He never saw Giuliano, his younger son. Infrequent letters were a poor substitute for direct physical and emotional contact with his children. With his zest for teaching and strong need to have a shaping influence on his two sons, Gramsci probably felt the loss of contact with his two boys even more acutely than with his wife. He could rationalise his wife's long silences but there was no way he could rationalise the void he felt as a father, the yearning for closeness with his sons that he was destined never to have. A sentence from one of Tania's letters alludes touchingly to Gramsci's pain every time she mentioned his two sons to him during her visits at Turi. After asking him whether he liked several photos of his sons she had recently sent him, she wrote:

You know, I would like to remind you of your own words, of something you said when I was afraid to visit you at San Vittore prison, in the same way I was afraid to see Julca and Eugenia arrive in Rome, do you remember? Well, you wrote to me 'it is painful to see each other in prison, but it is worse never to see each other'. I have always noticed your pain whenever I told you something about your little boys, but isn't it better to talk about them than to keep silent?[26]

Letters such as this one, and many of Gramsci's own letters to and about his sons, suggest that he felt a stronger sense of identification with the paternal anguish of Cavalcante than with the proud defiance of Farinata.

But there *was* also a political as well as personal aspect to Gramsci's suffering. His letters from prison during the years 1928 to 1932 bear the imprint of a man who possessed

---

25. Gramsci 1994, Vol. II, p. 133.
26. This letter is dated 4 December 1928.

intelligence, broad experience, and clarity of vision that were rendered powerless by the circumstances of his immediate physical existence. Not only was he a prisoner; he was also gravely ill. Let us recall, here, what Gramsci said in 1918 of the blind Tiresias. Now, a little more than a decade later, in prison, he returned to the insights he had had in 1918 concerning the relationship between 'limpid clarity' of thought in Tiresias and his 'blindness' to everything that was immediately present. But in the paragraph of the *Prison Notebooks* which refers back to that article, two small but significant changes have been made by Gramsci. Instead of speaking of Tiresias's blindness alone as the price he paid for his gifts of prophecy, Gramsci adds the word 'infirmity' as the price demanded for such gifts, according to popular tradition, by 'the natural order of things'. Instead of characterising the sin committed by Cavalcante and Farinata as the desire to 'see into the beyond', beyond the grave, now, in prison, he writes simply of 'seeing the future'. The part of this paragraph of the *Notebooks* that concerns us here reads:

> In literary tradition and in folklore, the gift of foreknowledge is always connected with the present infirmity of the seer, who while he sees the future does not see the immediate present because he is blind.[27]

Clearly the wording of this paragraph bears more directly on Gramsci's own situation in prison than the article of 1918, while at the same time one could argue that the article of 1918 anticipates precisely the type of tragic dilemma in which Gramsci was to find himself a decade later.

Gramsci's contribution to Dante studies

Gramsci's analysis of the relationship between poetry and structure in the *Divine Comedy* demonstrated his ability to draw creatively from his predecessors while at the same time adding insights and clarifications of his own and stimulating others to begin a process of critical revision of long-accepted judgments. In this sense, he fulfilled one of the tasks he assigned to the engaged intellectual, which was to mediate between past and present, but also to move forward for the purpose of creating new values, of charting new pathways for the cultural advancement of society.

In the few but extraordinarily dense pages he devoted to his analysis of Canto X, and in letters that refer to his reading of Dante, Gramsci made clear that he drew primarily on three literary and philosophical sources: 1) the meticulous archival research of literary scholars belonging to the positivist school; 2) the Italian neo-idealist tradition; 3) Marxism, if understood as a philosophy based on a dialectical conception of life in all of its manifestations and not only in its specific applications to the study of art and literature.

---

27. Gramsci 1996, Vol. II, p. 256.

As already noted, Isidoro Del Lungo, who called Canto X 'one of the most humanly and historically dramatic cantos of the *Divine Comedy*',[28] provided Gramsci with the crucial piece of information, the date of Guido Cavalcanti's death, that first allowed him to grasp the inner structural relationship between Cavalcante's anguish as experienced *in atto* and the subsequent doctrinal explanation by Farinata in answer to Dante's question concerning knowledge of the future but not of the present. Another scholar formed in the heyday of positivism from whom Gramsci appears to have derived some assistance for his own analysis is Michele Barbi, whose position was that, despite the seminal work done by De Sanctis and Momigliano, there was still legitimate reason for 'the doubts and discrepancies' that exist in interpretations of certain features of Canto X.[29]

The Dante criticism that exerted a decisive influence on Gramsci's reading of the *Divine Comedy* was produced by the Italian neo-idealist school, whose first great exponent was Francesco De Sanctis. After De Sanctis, Benedetto Croce, in his dual role as teacher and adversary, and Luigi Russo, figured prominently in the development of Gramsci's critical perceptions, as did the German disciple and friend of Croce, Karl Vossler.

De Sanctis's 'militant criticism' is the predominant influence not only on Gramsci's reading of Canto X but on his general conception of the intimate link between history and literature, between lived experience and its distillation in poetic form, that underlies Gramsci's formulations on literary questions throughout the *Prison Notebooks*. It was De Sanctis who taught Gramsci that great works of literature such as the *Divine Comedy* orginated in and formed part of a general historical process, yet were also in some mysterious way independent of it, in that they possessed characteristics that made them appealing to sensitive readers in all ages. Under De Sanctis's influence, Gramsci could assimilate what was useful in Marxist philosophy for an understanding of art while holding fast to the belief that the timeless quality of certain works of the human imagination did not hinge on their creators' particular ideology. This quality lay, rather, in the intellectual coherence and in the emotional intensity with which the artist was able to give life to his personal vision of reality.

With specific regard to Canto X, De Sanctis's essay 'Il Farinata di Dante' was of capital importance to Gramsci.[30] For example, it was De Sanctis who recalled to Gramsci's mind the idea that excruciating pain such as that experienced by a parent at the death of a child had often been expressed in classical times, and was again expressed in Canto X by Dante, by not revealing the face of the sufferer. On this point, De Sanctis said:

> If you want to render sorrow sublime, cover Agamemnon's head with a veil before the sacrifice of Iphigenia, or have a man fall, like a dead body, and above all remove him

---

28. Del Lungo 1900. (Get page number)
29. Barbi 1924, p. 207.
30. The essay first appeared in 1865 but in its final form in De Sanctis 1872. The text I cite is De Sanctis 1969, pp. 100–26.

from my sight: the less I see the more I imagine. Of such a nature is the sudden collapse of Cavalcante, who disappears into his tomb after concluding that his son was dead.

The work by Croce that caused Gramsci to rethink the whole question of the relationship between the doctrinal and the poetic features of the *Divine Comedy* is *La poesia di Dante*, which appeared in 1920. Gramsci believed that Croce's notion of art as essentially lyrical and intuitive was difficult to refute unless one was able to apply an entirely different set of criteria not only to the study of art, but to human history in all its aspects. For Gramsci, these were to be found in Marxism, but needed to be refined and purified of their crudely positivistic and crudely materialist versions. In short, what was needed not only to read Dante properly, but also to interpret life in its perpetual movement was a dialectical approach to reality. Dialectics, as applied concretely to a work of art such as the *Divine Comedy*, held the solution to the problem of how, after the Crocean theory of aesthetics had imposed itself, to rebuild a conception of art that restored the unity of poetry and structure. As we have seen, Gramsci felt that he had made a small contribution to this process of restoration in his interpretation of Canto X.

Gramsci was indebted to others, but it can also be said that he stands in a pivotal position with respect to the history of Dante studies since the appearance in 1950 of *Letteratura e vita nazionale*. The names of literary scholars and critics whose reading of Dante, especially of Canto X, reflects Gramsci's influence are numerous. Among them are Sebastiano Aglianò, Bartolo Anglani, Rino Dal Sasso, Galvano Della Volpe, Guido Guglielmi, Armanda Guiducci, Francesco Mattarese, Rosso Morttano, Giorgio Padoan, Dario Rastelli, Mario Sansone, Natalino Sapegno, Simonetta Piccone Stella, Niksa Stipcevic, and Odoardo Strigelli.[31]

There is a division of opinion among these scholars, between those who agree with Stella and Della Volpe that Gramsci's analysis not only illustrates the distortions and incongruities imposed by the Crocean distinction between poetry and structure but also reclaims for art its rational and intellectual component, and those, like Sansone and Anglani, who credit Gramsci with provoking a crisis in the 'traditional criticism' of Dante, but who do not think that he added anything substantially new to what had already been said by Luigi Russo during the years 1927–9, and by Croce in his revised thought on the relations between poetry and structure in *La poesia* (1936).

Because of the abundance of Marxist literary studies in Italy since the end of World War II, it is easy to forget that Italian Marxist thinkers of earlier periods had not devoted serious attention to the place of art in the philosophy of dialectical materialism. Aesthetic questions were neglected by Antonio Labriola, and Croce, after a brief period of interest in Marxism in the 1890's, gave the study of aesthetics a radically anti-Marxist, anti-materialist direction that dominated the Italian literary scene for over four decades.

---

31. The reader will find these scholars and their writings on Gramsci and Canto X in the References.

In this historical context, Gramsci's solitary reflections on Canto X assume an importance that in other circumstances they might not have had.

Gramsci gave strong impetus to the revival of Marxist literary studies and cultural criticism after World War II. Even scholars who tend to regard his writings on literature as being of minor importance admit that those few pages on Canto X have had a powerful resonance. Bartolo Anglani identified the reason for this resonance when he referred to Gramsci's pages on Canto X as an example, a case study of the general reappraisal of the place of art in Marxist philosophy. Gramsci stimulated the production of critical work that, since the early 1950s, has been fruitful and vivifying. Giorgio Padoan made this point succinctly when he said that Gramsci's 'little discovery' concerning Canto X, together with some of his other scattered observations on literary questions in the *Prison Notebooks* and the *Letters from Prison*, was one of the main reasons for the 'crisis of traditional criticism in Italy',[32] by which he meant criticism that separates imagination from intellect, intuition from reflection, and 'poetic' values from their connections and interactions with an articulated or implicit configuration of ideas that inhere in the 'structure' of works of literary art.

---

32. Padoan 1959, pp. 12–39.

Chapter Six
Gramsci's Path from 'Ploughman' to 'Fertiliser' of History

My focus in this essay is on the changes that took place in Gramsci's mind concerning his role in revolutionary struggle when, after three years of work as Italian representative of the Communist International in Moscow and Vienna, deputy to the Italian parliament, and general secretary of the Communist Party of Italy from 1924 to 1926, he became a political prisoner subjected to that 'grinding attrition' of prison life whose ruinous effects he openly acknowledged.[1] That something changed in him in prison is certain; but we need to specify it, and to determine, as precisely as possible, whether and how this change affected the way in which he conceived the notion of political will and the relationship between political will and the struggle for a new socialist order.

I refer in the title of this essay to a passage in the *Prison Notebooks* where Gramsci employs images of the ploughman and of fertiliser to evoke the 'molecular change' that his personality had undergone in prison.[2] The pertinence of this passage to the psychological situation of Gramsci in prison seems clear: instead of being a 'ploughman' of history, a role he had played before his imprisonment, he was now acting as a 'fertilising' agent, a function to which, he says, he had adapted himself 'philosophically'. The passage is worth citing in its entirety. Referring presumably to his communist comrades with the pronoun 'they', Gramsci expressed himself in these terms:

1. Gramsci 1975, Vol. II, p. 1126. If the notebook from which quotes are taken has not yet appeared in English, I have cited the 1975 Italian edition with the relative volume number, as in this case.
2. Gramsci 1975, Vol. III, pp. 1762–4.

A dialogue. Something has changed, fundamentally. This is evident. What is it? Previously, they all wanted to be plowmen of history, to play the active parts, each one of them to play an active part. Nobody wanted to be the 'fertiliser' of history. But is it possible to plow without first manuring the land? So plowmen and fertiliser are both necessary. In the abstract, they all acknowledged this. But in practice? 'Fertiliser' here and 'fertiliser' there really meant [for many of us] to retreat, to return to darkness, to the ill-defined. Now something has changed, since there are those who adapt themselves 'philosophically' to being fertiliser, who know that is what they must be, and they adapt themselves to it. It is like the problem of the proverbial dying man. But there is a big difference, because at the point of death what is involved is a decisive act that lasts an instant; whereas in the case of fertiliser, the problem is a long-term one, and poses itself afresh at every moment. You only live once, as the saying goes; your own personality is irreplaceable. You are not faced abruptly with an instant's choice on which to gamble, a choice in which you have to evaluate the alternatives in a flash and cannot postpone your decision. Here, postponement is continual, and your decision has continually to be renewed. Therefore, it can be said that something has changed. It is not even a matter of living for one day as a lion or a hundred days as a sheep. You do not live like a lion even for a minute, anything but: you live like something less than a sheep for years and years and you know that you must live that way. The image of Prometheus who, instead of being attacked by the eagle, is devoured by parasites. The Jews were able to imagine Job: Only the Greeks could imagine Prometheus; but the Jews were more realistic, more pitiless, and they also endowed their hero with greater distinctiveness.[3]

It would be difficult to find a more appropriate metaphor than the one Gramsci used in this 'autobiographical note' to characterise his psychological situation and his choice of role during the ten years of his imprisonment. In this passage, Gramsci observes that 'Nobody wanted to be the fertiliser of history. But is it possible to plow without first fertilising the land?' Here we have a formulation that evokes the Gramscian theory of 'war of position' and of 'hegemony' which, from about 1930, he saw as a long and arduous task to be carried out *before* the triumph of socialism, not after.

In prison, Gramsci found two ways to make himself a 'fertilising' agent of revolution. One of these, from 1929 to 1935, was the extraordinarily rich intellectual diary he kept in his cell that became known after World War II as the *Prison Notebooks*. The other was in the lively but short-lived dialogues he initiated with some of his fellow communist prisoners. Aurelio Del Gobbo recalls that when Gramsci talked about Marxist theory, 'everyone listened to him and never interrupted him',[4] and Girolamo Li Causi states that 'the conversations with Gramsci were an inexhaustible source of intellectual and ideological enrichment'.[5] As an organiser and man of action, recalled Alfonso Leonetti, 'you

---

3. Gramsci 1975, Vol. II, p. 1128.
4. Mammucari and Miserocchi (eds.) 1979, p. 50.
5. Quercioli ed. 1977, p. 152.

learned from Gramsci how to throw yourself head long into the struggle, to change the world and bury capitalism'.[6] These testimonials are sufficient to suggest that, at least in the first two to three years of his imprisonment, up to the time when his views of social-ist revolution as a long-term political project alienated him from his comrades, Gramsci found ways to remain intellectually engaged in political struggle. But by 1930, something began to change in his attitude toward the outside world and toward himself as a person compelled to adapt his thinking to a whole new realm of being. To appreciate the nature of this change, a review of Gramsci's activities during the three years when he was a true 'ploughman' of history should be helpful.

Gramsci as leader of the Communist Party of Italy (1924–6)

On 14 August 1924, Gramsci was elected general secretary of the Communist Party of Italy, a responsibility that he fulfilled with unflagging devotion. Energetic, capable of explaining abstract ideas to his comrades, and above all politically and morally commit-ted to the struggle for socialism, Gramsci lived the period of about three years prior to his incarceration with exceptional fervour.

Even amidst the widespread demoralisation among anti-fascist groups in the mid-1920s, Gramsci never doubted the efficacy of Communist praxis in the face of the Fascist challenge. Though restrained by the 'pessimism of his intelligence', the 'optimism of his [political] will' never waned after he assumed leadership responsibilities in the PCd'I. It was an optimism reflected, for example, in the recollections of a young militant anti-fascist of that time, Renato Cigarini, who in 1924 was still wavering in his political choices. Of his meeting with Gramsci, Cigarini recalled that

> 1924 was in fact the moment of defeat of the Italian working class, the Chambers of Labour were being burned down, the leagues destroyed. I was opposed to those who had won and I was not an optimist, on the contrary I was more pessimistic than he; I thought that the struggle would be long and difficult. Gramsci convinced me: [he said to me] 'Because of all the risks and sacrifices you have faced, if you still want to go in that direction it is worth the trouble, but in the Communist Party you can find a place to fight better, with more effect and also with certainty about the future'.[7]

It would be wrong, of course, to conclude, on the basis of this and other similar episodes, that Gramsci did not suffer from doubts and anguish about the future in these years. But anyone who reads his writings from 1923 to 1926 must be struck by the tone of con-fidence and, if not of 'certainty about the future', of hope in the possibility of organiz-ing an opposition, headed by the Communists, able not only to overthrow the Fascist government but to obtain an effective hegemony over the other active political forces

---

6. Mammucari and Miserocchi (eds.) 1979, p. 56.
7. Quercioli (ed.) 1979, p. 139.

in 1924 and 1925. It was in this context that his concept of political will was transformed from a somewhat impulsive and generic voluntarism – which had been characteristic of Gramsci as a young socialist in Turin during and after World War I[8] – into a well thought-out conviction based, moreover, on his belief that he had the full support of the Third International, some of whose major figures he had come to know during his year-and-a-half stay in the Soviet Union from May 1922 to November 1923.

Gramsci experienced crises of loneliness, discouragement, and anguish during these three years, but these crises were overcome and integrated in a conception of militant struggle that he believed could deliver a mortal blow to the heart of the Fascist beast, provided – and this was the crucial condition of any and all political stances assumed by Gramsci as a leader and then head of his party – that there was the collective will to strike it in a coherent and decisive manner. It was necessary, he said, that passive resistance be transformed into active will, that analysis of the structural deficiencies of Fascism become a means to undermine and subvert the régime at its very foundations.

Gramsci's anti-fascist writings during these three years are marked by an exceptionally decisive tone. They exude a sense of confidence that the Fascist government could be toppled by the coordinated actions of a unified political opposition led by the Communist Party. In 1922, he had been won over to the Leninist-Trotskyist line of a united front against Fascist and capitalist reaction. This feeling of international solidarity allowed him to take a number of hard-line positions: his call for a general strike in the days following the Matteotti assassination on 10 June 1924, to which he subsequently added other demands: the disbanding of the Fascist militia, the resignation of the Fascist government, the establishment of a new political leadership for the country. The Italian Communist leader Camilla Ravera recalls that after the Matteotti assassination, Gramsci 'was convinced . . . that a popular movement that assumed responsibility for resolving the problem and with precise and realisable objectives might really have been able to free Italy from a régime that was effectively abhorred by so many people'.[9]

What existed in a pure state in Gramsci during these three years prior to his imprisonment was a revolutionary commitment that he wanted to join to a tightly disciplined and ideologically unitary praxis. In his communications from Vienna, where he was stationed in 1923 and early 1924, Gramsci insisted on 'the need for a tactical line that leads in the shortest time possible to an organic grouping of revolutionary elements around the Communist Party'.[10]

On 10 January 1924, again from Vienna, he declared himself convinced that 'the present situation is more favourable to the successful outcome of revolution than had been that of 1919-1920'.[11] The Party could no longer tolerate, he said in the early months of 1924,

---

8. Gramsci's early writings, such as 'The Revolution against *Capital*' of 24 December 1917, are often marked by a 'voluntaristic' point of view.

9. Quercioli (ed.) 1977, p. 167.

10. Gramsci 1992, p. 137.

11. Gramsci 1992, p. 172.

that a state of passivity and renunciation be allowed to determine 'the birth of political grouplets bent on splitting off and undermining revolutionary ideology'. Together with the word 'revolution', the words 'will' and 'hegemony' begin to appear in his writings of this period, words that will become key terms in the *Prison Notebooks*, but with the difference that will and hegemony were used by Gramsci from 1924 to 1926 as terms of a struggle whose outcome would be decided within a relatively short span of time. Even while acknowledging both the qualitative and the quantitative deficiencies of his Party, the perspective on time that governed his way of evaluating the political struggle before prison amounted to a matter of years, even of decades, but not of entire historical epochs. In a letter sent to his comrades in Rome from Vienna on 9 February 1924, Gramsci expressed himself in the following manner:

> It is a common opinion that a resumption of proletarian militancy can and must occur only to the benefit of our party. I believe however that in such a resumption our party will still be a minority, that the majority of the working class will go with the reformists and that the democratic liberal bourgeoisie will still have a lot to say. That the situation is actively revolutionary I do not doubt and therefore that within a limited span of time our party will have the majority with it; but if this period will perhaps not be long chronologically it will undoubtedly be dense with successive phases, which we will have to predict with a certain exactness in order to be able to maneuver and not to fall into errors that would prolong the experiences of the proletariat.[12]

One of the tasks of the PCd'I, Gramsci thought, was to attract to its ranks 'the overwhelming majority of the Milanese proletariat', without which 'we cannot win and maintain the revolution in all of Italy'.[13]

We should not give too much weight to such expressions of revolutionary optimism on Gramsci's part during these 'years of iron and fire', as he called them. He was certainly aware of the difficulties that impeded the realisation of a socialist order in Italy; he knew how difficult it would be to acquire decisive influence among the majority of the masses influenced by the Italian Socialist Party and began to formulate the ideas that would lead him, in prison, to the theory of 'war of position' – involving a prolonged ideological as well as political struggle by the proletariat against its class enemies – as a tactic appropriate to a period of long waiting and of patient and careful educational work. He saw all around himself a 'vast and terrible world' filled with threats and dangers. He shunted back and forth between hopes and disappointments, between moments when the reality of the socialist revolution in Russia led him to ask 'why should our country be excluded from this process of general renewal?'[14] and other moments when he saw before him only chaos and the unknown, a maelstrom without predictable outcomes.

---

12. Gramsci 1992, p. 236.
13. Ibid.
14. Gramsci 1992, p. 312.

However, notwithstanding these qualifications, it does not seem reasonable to deny that, during the years 1924 to 1926, above all in his official writings as head of the Communist Party of Italy, Gramsci was, both as theorist and as man of action, a loyal adherent to what he called a 'Leninist stabilisation' of Communist practice not only in Italy but throughout Europe. The theoretical and organisational standards that Gramsci applied to his own Party were the ones established by the Russian Communist leadership. The Communist Party, Gramsci wrote in a report of May 1925 (but published only in 1931)[15] must improve its organisation and raise the intellectual level of its members who 'will guide the revolution and administer the proletarian State'. The Party, he said, 'represents' the interests of the entire working class but 'carries out' the will of only a particular part of the masses, of the most advanced part, the proletariat, 'that wants to overthrow the existing régime with revolutionary means to found communism'. It struggles to unify the will of the masses in a socialist direction, and 'knows that it cannot have the bourgeoisie as an ally in this struggle that is precisely a struggle against the bourgeoisie'. It is a struggle on two fronts, against Fascism and against the 'Aventine secession',[16] [a struggle] that aims to crush reaction and to create a new State by establishing its dictatorship.

It is important to note that in his report on the Third Congress of the PCd'I held in Lyons from 20 to 26 January 1926,[17] Gramsci congratulated the majority of his Party for having placed itself squarely on the ground of the International and of Leninism, and praised his comrades who were working for a higher and higher level of 'homogeneity, cohesiveness and ideological stabilization'. Almost all the themes and the essential tone of this report echo the phraseology and the mentality of the Russian Bolsheviks of the 1920s, after the seizure of power by the group around Stalin.

The climate of expulsions and of intransigent boiler-plate formulations against which Gramsci protested in his letter of 15 October 1926 to the Central Committee of the Russian Communist Party was, for as long as he remained free, the same climate in which he agreed to function and because of which he rejected the platform of the right wing of the PCd'I, as can be seen at the end of his report on the Lyons Congress. The three unacceptable points in the position of the Right led by Angelo Tasca were, said Gramsci, the statement that the workers' and peasants' government can be established on the basis of the bourgeois parliament; that social democracy must not be regarded as the left wing of the bourgeoisie, but as the right wing of the proletariat; and that in the evaluation of the bourgeois state it was necessary to distinguish the function of a pressure group of

---

15. This report was not included in the English-language edition of Gramsci's writings in 1925. My source, therefore, is the Italian edition, Gramsci 1967, Vol. II, pp. 598–603.

16. 'The symbolic Aventine of 1924–6 was that part of the anti-fascist opposition which abandoned its parliamentary seats on 27 June 1924, in protest against the Fascist assassination of Giacomo Matteotti, leader of the Unitary Socialist Party'. The term 'Aventine' referred to an event of about 500 BC, 'when the Roman plebs withdrew to the Aventine hill as a sign of protest against the patriciate'. See Coppa (ed.) 1985, pp. 24–5.

17. See 'The Italian Situation and the Tasks of the PCI (Lyons Theses)' in Gramsci 1978, Vol. II, pp. 340–75.

one class on another from the economic function of producing commodities that meet certain general needs of the society. While the first and second of these elements were contrary to the decisions of the Third Congress, the third point, Gramsci said apodictically, was 'outside the Marxist conception of the State'.[18] Dogmatic assertions and rigid criteria of Communist action such as these, if not entirely absent from the prison writings of Gramsci, will effectively be transcended by him in prison, and not only for obvious reasons of censorship and of political caution.

Gramsci in prison

There is an organic connection between the prison experience of Gramsci, which began on 8 November 1926 and ended at his death on 27 April 1937, and the different way – different, that is, from the positions he took from 1923 to 1926 – he conceptualised the theme of political will in relation to his perspective on the struggle for socialism.

This does not mean that Gramsci disavowed all of the ideas that he had tenaciously defended in the pre-prison years. It is not difficult to find in his pre-prison writings prefigurations of ideas that will have a more articulated and comprehensive development in the prison notebooks and letters. But the distinctively reflective character of the prison notes stands out clearly if compared with the certainties, the unshakeable convictions, the powerful assertions that appear in the writings cited above. Despite acute physical and spiritual pain in prison, Gramsci maintained the integrity of his personality up to his death, but, at the same time – and this can seem paradoxical – the 'grinding attrition' of prison life, above all after he became prisoner #7047 in Turi, in July of 1928, set off in him a transformative psychological process that contributed to forming the new foundations of his political thought in prison.

I think that Valentino Gerratana was correct when he pointed out that, after the failure of the factory council movement in the early 1920s, and after 'the unhappy outcome of the new initiative [taken by the Communist Party of Italy] from 1924 to 1926 to counteract the involutional tendencies of the Italian political situation', Gramsci made a concerted effort in prison to rethink the terms of the struggle for socialism in a moment of dispersion and pulverisation of the workers' movement.[19] This is a sound judgment, but it does not suffice to fully explain the reasons for Gramsci's rethinking. We should remember that prisoner #7047 had been the general secretary of the Communist Party of Italy, a deputy to the Italian parliament, a respected journalist feared by many, and a delegate to the Communist International. Suddenly, all of these avenues of political action were no longer available to him; his space was reduced to the dimensions of his cell and the prison courtyard; time was now measured in accordance with a routine

---

18. Gramsci 1967, Vol. II, p. 663.
19. Santucci (ed.) 1987, p. 233.

entirely imposed on him, as on all prisoners, but perhaps in a more painful manner on him, inasmuch as his life up to then had been almost wholly devoted, at the cost of enormous sacrifices, to a struggle that now seemed ill-fated and remote.

Most people who are knowledgeable about Gramsci are familiar with the words with which he tried to explain to Tania Schucht the mentality typical of the prisoner, but it is worth citing them again in order to highlight the difference of perspective between his life before and after imprisonment:

> I am obsessed (this is a phenomenon typical of people in jail, I think) by this idea: that I should do something *für ewig*, following a complex concept of Goethe's that as I remember tormented our Pascoli a great deal. In short, in keeping with a set program, I would like to concentrate intensely and systematically on some subject that would absorb and provide a centre to my inner life.[20]

This fragment of a letter written from San Vittore prison in Milan on 19 March 1927 contains many of the elements of Gramsci's intimate life as a political prisoner: the often obsessive nature of his thought processes, his effort to understand his situation as an imprisoned man, his preoccupation with material time as seen against the notion of the eternal, his identification with kindred souls across space and time (Goethe and Pascoli), and finally his need to regulate his inner life according to a coherent plan of study. We see emerging here an aspect of Gramsci's personality that had only rarely expressed itself in the world of active politics; an aspect whose core principle transcended the normal positive limits of time as measured by a man of action. Indeed, this same letter should be read together with those of 14 January and 9 February 1929, where Gramsci revealed a new conception of writing: no longer was it primarily a means of militant journalistic commentary, but had now become his 'greatest aspiration' and the means with which he would redeem his loss of freedom.[21]

In prison, deprived of any immediate opportunity to influence the course of human affairs, Gramsci's sense of time became, paradoxically, both more intimate and subjective, yet at the same time more oriented to distant horizons. Explaining to Tania why 'every book, especially if it is a history book, can be useful to read', he observed that even 'in any small unimportant book one can find something useful... especially if one is in our situation and time cannot be measured with the normal yardstick'.[22] In a letter to his wife of 20 May 1929, after alluding to his suffering in the first two years of his imprisonment because of delays in correspondence and the lack of answers to the questions that he had asked, Gramsci added these words of clarification concerning his present state of mind:

---

20. Gramsci 1994, Vol. I, p. 83. For a perceptive analysis of the expression *für ewig* as used by Gramsci, see Francese 2009.
21. Gramsci 1994, Vol. I, pp. 241, 245–6.
22. Gramsci 1994, Vol. I, p. 263.

> Then time passed and the perspective of the prior period moved further away; every-
> thing that was accidental, transitory, in the realm of emotions and of will gradually
> vanished and only the essential and permanent reasons of life remained.[23]

This is, it seems to me, the sense in which Gramsci, as a historicist, used the Goethean phrase *für ewig*, meaning literally forever, for all time, but that probably designated something closer to 'in the long term, or far in the future'.

In a memorable letter to his sister Teresina, which I also cited in Chapter Four, Gramsci spoke of the difficulty that he had experienced in explaining his political and moral convictions to his mother:

> There is a whole realm of emotion and ways of thinking that forms a kind of abyss
> between us. For her my incarceration is a dreadful misfortune, somewhat mysterious in
> its concatenation of causes and effects; for me it is an episode in the political struggle
> that was being fought and that will continue to be fought not only in Italy but through-
> out the world, and for who knows how much longer.[24]

Three and a half years later, on 24 August 1931, in a letter to his mother, Gramsci made a distinction between 'the immediate struggle' in which he was, of course, a loser, and, implicitly, the struggle in the long term, which extended vaguely towards the far-off future but which held some promise for ultimate vindication:

> I never speak [to you] of the negative aspect of my life, first of all because I do not want
> to be pitied; I was a soldier who had no luck in the immediate struggle, and combatants
> cannot and must not be pitied if they have fought not because they were forced to do
> so but because that's what they consciously set out to do.[25]

It is not that Gramsci renounced in prison the idea of political will and political and moral energy aimed at a revolutionary end; what changed in him, as has been said several times, was his perspective on the means and the forms of struggle applicable in an epoch dominated by anti-socialist reaction. He was in search of a new equilibrium between the impulses of the will and the goals to be reached, an equilibrium and a *raison d'être* that did not depend on rapid and decisive interventions but rather on more far-reaching, more objective analysis, to be carried out on the ideological, cultural, and philosophical fronts as well as organizational and political, in any event conceived differently from those advocated up to 1926.

In a letter of 2 November 1931, Gramsci referred to a summation of his speech at the Lyons Congress, insisting, in relation to the accusations against him at the trial before the Fascist Special Tribunal in 1928, that in that speech he had 'peremptorily' stated that in Italy

---

23. Gramsci 1994, Vol. I, pp. 265–6.
24. Gramsci 1994, Vol. I, p. 177.
25. Gramsci 1994, Vol. II, p. 58.

'the work to be done was that of 'political organisation' and not 'insurrectional attempts'.[26] Nevertheless, despite this denial of 'insurrectional' aims, what Gramsci called for in that speech was a shift of emphasis, not a true change of course by the PCd'I and not even a definitive renunciation of armed conflict. His point of view and mindset from 1931 to 1936 stands in sharp contrast with the 'peremptory', militant and aggressive tone of voice he used in that Lyons speech, when Gramsci felt himself supported by the Comintern, and believed in the possibility of a collapse or overthrow of Fascism that might be close at hand.

There is another aspect of Gramsci's state of mind in prison that should be noted before looking briefly at several passages of the *Notebooks*. I am again referring to the question of will, which is problematised by Gramsci in prison in a radical manner. At times, he had the feeling that he was without impulses of volition of any kind, that he was sinking deeper and deeper into a realm of the ocean depths where there was an 'absolute immobility' and where 'even the most formidable storms no longer make themselves felt'.[27] But more often, he used a clearer and more explicit language, because for him will was a fundamental faculty of the human personality and a key concept underlying his vision of the political and moral worlds. To be virtually deprived of it, to find himself powerless in the face of initiatives taken by his loved ones that he had not approved beforehand was unspeakably painful, an insuperable obstacle which, in my view, contributed to modifying his conception of the relationship between subjective will and objective circumstances. Here is an example of his way of formulating the problem of the will in his prison letters, written to Tania on 25 January 1932 (a letter which I cite also in 'Gramsci's analysis of Canto X'):

> You still haven't well understood what the real psychology of an imprisoned person is. What causes one to suffer the most is the state of uncertainty, the indeterminateness of what is going to happen due to persons who are not prison guards, because this is added (but with a much different effect) to the condition of uncertainty and indeterminacy that is inherent in one's being incarcerated. After much suffering and many efforts at restraint, one becomes used to being an object without will and without subjectivity vis-à-vis the administrative machine that at any moment can ship you off in any direction, force you to change ingrained habits, etc., etc., so if to this machine and its irrational stops and starts you also add the irrational and chaotic activities of one's relatives, the incarcerated man feels crushed and pulverised.[28]

In the *Notebooks*, and in his conversations and 'lessons' with his comrades in prison, which have been gathered into two useful volumes for the reconstruction of his prison

---

26. Gramsci 1994, Vol. II, pp. 96–7.
27. Gramsci 1994, Vol. I, p. 229.
28. Gramsci 1994, Vol. II, p. 133.

experiences,[29] Gramsci remained faithful to several basic facets of his vision of the world, but they are expressed in a much more nuanced language than in the past and integrated into an analysis of the prospects for socialism that takes into account the new political realities on a global scale. His criticism of the Italian Socialist Party and of the parties of the Aventine secession, remained what it had always been, which Gramsci encapsulated in the parable of the beaver who, 'pursued by hunters who want his testicles for the extraction of medicinal substances, tears off his own testicles to save his life'.[30] As in the past, he insisted on the discipline, the rigour and the united will of the Party. But then, in the midst of reflections and observations of this type, Gramsci added a note whose nucleus of thought is articulated with greater boldness and clarity than in the past:

> The scholastic and academic historico-political conception: the only authentic and worthy movement is one that is one hundred percent conscious and that, furthermore, is governed by a preestablished, minutely detailed plan or (and this amounts to the same thing) corresponds to abstract theory. But reality is teeming with the most bizarre coincidences, and it is the theoritician's task to find in this bizarreness new evidence for his theory, to 'translate' the elements of historical life into theoretical language, but not vice versa, making reality conform to an abstract scheme. Reality will never conform to an abstract scheme, and therefore this conception is nothing but an expression of passivity. (Leonardo knew how to discover number in all the manifestations of cosmic life, even when the eyes of the ignorant saw only chance and disorder.)[31]

We are at the opposite pole, here, from the form of determinism and the trust in objective 'laws of development' that were supposed to be inherent in the historical process of capitalism transforming itself into world socialism. When Gramsci said that it was necessary to adapt theory to events and not events to theory, he was taking a position implicitly opposed to a tendency of the orthodox Marxist Left of the Third International, which did not like formulations of this kind.

This conception of reality that gives ample space to 'the most bizarre coincidences' should be placed next to the notion of predictability that predominates in the *Notebooks*, a notion that, in accord with Gramsci's non-reductive philosophy of historical materialism, allows for only the most general predictions, such as the inevitability of class conflicts, but never of the outcome and results of these conflicts.

The question of the predictability of historical events is examined by Gramsci under the general category of 'concept of science' that, in its positivistic forms, is one of the main targets of his cultural and political criticism. Note 15 of Notebook 11 on the *Popular [Sociological] Essay* by Nikolai Bukharin contains the essence of Gramsci's argument in this regard; the vision of history implicit in it must not be separated from the new

---

29. Quercioli (ed.) 1977, and Mammucari and Miserocchi (eds.) 1979.
30. Gramsci 1996, Vol. II, p. 40.
31. Gramsci 1996, Vol. II, p. 52.

problematic of the will and from concerns about time mentioned above. Here, we are inserted into a discourse in which the sense of the unknown and the unpredictable that appears so often in the prison letters occupies a very important place. Moreover, we are looking in this discourse at a conception of history for which 'the concrete moments' of reality 'cannot help but be the results of contrasting forces in continuous movement, [which are] not reducible to fixed quantities, because in them quantity continuously becomes quality'.[32]

This statement leads a little further on in the pages dealing with Bukharin's work to two other judgments that seem to me to be anything but orthodox if read in the context of the new 'scientific' dogmatism that accompanied the involutional drift in the Soviet Union in the early 1930s, and consequently within the Communist Parties faithful to the Comintern. First of all, Gramsci establishes a series of requirements for science, or better for the individual scientist, that basically form part of a methodology that I would call 'open' and 'liberal' in the sense of being free of a priori judgments and dogmatic presuppositions. One can say, Gramsci writes, that someone is not a scientist who

> demonstrates little command of his particular criteria, who does not have full understanding of the concepts he is employing, who has little information and understanding of the preceding state of the questions involved, who is not very cautious in his statements, who does not move forward in a logical but rather in an arbitrary and disconnected way, who does not take into account the gaps that exist in the knowledge that has been acquired but omits mentioning them and rests content with purely verbal solutions or connections instead of declaring that what is at issue are provisional positions that can be taken up again and developed at a later date etc. (Each one of these points can be developed, with suitable examples.)[33]

The criticism levelled by Gramsci against a mentality uncritically tied to a positivistic form of scientism coincided with his new emphasis in his prison notes and letters on the theme of socialist revolution (and of political will) understood as part of a historical process and not as events that happen once and for all. The temporal perspective implicit in the theory of war of position led him then to the proposal – the famous (or infamous, depending on one's point of view) 'sock in the eye' – of a Constituent Assembly to replace the theory advanced by the Comintern in the early 1930s of an immediate thrust for power, without intermediate attempts at collaboration and coalition with other antifascist groups and parties.

Most of Gramsci's fellow communist prisoners in Turi adhered to the Comintern position of the early 1930s, that the time was ripe for a decisive seizure of power by Communist Parties loyal to the Third International. The rift resulting from this controversy led to the expulsion or isolation of thousands of Communists who were now deemed to

---

32. Gramsci 1975, Vol. II, p. 1403.
33. Gramsci 1975, Vol. II, pp. 1404–5.

be incorrigibly deviationist. It was one of the issues that divided the Russian party into irreconcilable factions, leading to the exile of Leon Trotsky and the subsequent founding of the Fourth International. Although not friendly to some of the tenets of Trotskyism, Gramsci was in agreement with Trotsky concerning the urgent need of the Communist Left to band together with class and political allies to defend itself against right-wing fanaticism in Italy, Germany, and elsewhere.

Two novel features of Gramsci's thought in prison are his emphasis on the international situation facing the socialist forces, which emerges in the oft-quoted pages of the *Notebooks* on the 'relations of force' that need to be taken into account in developing an effective policy for the communist movement, and the concurrent development of his theory of hegemony, in relation to which his ideas concerning the role of intellectuals acquires great importance. It is not possible here to discuss these and other innovations of Gramsci's thought in prison; I will limit myself to a few of the arguments he developed from 1928 to the early 1930s, as reported by his Party and prison comrades.

As a framework for these references, Anne Showstack Sassoon has illuminating things to say about Gramsci's politics in prison, especially in relation to the theory of war of position, namely that this theory represents a deepening and an enrichment of a theme that had remained only lightly sketched prior to Gramsci's imprisonment. Sassoon argues that 'it is a false dichotomy to identify the war of movement with an offensive struggle and the war of position with a defensive one'. The two wars are not 'two separate moments' but part of 'a single dialectical process'.[34] What is involved, here, is a change of historical perspective that conditioned Gramsci's thought, not an absolute and permanent repudiation of the ideas that he had expounded in the years 1924 to 1926.

Looked at from this point of view, it becomes clear that in outlining his theory of a war of position and the proposal for a Constituent Assembly, Gramsci was trying to adapt his theory to historical events, and not historical events to his theory. This complex question often engaged Gramsci and his prison comrades in some heated internecine debate.

The increasingly wide gap between Gramsci and the official line of the PCd'I is remembered, unanimously, by the men who shared his fate at Turi. As mentioned earlier, Gramsci conducted a series of conversations and 'lessons' that, as recalled by Giovanni Lai, dealt with such topics as the class character of Fascism, intellectuals in modern society, the southern question, the function of the party in the struggle for socialism, the hypothesis of a period of democratic transition after the fall of Fascism, and the motor forces of the revolution in Italy, which would require the convocation of a Constituent Assembly in which all of the anti-Fascist forces would take part.

Serious consideration of this question falls outside the bounds of this essay. My aim is simpler, that of indicating the new ways of thinking and the new ideas of a political prisoner who wanted to discuss issues, to analyse and evaluate the different positions of the parties, and to impress on his orthodox comrades' minds that

---

34. Showstack Sassoon 1987, p. 193.

one must be fair with one's adversaries, in the sense that it is necessary to strive for an understanding of what they really mean and not fix one's attention maliciously on the superficial and immediate meanings of their expression. This is how we should conduct ourselves, if our aim is to raise the tone and the intellectual level of one's own followers and not the immediate one of creating a desert around oneself, with whatever means and manner [are available].[35]

This last passage, taken from Notebook 11, dated 1932–3, probably reflects the polemics and accusations of 'social-fascist' and 'opportunist' levelled against Gramsci at Turi by some of his comrades, who wanted at all costs to be 'plowmen' of history in a moment, a rather long one, in which Gramsci had adapted himself 'philosophically' to being its 'fertiliser'.

---

35. Gramsci 1975, Vol. II, p. 1405.

Part Three

Comparative Perspectives on Gramsci

Chapter Seven

Antonio Gramsci and C.L.R. James: Some Intriguing Similarities

An intriguing aspect of C.L.R. James studies in recent years has been the frequency with which various critics and scholars have compared him to Antonio Gramsci. The parallels and similarities between these two seminal thinkers of the twentieth century are, in fact, quite striking, and deserve some commentary.

James and Gramsci had different political affiliations and loyalties. Gramsci was a leader of the Communist Party of Italy and deeply committed to the policies of the Third International, which he himself helped to develop. James was a neo-Trotskyist who for most of his life rejected out of hand the idea that Soviet society was in any way socialist. Yet if we look closely at the full spectrum of Gramsci's writings on Soviet socialism and on bureaucratic centralism, it is clear that he agreed with some of James's reasons for repudiating the Stalinist régime. But he was able to accommodate a much wider range of possible 'socialisms' within his overall conception of world politics than was James. This trait allowed him to temper his fears of the involutional and anti-democratic drift of the Soviet régime with a series of historical and pragmatic arguments having to do with the global struggle against capitalism (in which he believed the Soviet Union played an indispensable role), while for James the Soviet Union was simply a 'monstrous tyranny' that embodied all of the evils of capitalist exploitation in the form of bureaucratic 'state capitalism'.

In my view, what James and Gramsci shared, above and beyond their choices of political affiliation, was a conception of life that connected Marxism to humanism. They both thought of Marxism not only as an irreplaceable analysis of the capitalist economic system, but also as a comprehensive critique and clarification of the alienated socio-political relations typical of bourgeois society. They were both alarmed by and sought to correct the tendency of many self-styled Marxists to interpret and apply Marxist theory in a mechanistic manner. This is why they both had a penchant for verbal images connoting or symbolising organic life forms and processes.

The humanism of James and Gramsci rested essentially on the premise that the human species is not motivated solely by material needs but also, and crucially, by a striving for creative individual expression in all areas of life. In this sense, it is no accident that they were both mindful of Marxism's Hegelian origins, not in order to deny the relevance of the materialist turn taken by Marx but rather to insist on the dialectical vision of life that Hegel had transmitted to Marx,[1] a vision that integrates subject and object in a totalising (not a totalitarian) synthesis. For James, Hegel was the necessary point of departure for any and all philosophical work worthy of the name. For Gramsci, the Hegelian dialectical breakthrough had made possible the thought of two of his Italian forebears, the Marxist philosopher Antonio Labriola and the literary critic and historian Francesco De Sanctis.

James and Gramsci both believed that Marxism would retain its vitality and relevance only by opening itself to new currents of thought and experience. They both extended their investigations into the socio-political and cultural trends of nineteenth- and twentieth-century life beyond the boundaries of class and race to take into account other sources of human identity. For this reason, they played a fundamental catalytic role in modern social theory in that innovative lines of inquiry which they initiated have been subsequently developed fruitfully by their intellectual descendants in many parts of the world. Two names come readily to mind: that of Stuart Hall, a founder of cultural studies who is indebted to both thinkers for his own critical orientation; and that of Edward Said, who repeatedly acknowledged the influence that both James and Gramsci had on the main directions of his own work as a cultural critic and historian for whom literary studies were inextricably intertwined with the investigation of such phenomena as colonialism and neocolonialism, racism and imperialism. This can be seen above all in Said's *Culture and Imperialism*.

Gramsci's concept of the *national popular* dimension of the struggle for socialism had its counterpart in James's gradual evolution towards what one James scholar, Patrick Ignatius Gomes, calls 'Marxian populism'.[2] The formation of a 'national popular' culture was for both thinkers a necessary component of socialist ideology. For Gramsci, one of the deficiencies of Italian national development was precisely the lack of a closely interconnected and fruitful relationship between the intelligentsia and the common people, while for James, especially after his return to Trinidad in 1958 following a twenty-year

---

1. However, on this point, Marx was explicit in distinguishing his dialectical method from that of Hegel. See Marx's 'postface' to *Capital*, Vintage Press: 1977, Vol. I, p. 102.

2. See Gomes 1980.

absence from his native land, a task of primary importance for Trinidadian intellectuals was to help forge a strong bond among the island's diverse races and classes within the larger framework of a political federation embracing all the countries of the Caribbean archipelago. James was as deeply immersed in the critical study of Caribbean creative writing as Gramsci was in the study of Italian literature, for both saw in their respective literary traditions a valuable record of their countries' social history. Literary study was a means through which to understand the mind and spirit of a people in historical context.

The notion of the 'national popular' presents nettlesome problems from a Marxist point of view because it embraces sectors of the population that orthodox Marxists do not usually see as appropriate agents of radical social transformation. Be that as it may, what Gramsci and James had in common was their resolute adherence to a conception of the people that included not only workers and peasants, but all people whose way of life and outlook were conditioned by the need to cope with the burdens of everyday human existence. James habitually called them 'the great masses of people' or, more simply, 'ordinary people', and Gramsci, when considering the prospects for radical change in Italy, did not always restrict himself to the working class as its agent, but spoke, instead, of 'the creative spirit of the people'.

Both Gramsci and James looked favourably on the idea of 'the people' as eloquently evoked by Abraham Lincoln at the end of the Gettysburg Address. This is why James was able to see the struggle of black people in America as having an independent significance of its own which revolutionary socialists should recognise and incorporate into their programme of action; and why in the 1930s Gramsci rejected a strictly class-based conception of the anti-fascist movement in favour of a more expansive and ecumenical view of how various political groups might struggle together against a common enemy.

Gramsci and James both had an abiding interest in the history, roles and functions of intellectuals. This is a subject where one finds a plentiful admixture of political and literary themes common to both thinkers. In the early phase of my research on James, I was tantalised by his use of the phrase 'organic intellectual' in his commentary on Shakespeare's *Hamlet*.

In a section of the *Prison Notebooks* dealing with the formation and function of intellectuals, Gramsci distinguishes between 'organic' and 'traditional' intellectuals, the former characterised by their function as representatives of a particular social group or class.[3] At first, I thought that James must have been aware of Gramsci's formulation when he, James, used it in his 'Notes on Hamlet', where he asserts that in the Elizabethan era 'the intellectual was an organic part of rationalist society and Hamlet is the organic intellectual'.[4] But I have found no unimpeachable evidence in James's writing of

---

3. See Gramsci 1971, pp. 5–23.
4. James 1992, p. 245.

a direct Gramscian influence, which in a way makes his use of the phrase all the more fascinating.

While Gramsci and James shared an interest in the role of intellectuals in political life, their ways of addressing the question were quite different.

James's writings on intellectuals are sometimes quite biased, scornful, and emotionally charged, while Gramsci's approach is usually cool and impersonal, considerably more 'social scientific' in tone than James's. Gramsci, to be sure, was capable of animus in his writing, and he could be sternly acerbic and contemptuous, especially in his judgments of Italian intellectuals he grouped under the rubric 'Lorianism' in his commentaries on writers (most often literary intellectuals) guilty of sanctimony, hypocrisy, superficiality, and other defects. Nevertheless, in the *Prison Notebooks*, he tended to deal with the problems that interested him from a rather detached perspective. James, on the other hand, at least when intellectuals were the topic of discussion, let himself go with abandon. Consider, for example, Chapter V of his study *Mariners, Renegades & Castaways* on Herman Melville's *Moby Dick*, which James wrote during his six-month detention on Ellis Island in 1952. In this chapter, entitled 'Neurosis and the Intellectuals', James was in an especially bilious state of mind as he diagnosed the cause of the pervasive doubt and confusion afflicting mainly 'a special class of people, chiefly intellectuals and the idle rich who cannot decide what attitude they should take to a changing society'.[5] But indecisiveness was only a minor symptom of a grave spiritual illness which James saw as endemic to modern intellectuals, especially literary intellectuals. Suffice it to say that an angry James characterised many of the canonical literary works of the twentieth century as 'a catalogue of misery or self-centred hopelessness'.[6] It should be noted, however, that eleven years later James acknowledged that his judgments concerning intellectuals and other questions taken up in his study of Melville were challengeable, and in need of revision, because of their overly politicised character.[7]

Probably the strongest link between these two great figures was their attachment to the idea of organicism as the foundational principle on which to build a fully integrated conception of life that was at once dynamic and fertile. This idea was not at all in conflict with Marxism, as alleged by some scholars. In fact, it is likely that it was from Marx himself that Gramsci especially, but James as well, borrowed the idea, as it regarded the study of society. In the concluding paragraphs of his preface to the first edition of *Capital*, for example, Marx argued that more and more people had become aware that 'the present society is no solid crystal, but an organism capable of change, and constantly engaged in a process of change'. Moreover, he made it very clear that his aim was 'to

---

5. James 2001, p. 91.
6. Among these were *The Waste Land, Journey to the End of the Night, Darkness at Noon, Farewell to Arms, The Counterfeiters,* and *Remembrance of Things Past.*
7. In a letter to Ronald Mason, a Melville scholar, dated 8 October 1963.

reveal the economic law of motion of modern society', implying that society changed and developed in ways that were analogous to those found in nature.

Marx left himself open in this last statement to the claim that his method was undermined by a subtle form of determinism, inasmuch as he seemed to have left out the role of conscious human volition in his notion of organic processes. It is not within my competence to make any pronouncements on this question, but I can say with confidence that both James and Gramsci, basing themselves on an understanding of society as what Marx called 'an organism capable of change',[8] were explicit in connecting human initiative and creativity to Marx's formulation that viewed the development of the economic formation of society as 'a process of natural history'. In any event, the natural and the organic, for Gramsci, was inextricably linked to the concept of change, as Marx had said; but for the Sardinian communist, change did not unfold in accordance with a so-called 'economic law of motion of modern society'. James, too, rejected the notion that what was natural and organic, at least in the realm of human activity, could be understood as a process undirected by subjective human agency.

The youthful Gramsci of 1916 who penned the wonderful essay 'Socialism and Culture' was father to the man who viewed his own life as part of a living, organic process of struggle fraught with uncertainty precisely because the outcome of events was always the result of clashing interests and perspectives, part of a vast tapestry composed of many and diverse wills and purposes.

It will be helpful to look now at a few of the critical writings on James where Gramscian terms and concepts are germane to the authors' main arguments.

Bill Schwarz's 1994 review of *American Civilization*, which James wrote in the early 1950s, is a good example. Schwarz sees suggestive parallels between the life trajectories of Gramsci and James, most importantly their insular origins (Sardinia and Trinidad), their deepening consciousness of belonging to a 'colonised' people, and their embrace of Marxism after their arrival in the 'imperial centres' of Britain and Italy (London and Turin), where both encountered for the first time an organised industrial working-class movement. Schwarz sees these parallels from a rather strongly Eurocentric viewpoint:

> The intellectual traffic across the old empires clearly possesses a prodigious unwritten history, and James represents one moment in this larger story. In my own mind I've always thought of James in this context in parallel with Gramsci: close enough in birth to be of the same generation (1891 and 1901), moving by virtue of the structures of colonial education from periphery to centre – Gramsci an impoverished Sardinian nationalist, James a luminary in the largely unknown, tiny Trinidadian literary renaissance – and then, when abruptly confronted by the internal culture of the metropolis, each

---

8. See Marx's 'postface' to the second edition of *Capital*, Vol. I.

moving to Marxism: Gramsci to the Socialist Party and thence the Third International, James to Trotskyism.[9]

At the beginning of his study *Caliban's Freedom – The Early Political Thought of C.L.R. James* (1997), Anthony Bogues argued that both Gramsci and James had been engaged in the 'massive project of reconstructing Marxism'. His argument, which recalls a similar generational divide in Perry Anderson's *Considerations on Western Marxism*, takes off from the premise that there was a profound difference between the generation of Marxist thinkers to which Lenin, Rosa Luxemburg and Leon Trotsky belonged and the next generation, which included Gramsci and James (born respectively in 1891 and 1901). Bogues thinks that James's contribution to Marxist renewal took place in basically the same historical context as that of Gramsci, and was motivated by a similar impulse to reestablish the dialectical and humanistic foundations of Marxism. The paragraph in which Bogues proposes this comparison is worth quoting in its entirety:

> In 1940, having recognised the limitations of the Trotskyist movement, James attempted the massive project of reconstructing Marxism for the immediate post-World War II period. Here, his aim was similar in some respects to that of the Italian Marxist thinker Antonio Gramsci. Within the classical Marxist revolutionary tradition, the major political thinkers and activists of the early twentieth century, Lenin, Rosa Luxemburg and Leon Trotsky, had operated from the foundation of the success of the Russian Revolution and its immediate aftermath. Gramsci, on the other hand, wrote his major essays during the 1920s and 1930s, when the revolutionary temper had begun to subside, and within the framework of emerging new tendencies which were restructuring capital. Gramsci's central objective was the survival of the 'philosophy of praxis' (his phrase for Marxism) and the core of his work – *the role of consciousness* and the development of the notion of hegemony – was an attempt to explain the failure of the proletarian revolution in Europe. By focusing on consciousness, he was battling against mechanical determinist currents which had by then affected the character of Marxism.[10]

Later on in his discussion, in a chapter entitled 'The New Universals', Bogues restated his conviction that James and Gramsci had two things in common: their 'approach to the philosophy of Marxism and history', and their conception of 'consciousness' in the working-class movement. I would agree that 'consciousness' and 'subjectivity' are key components of the Marxism of both Gramsci and James. This is a point which Bogues finds exemplified in Gramsci's youthful essay of 1916, 'Socialism and Culture', which has its counterpart in several of James's writings.

Bogues wanted to establish James's contribution to the discourse of 'Western Marxism' (James is not mentioned in Perry Anderson's *Considerations on Western Marxism*), a contribution he felt was not yet sufficiently appreciated by students of James's work. But

---

9. Schwarz 1994, pp. 174–83.
10. Bogues 1997, pp. 1–2 (author's italics).

at the same time, Bogues insisted on a crucial difference between Gramsci and James. Gramsci's political thought was a creative adaptation of Marxism-Leninism to the realities of power relations in the 1930s, while for James, Bogues maintains, even more than classical Marxism, the black radical tradition lay at the core of his thought. This is a leitmotif of Bogues's *Black Heretics/Black Prophets*, which places far greater emphasis on the racial origins of James's radical worldview than do many others who have looked at this aspect of James's life. It is certainly true that from 1939 on, James did see black liberation struggles as an independent regenerative force for progressive change, not only in the United States but throughout the world.

Gramsci figures prominently in John Martin's 1995 dissertation *American Class and Race Relations: An Intellectual History of the American Left*, and in Grant Farred's *What's my Name? Black Vernacular Intellectuals* (2003).

Martin argued that what James had in common with Gramsci was his belief in 'the self-governing capacity' of ordinary people. This is true as far as it goes, but Gramsci's theory of workers' self-actualisation was rooted in a highly specific movement, the workers' council movement in Turin of the years 1919 to 1924. In other words, for Gramsci, it was workers' power that mattered, not that of a vaguely defined social movement.

Farred's analysis of the Gramsci-James connection is marked by the affinity he sees between 'Gramsci's organicism, and James's conception of self-movement, of emancipatory initiative, in opposition to all forms of mechanism and bureaucracy.[11] Also worthy of note is the way in which Farred locates figures such as Mohammed Ali and Bob Marley as popular 'vernacular' intellectuals quite conscious of culture as 'a terrain crucial to ideological struggle'. Farred thinks of his own work as informed by 'Gramsci's democratic discourse', by which he means, among other things, Gramsci's belief that 'all men are intellectuals', inasmuch as he thought that there was an inherent need in all human beings to form a more or less coherent picture of the world, whether one was a highly educated systematic thinker or a plain person with common-sense notions about what is and is not important. As far as his view of James was concerned, Farred considered him from a Gramscian point of view as the author of works in which 'traditional' and 'organic' intellectuals confront each other, recognise their points of intersection and divergence, and comprehend how such an encounter complicates their position in relation to their community.

Although Cameron McCarthy never mentions Gramsci's name in his excellent essay 'Mariners, Renegades, and Castaways: C.L.R. James and the Radical Postcolonial Imagination',[12] he nonetheless draws upon Gramscian categories of investigation in trying to understand what distinguishes three types of 'intellectual exemplars', which he calls the 'organic/subaltern intellectual', the 'authoritarian or resentful intellectual', and the 'contextual/revisionary intellectual'.

---

11. See Farred 2003.
12. McCarthy 2001, pp. 86–107.

McCarthy's first category includes such figures as the Haitian revolutionary leader Toussaint L'Ouverture, whom James depicted so vividly in *The Black Jacobins*, and the polyglot, racially diverse crew members of the Pequod in Herman Melville's *Moby Dick*. These are 'intellectual' types who emerge directly from the masses and seem inextricably bound to them. *Seem* inextricably bound to them because as James describes the final years of Toussaint's leadership of the San Domingo slave revolt, it is clear that Toussaint lost close contact with his followers and eventually tied his own fortunes much too closely to those of the French Republic, which subsequently led to his imprisonment and death in the France of Napoleon Bonaparte.

The second type of authoritarian or resentful intellectual, which Melville incarnated in the figure of Captain Ahab, reminds one of the personality types described by Fritz Stern in *The Politics of Cultural Despair*, and of Gramsci's reaction to Benito Mussolini, whose demagoguery exploited so effectively the personal and national resentments of his countrymen.

The third type, the contextual or revisionary intellectual, is, in McCarthy's view, represented by James himself. By this he means that James combined in himself both the learning handed down by the avatars of Western civilisation while, at the same time, developing the 'magic arts of interpretation' with which he led a deconstructive assault on 'the taken-for-granted and naturalised terrain of the West'. For McCarthy, James succeeded in overcoming the barriers erected by bourgeois society between intellectuals and the masses.

Others have pointed out parallels and similarities between Gramsci and James: Anna Grimshaw and Keith Hart, Aldon Nielsen, and James's longtime friend and co-militant, Grace Lee Boggs, come to mind. In most of these cases, the comparisons serve merely to orient the reader to particular features of James's thought. Boggs often refers to James as 'an organic intellectual' whose 'spiritual leadership' stimulated his comrades in the Johnson-Forest Tendency to transcend the bourgeois separation between material and intellectual labour.[13] As far as I know, she did not elaborate on this point. However, in view of the fact that Boggs, second only to Raya Dunayevskaya and James himself, applied her philosophical intelligence to the political movement led by James, and helped James to deepen his grasp of many of the problems with which he deals in *Notes on Dialectics* and other writings, her comments assume a special importance in this brief survey of the Gramsci-James connection.

James was an eclectic thinker who drew his ideas from diverse sources. The fact that in his revolutionary response to the crisis of modern civilisation he employed methods and reached conclusions that were so akin to those of Gramsci is testimony to their common affiliation – despite their sharp differences in political orientation vis-à-vis the Soviet Union – with Marxist humanism. This, in any case, is the informed opinion of the historians, political scientists, and educators I have discussed, and with which I concur.

---

13. See Boggs 1993.

Chapter Eight

On the Qualities of Intellectuals: Antonio Gramsci, Edward Said, and Betty Friedan

The word 'intellectual' generally designates an individual who expounds ideas and theories, and who expresses this proclivity as a normal part of his or her professional and personal life. As used in this sense, the word began to appear in the writings of late eighteenth- and early nineteenth-century writers and thinkers. William Wordsworth and William Hazlitt, for example, were conscious of the novelty of the word as used to characterise individuals who employ their intelligence to examine, clarify, argue, advocate, and theorise points of view related to areas of broad general interest.

For the sake of my argument, I am going to make an assumption with which not everyone will agree, namely that not only are the five activities I mention above what intellectuals essentially do, but that these activities, as I define them, give a special place and distinction to the life that intellectuals lead.

I build my argument on a few selected writings of three twentieth-century thinkers who, in my view, exemplified intellectual life as I define it. They are Antonio Gramsci, Edward W. Said, and Betty Friedan, all of whom were leading theorists of the political movements of which they were a part. Gramsci was a communist who considered it his responsibility not only to advance the cause of the world Communist movement, but also to develop and apply a critical methodology built primarily on Marxist foundations. Edward Said brought singular acumen and learning to the task of giving a voice to Palestinians who suffered the consequences of a historical injustice that remains, to this day, uncorrected. Betty Friedan was a militant feminist who, like Gramsci and Said, took her responsibility as a writer and thinker as seriously as she did the cause to which she was dedicated.

After a few brief considerations on the question of political engagement, my plan in the following pages is to offer some commentary on how these three figures developed their arguments while, at the same time, remaining within a methodological framework that is compatible with intellectual work as I conceive it. From the point of view I advance here, Gramsci, Said, and Friedan, together with their strong allegiances to specific political parties, movements and causes, were also independent critical intellectuals.

The question of engagement

I am strongly inclined to think that what intellectuals do cannot be adequately defined by the inherent nature of the causes or values that they favour in their writings and related activities. For my purposes, the fact that advocacy is one of the things that intellectuals often do is of primary importance, not the specific content of the causes they advocate. Once we begin to make ethical and moral demands about the content and character of what intellectuals have to say in support of or in opposition to this or that cause or position, we run the risk of allowing our partisanship to obfuscate and override the role of intellectuals as I define it.

I realise, of course, that this claim raises some serious questions about how we should go about judging certain intellectuals who have identified themselves with causes and movements that, from a liberal point of view at least, make them irrelevant to the kind of questions that I want to raise. It seems quite natural, for example, to believe that there can be no consideration whatsoever of Fascism as a body of ideas that intellectuals can profitably debate. Yet from the point of view that I advance here, it is necessary to separate the messenger from the message and to realise that a right-wing intellectual can present his or her ideas, can examine, clarify, argue, advocate and theorise a body of ideas in such a way as to earn the right to be called an intellectual. We are not obliged to think that everything that our ideological opponents have to say is inherently unsuitable to intellectually responsible discourse.

Engagement became a matter of burning concern during but especially after World War II, when Jean-Paul Sartre and his existentialist colleagues confronted the atmosphere of despair and inaction that had marked French society in the years between the two great wars. He argued that the crisis undermining French society had already had its corrosive effects before the outbreak of World War II, because decisive action in opposition to war and oppression depended on a choice between resistance and passivity, and that choice hinged in turn on one's stance vis-à-vis the question of personal responsibility to take positions not only in theory but in fact. Too many intellectuals, Sartre said, had betrayed themselves and their function in society, which was not only to develop a criticism of institutions and practices, but to change them. Marx bequeathed this point of view to Sartre, but Sartre made more of it than Marx, inasmuch as he saw it as a matter of spiritual life and death for the individual person. In other words, Sartre saw the crisis as not only economic in nature, but personal and existential, in that human beings could not free themselves from doubt and despair by relying on any preconceived system of ideas. Each day, each moment of life demanded that the individual choose his or her course of action, but always within the context of unique 'situations'. Situations were always composed in large measure of unpredictable circumstances that foreclosed reliance on already determined, self-justifying 'essences'.

Sartre's epochal philosophical undertaking was to restore to human beings their sense of themselves as participants in an open-ended adventure in which they became protagonists of their lives. His aim was to 'focus on the free, responsible agent who can make something out of what has been made of him'.[1] There could be no escape from the responsibility to be fully human in thought and action. In that sense, one can speak of Sartre's humanism, his conviction that we do honour to ourselves when we act as self-determined human beings, not as actors in an already determined universe governed by sub-human or superhuman essences.

Antonio Gramsci on the function of intellectuals

We come now to a line of inquiry and reflection that has upset common opinion regarding the question of engagement and, above all, some of the things I have said thus far concerning who intellectuals are and what they actually do. I am referring to the pages of his prison notebooks where Gramsci discusses the topic under consideration in this essay, but from a perspective that differs markedly from the one that I have proposed.

Not only does Gramsci reject the notion that intellectuals are to be seen as a group apart from the common run of humanity in terms of how they conduct themselves in society and perform the tasks to which they are customarily dedicated; he also poses the question of intellectuals as a problem of determining the context in which they operate. He takes the position that the proper context in which to look at the question of intellectuals is the world of work, particularly as it involves the performance of tasks that, far from being in any way removed from the practical needs of society, make these needs the object of their activity.

Without excluding the occupations customarily thought of as inherently intellectual in nature – writers, academics, journalists, and so on – Gramsci redefines the meanings of the word 'intellectual'. He does so by moving away from conventional categories and insisting on two points: 1) intellectuals have a social function like everyone else, in that what they have to say, write, and advocate always serves the practical and worldly

---

1. Flynn 1984, p. 3.

purposes of specific social groups or classes, who feed off what intellectuals offer them for the purpose of erecting a structure or framework of ideas capable of winning the loyalty of the masses of people; 2) the usual concept of intellectual in the abstract academic sense needs to be considerably enlarged by extending its applicability to include technically and professionally trained people in various fields of endeavour, from social service workers to pharmacists; from scientists to administrators; from public relations specialists to individuals who promote the work of political parties and religious communities. This expanded conception of intellectuals explains why one of the most important sections of the *Prison Notebooks* is on the topic 'intellectuals and the organisation of culture'. The key word, here, is 'organisation', inasmuch as it connotes the more or less systematic and rational planning that intellectuals do, as Gramsci re-defines them.

What ties together the types of work mentioned under category two is that they are all seen as crucial to the functioning of the entire society of which they are a part; the whole structure of society rests on the resources, skills, technical know-how, and administrative abilities that these occupations make available to the class or classes to which they are bound by common interests. They are the binding agent of societal networks, and are rewarded with suitably high salaries and privileges. They all perform what Gramsci considers 'intellectual' functions, in that they provide a body of ideas that serve to legitimate a given class structure and set of power relations.

This conception of intellectual work forms part of Gramsci's theory of hegemony; a theory that, in the final analysis, brings us into touch with the Marxist concept of class struggle. Gramsci placed his analysis of the function of intellectuals within a larger framework that he and other Marxist intellectuals called the 'philosophy of praxis', which hinges on the unity of thought and action, of theory and practice. It was the central pillar on which his adherence to the philosophy of historical materialism was based.

But I would argue that it was precisely in his interpretation of historical materialism that Gramsci distinguished himself from many communist intellectuals of the twentieth century. He was emphatic about the need to differentiate history, as the infinitely complex record of human struggle, experience and creative endeavour in all realms of life, from the material dimension of reality, within which human beings interact and contend with the forces of nature, of which human nature is a part. He wanted to get away from the notion, fairly common in the Marxist movement of his day, that human behaviour was just as constricted and determined by the material bases of life as that of all other creatures. His aim was to open up Marxists to a non-reductive understanding of history. Gramsci was sensitive to the creative powers of human beings, and rejected modes of thinking that were mechanical or positivist. He returned to the Hegelian-Marxist theory of dialectics and used it as a fundamental pedagogical principle on which to base the education of the working class, whose cause he championed throughout his life.

Another facet of Gramsci's theory of intellectuals resides in his belief that, by virtue of their common humanity, all human beings are intellectuals, in that they work out ways of conceptualising reality and deal with questions having to do with the conduct of life. What distinguishes professional intellectuals is that they perform intellectual work as part of their essential function in society.[2] On the one hand, he thought, 'there is no human activity from which every form of intellectual participation can be excluded: *homo faber* cannot be separated from *homo sapiens*'. On the other hand, Gramsci argues, one can say that while 'All men are intellectuals ... not all men have in society the function of intellectuals'. Gramsci wanted to pin down his definition to the notion of function; it is what one does within a given system of social relations that matters, not the intrinsic nature of intellectual activities, as I have proposed. On this point, he clarifies the difference between the conception of intellectuals that I have outlined above and his own in the following manner:

> What are the maximum limits of meaning of the term intellectual? Can one find a unitary criterion to characterise equally all the diverse and disparate activities of intellectuals and to distinguish these at the same time and in an essential way from the activities of other social groupings? The most widespread error of method seems to me that of having looked for this criterion of distinction in the intrinsic nature of intellectual activities, rather than in the ensemble of the system of relations in which these activities (and therefore the intellectual groups who personify them) have their place within the general complex of social relations. Indeed the worker or proletarian, for example, is not specifically characterised by his manual or instrumental work, but by performing this work in specific conditions and in specific social relations (apart from the consideration that purely physical labour does not exist and that even Taylor's phrase of 'trained gorilla' is a metaphor to indicate a limit in a certain direction: in any physical work, even the most degraded and mechanical, there exists a minimum of creative intellectual activity). And we have already observed that the entrepreneur, by virtue of his very function, must have to some degree a certain number of qualifications of an intellectual nature although his part in society is determined not by these, but by the general social relations which specifically characterise the position of the entrepreneur within industry.

In this passage, Gramsci makes a case for thinking about intellectuals in terms of their function in society, not, as I have done, in terms of 'the intrinsic nature of intellectual activities'. He grounds his analysis on the principle that one must understand the ways in which any kind of work, including intellectual work, fits within the 'specific conditions and in the specific social relations' that make up the warp and woof of any society. Therefore, on the basis of this conception of things, one is obliged to study these conditions and social relations in order to arrive at judgments about different human activities at particular moments in history.

---

2. Quotes and discussion on intellectuals are taken primarily from Gramsci 1971, pp. 5–23.

Gramsci's point of view is compelling, yet I am convinced that it is possible to connect and reconcile his functional conception of intellectuals with the argument that I advance in this essay, which is that there *is* something intrinsic in intellectual activity that sets it apart from other pursuits.

Gramsci's writing has qualities that belie his argument that we should base our evaluation of what he has to say on his specific function in Italian society, that of an agent of the communist revolution, from about 1919 to his death in 1937. In my opinion, it is not his function as Communist Party leader and organiser that gives his writing its special appeal and persuasiveness. The fact that he used his literary training and skills to pen some memorable essays, articles, letters and notes on behalf of a particular movement within the 'specific conditions and specific social relations' prevailing in Italy in the 1920s and 1930s is of great historical importance, but this fact tells us little about what gives his writing, in these specific conditions and social relations, its distinction.

The qualities that we are looking for are to be found in something that the idea of function does not embrace, which is the exquisitely interactive, dialogic nature of his writing, and the way in which he builds his analysis in a variety of fields, mainly history, politics, literature, and philosophy. The tone throughout the *Prison Notebooks* is that of a man engaged in critical inquiry, of someone who feels the weight of centuries of thought, of a man who, steeped in the arts of debate and public speaking, was eager to perform the tasks that I have associated with most intellectual activity, those of examining, clarifying, advocating, arguing, and theorising ideas and positions, all of which Gramsci carried out in a careful and stimulating way. How else can we explain why his writing appeals to readers coming from so many different backgrounds and ideological orientations? Upon reading sections of the notebooks that interest us, we feel enriched and enlightened. We feel that we have partaken in a rather elegant disputation, not bludgeoned by a single overpowering point of view. We are not discomforted by our feelings of confusion and uncertainty, for we intuit that Gramsci would not look down on us by reason of our need for further exemplification and clarification. When we open the *Prison Notebooks*, we do not enter the realm of the absolute, even in those passages, and there are many of them, where he goes about exposing the superficiality and harmfulness of certain writers and schools of thought which were gaining followers in Italy and elsewhere at the time he was composing his notebooks (1929–36).

Edward W. Said and the question of Palestine

Edward W. Said also gives us the chance to consider the possibility of leading an intellectual life while, at the same time, maintaining a commitment to political and moral causes, which in his case was primarily the liberation of the Palestinian people. It is no accident that Said found Gramsci's writing so attractive. He understood its philosophical nuances, its method of coping with difficult and controversial ideas, and its deployment of rhetorical strategies that derived from study and analysis, not from a desire to annihilate his opponents.

There is a passage in his essay 'The Public Role of Writers and Intellectuals', where Said articulates his opposition to the official line of various US government agencies and special interest groups (with particular regard to the politics of the Middle East), while making it clear that he wants to advance his own point of view in a dialogic manner, for the purpose not of shutting down debate of the issues at hand but of 'initiating wider discussion' of them. Note the various uses of the word 'intellectual' in the following passage, where Said differentiates himself from what he calls 'policy intellectuals':

> It should be obvious by now that for an intellectual who is not there simply to advance someone else's interests, there have to be opponents that are held responsible for the present state of affairs, antagonists with whom one must directly engage.
>
> While it is true and even discouraging that all the main outlets are . . . controlled by the most powerful interests and consequently by the very antagonists one resists or attacks, it is also true that a relatively mobile intellectual energy can take advantage of and, in effect, multiply the kinds of platforms available for use. On one side, therefore, six enormous multinationals presided over by six men control most of the world's supply of images and news. On the other, there are the independent intellectuals who actually form an incipient community, physically separated from each other but connected variously to a great number of activist communities shunned by the main media, and who have at their actual disposal other kinds of what Swift sarcastically called oratorical machines. Think of the impressive range of opportunities offered by the lecture platform, the pamphlet, radio, alternative journals, occasional papers, the interview, the rally, the church pulpit, and the Internet, to name only a few. True, it is a considerable disadvantage to realise that one is unlikely to get asked on to PBS's News-Hour or ABC's *Nightline* or, if one is in fact asked, only an isolated fugitive minute will be offered. But then, other occasions present themselves, not in the sound-bite format, but rather in more extended stretches of time. So rapidity is a double-edged weapon. There is the rapidity of the sloganeeringly reductive style that is the main feature of expert discourse – to the point, fast, formulaic, pragmatic in appearance – and there is the rapidity of response and format that intellectuals and indeed most citizens can exploit in order to present fuller, more complete expressions of an alternative point of view.[3]

In this passage, Said sets up a series of antitheses, one pole of which he identifies with the 'State Department' establishment, the other with an opposition limited in its means of communication but ready to utilise the tools of intellectual discourse with which to

---

3. Said 2004, pp. 132–3.

develop 'an alternative point of view'. He is concerned not only with advancing his own understanding of the issues involved, but also with his mode of argumentation. Implicitly, he is making a case for distinguishing between two approaches to the problems of the Middle East, one emanating from State agencies, the other from 'independent intellectuals' attached to various 'incipient or activist communities'. Said was anxious to place his knowledge and point of view at the service of 'communities' of likeminded people interested in maintaining an intellectually responsible, carefully argued level of analysis, using the same linguistic resources of the State Department, but in a 'fuller and more complete manner' that aims to 'initiate wider discussion' of the issues.

Underlying this distinction between official state-sponsored discourse and that of 'activist communities' armed solely with their convictions, is Said's determination, derived in part from the ideas of the French sociologist Pierre Bourdieu, to disavow building an 'alternative point of view' on the thought of a 'single great intellectual'. What he is after, with Bourdieu, is the development of a democratically conceived 'collective intellectual'. In response to Bourdieu, Said wanted 'to stress the absence of any master plan or blueprint or grand theory for what intellectuals can do and the absence now of any utopian teleology toward which human history can be described as moving'. This guarded assent to a postulate of postmodernism appears in a number of Said's writings, much to the displeasure of his critics in the Marxist camp. Moreover, Said continues, the goals toward which we strive must be 'invented', not in the sense of 'creating something from scratch' but rather by 'hypothesizing a better situation from the known historical and social facts'.[4]

Despite his passionate advocacy of the Palestinian cause, Said argued from within a discursive universe very far away from that of many of his co-militants. His ability to carry on his struggle while fulfilling the responsibilities and functions of the intellectual can be seen even in one of his angriest and most impassioned denunciations of Israeli government policy vis-à-vis the Palestinian people: his 1979 book *The Question of Palestine*. I'll limit my remarks here to three aspects of this book. The first is that Said does not argue from the point of view of those Palestinian militants who deny Israel's right to exist. On the contrary, he shows an appreciation of the historical events that led to the creation of the state of Israel, and recognises the reasons why what began as an ideal, embodied in the word Zionism, became a resolve to deal with the causes of genocidal anti-Semitism by giving world Jewry the opportunity either to live in or in some way to identify with an independent Jewish state.

The second point is his decision to focus his analysis on the twists and turns of political languages that serve particular interests and policies. Thus he builds a case against certain forms of Zionist ideology – which had long been based on the conception of Jews as victims – by employing that ideology against itself. He startles readers who have never

---

4. See Said 2004, pp. 119–44.

considered the possibility that Jews, too, could be oppressors, that Jews too could victimise other peoples. The title of Part Two of *The Question of Palestine* succinctly states his main theme: 'Zionism from the Standpoint of its Victims'. Said's purpose here is not, as has been claimed, to mystify or distort the relations between Israel and the Palestinians, but, instead, to redirect the attention of readers away from ingrained habits of thought toward new ways of thinking about Jewish-Palestinian and Jewish-Arab relations. He recognised that more than a century of Zionist commentary on this question had almost completely denied, at least in the United States, the possibility that Palestinians had rights in the land of their birth, that Palestinians, long the victims of European imperialisms, were now, in the wake of World War II, contending with deeply rooted prejudices on the part of their Zionist neighbours financially and politically supported by the United States. His arguments are not racial in nature, nor simply nationalistic, but historical, political, and experiential. He asked the question: how does it feel to be a Palestinian in a world that refuses to consider his or her people's rightful claims to autonomy and self-determination? His book is an attempt to answer this question.

The third point is that Said develops his arguments on the question of Palestine in an international context, as one of many chapters in the history of Western imperialism, where he picks up on themes elaborated much more fully in his *Orientalism* (1978). The question of Palestine, he maintained, must be understood against the background not only of East-West relations going back many centuries, but as an integral part of a cultural and literary history as important, in its own way, as the political and military dimensions of imperialism. He rejects an analysis of his subject from a unilateral standpoint. This alone, it seems to me, if not a validation of all of Said's arguments and attitudes, is certainly an attribute of his book that is worth our while to take under consideration, above all if we regard ourselves as intellectuals. What he is asking us to do is adopt a panoptic, multidimensional approach to his subject, which demands the characteristically intellectual habits and qualities that I have tried to outline up to now in my discussion.

Betty Friedan and the 'feminist revolution'

Before discussing some of the intellectually rich and challenging aspects of *The Feminine Mystique* (1963), I want to point out what I think are some of the book's deficiencies in terms of the qualities that I have identified as crucial to intellectual discourse.

First of all, while Friedan advances a series of persuasively reasoned arguments in the first half of her book, culminating in two of her best chapters, those on Sigmund Freud and Margaret Mead, in the second half she resorts more and more to a raw, acerbic, contemptuous language more suited to a stump harangue than to a work dealing with one of the great, not-yet-resolved issues of world civilisation. She speaks brazenly in Chapter Nine of the 'sexually joyless lives' of most American women who are devoted primarily to house and home. In Chapter Ten she asks, rhetorically, 'why so many American housewives around forty have the same dull and lifeless look', and wonders whether this look can be attributed to 'the deadly sameness of their lives'.[5] In the same chapter, she concludes her acidulous comments by acknowledging that there are many American women who find happiness in their role as housewives, only to add that 'happiness is not the same as aliveness or being fully used', and then topping off these opinions by noting that 'some decades ago, certain institutions concerned with the mentally retarded discovered that housework was peculiarly suited to the capacities of feeble-minded girls'.[6] Drudgery, boredom, lifelessness, triviality, above all emptiness, are among the characteristic features of what she persistently calls 'housewifery'. She uses this word in such an opprobrious manner that it almost sounds like a treasonous act committed by those American women who have exchanged the true excitement of active engagement with the world outside the home in favour of security and predictability. In the same vein, instead of remaining content with her initial comparison of the typical domestic life of the American housewife to a 'prison', she elects to go far beyond this already highly charged metaphor in the title of Chapter Twelve, 'Progressive Dehumanization: The Comfortable Concentration Camp'. This analogy reappears five or six times, revealing, I think, Friedan's tendency to 'progressively dehumanise' the women whom she was trying to influence.

Friedan was primarily concerned in her book with the two successive generations of women who attained maturity during or shortly after World War II. Born in 1921, she herself was a product of this era, and became a dutiful wife and mother devoted to her family before she found the courage to change her status in life. It is surprising, therefore, to discover that she had so little appreciation of the disruptions and losses that were caused by the war, and as a consequence paid so little attention to the yearning for stability that was widespread among both men and women in the 1940s and 1950s, the two decades that she mainly deals with in her book. Admittedly, as Friedan argues, the feminine mystique – which rested on a conception of woman as unsuited for the demands of business and the professions – represented a diminishment of possibilities for many women. It was retrogressive and even, in some cases, infantilising. She attacks the rationalisations underlying this conception with gusto and analytical intelligence. Nevertheless, it is puzzling that a woman as sensitive as Freidan was to historical movement and change was so indifferent to the emotional matrix in which the return to hearth and home took place after the war finally came to an end in 1945.

A second set of complaints that one might make about Friedan's mode of presenting her case for women's emancipation has to do with her failure to include in her book any serious consideration of American women who did not belong to the middle and upper-middle classes. During the years when Friedan composed her book (1957–62), women of

---

5. Friedan 2001, pp. 359–60.
6. Ibid.

the working class, black women in particular, were taking their place in the vanguard of political struggle in the United States. Here and there Friedan mentions these struggles, yet she remains somehow apart from them – not indifferent, but aloof and distant.

Nevertheless, there are several key passages of *The Feminine Mystique* that do explicitly link Friedan's cause to other revolutionary movements. One of these, in Chapter Four, entitled 'The Passionate Journey', can serve as a lead-in to a discussion of the authentically intellectual nature of her arguments and point of view. It deals with the 'myths, images, and stereotypes' that have long attached themselves to women's struggles in the United States. Friedan was keenly aware that the feminist movement, if it was to succeed in the long run, would require personal revolutions in thought and consciousness as well as changes in objective social relations. In this respect, she made clear her conviction that the feminist movement was a revolution, that in the process of bringing about real change 'there [would be] excesses, of course, as in any revolution, but the excesses of the feminists were in themselves a demonstration of the revolution's necessity'[7]. In passages such as this, Friedan enlarges our perspective beyond the needs and aspirations of middle-class women.

Friedan used her intellectual armoury in several different ways, all of which, in my view, entitle her to an eminent place among progressive and revolutionary thinkers in the United States. First, she applied her analysis to some of the most influential figures of contemporary civilisation, such as Sigmund Freud, Margaret Mead, Talcott Parsons, and several others. Her aim was to show how complicit these thinkers were in disseminating a view of woman's proper place in society that was misinformed, prejudicial, and harmful to the cause of human equality. Second, she drew creatively from the historical record of women who, from the late eighteenth century to the early decades of the twentieth century, had manned the barricades and joined forces with other efforts to fulfil the democratic promise of American society. In some instances, she dwells at considerable length on the lives and fortunes of bold, innovative women such as Mary Lyon, Lucy Stone, Margaret Fuller, Elizabeth Cady Stanton, Sojourner Truth and others. Third, she discussed the ideas of well-known thinkers whose psychological and social insights proved useful in buttressing her own vision of a liberated humanity. B.H. Maslow and Erik Erikson served her well in her effort to substantiate the logic and the necessity of her cause. Fourth, she drew upon a wide variety of written sources, especially women's magazines with large circulations, to document the ways in which the anti-feminist politics of powerful commercial interest groups was communicated through the 'stay-at-home' message of so much popular fiction.

In general, *The Feminine Mystique* is a highly literate book, replete with colorful illustrative examples drawn from a variety of literary and socio-political sources. These qualities are present in Chapter Five, 'The Sexual Solipsism of Sigmund Freud'. One of Friedan's arguments is that, like all thinkers, even the most brilliant and original, Freud

---

7. Friedan 2001, p. 146.

was the product of his time and place, and had in several instances mistaken historically-determined views for universal principles. Her claim was that 'the feminine mystique derived its power from Freudian thought'.[8] Much of what Freud believed to be biological and instinctual 'had cultural causes', and as such could be identified and dealt with in cultural and political terms. His concepts of 'penis-envy' and 'castration complex', she insisted, were 'postulated on the assumption that women are biologically inferior to men.[9]

In the chapter on Freud, Friedan relates attitudinal and psychological phenomena to networks of views and opinions that prevailed in American society in the 1950s. She approaches the work of Margaret Mead in similar fashion. While explaining the positive contributions that Mead made to women's conception of themselves 'as whole persons', and making clear the conditions in which women 'would be able to realise their full capabilities', Friedan pointed out as well that Mead's picture of liberated women was vitiated by another aspect of her mindset. Referring to Mead's *Male and Female*, she expressed this point of view:

> As an anthropologist, of course, Margaret Mead knew how far modern societies [had moved away from an overwhelming concern with the simple needs of hunger, thirst and sex.] And for all her words glorifying the female role, there are other words picturing the wonders of a world in which women would be able to realise their full capabilities. But this picture was almost invariably overlaid with the therapeutic caution, the manipulative superiority, typical of too many American social scientists. When this caution is combined with perhaps an over-evaluation of the power of social science not merely to interpret culture and personality, but to order our lives, her words acquire the aura of a righteous crusade – a crusade against change. She joins the other functional social scientists in their emphasis on adjusting to society as we find it, on living our lives within the framework of the conventional cultural definitions of the male and female roles.[10]

There is more than one way to expound a revolutionary interpretation of causes and struggles that are close to one's mind and heart. Friedan's way was to assess the condition of American women at a critical juncture of its history, and to find it wanting for reasons that she explicates artfully, in terms of their social, psychological, and political origins. Her exposition is at once conceptually persuasive and, for the most part, and despite the deficiencies that I mentioned above, rhetorically effective.

If, as I have argued, Antonio Gramsci, Edward Said, and Betty Friedan were intellectuals of a high order, it seems reasonable to think that there is much more to the fully realised intellectual life than the ability to articulate a particular cause or position. Other

---

8. Friedan 2001, p. 166.
9. Friedan 2001, p. 181.
10. Friedan 2001, p. 219.

traits of character are involved, among which are an historical perspective on whatever issues one is dealing with, an appreciation of difference as a basic ingredient of human thought and behavior, a willingness to engage in debate and discussion with one's adversaries, and – at least where political and moral values are at stake – a world outlook that is comprehensive and universal in scope.

Chapter Nine
Gramsci in the Caribbean

In a preface to his *Intellectual History of the Caribbean*, Silvio Torres-Saillant makes two observations that are pertinent to the question of Gramsci's influence on Caribbean thinkers. First, he tells us that the ideas he foregrounds in his book 'occur in the wake of a human chronicle that opens with the conquest [in 1492] and the colonial transaction, going through successive stages of domination, insurrection, resistance, adaptation, and nation building'. Second, concerning our own moment in time, Torres-Saillant speaks of the Caribbean region's 'pervasive economic decline, with the attendant diasporic uprooting that has increasingly widened the contours of the Antillean world through the rise of enclaves in urban centres of Europe and the United States'.[1]

Although he did not focus his interest specifically on the Caribbean archipelago, Gramsci had so many important things to say about colonial and class oppression, and about forms of resistance to oppression that it comes as no surprise to discover that his writings have been used by thinkers concerned with unjust and exploitative power relations in many parts of the world, including the Caribbean. Terms and concepts associated with Gramsci, such as hegemony, national-popular, organic intellectual, passive revolution and others have turned out to be both convenient and useful analytical tools that have served the interests of radical and Marxist intellectuals throughout the Caribbean.

On the basis of this historical perspective, my aim is to describe briefly how a number of Caribbean intellectuals,

---

1. Torres-Saillant 2006, p. 7.

from the Trinidadian C.L.R. James to the Jamaicans Stuart Hall and Tony Bogues, from the Cubans Juan Jorge Luis Gonzalez and Ilyanas Mena Fernandez to the Guyanese Walter Rodney, have responded explicitly or implicitly to Gramsci.

The Cuban intellectuals I cite are, as far as I know, living and working in Cuba, but the diasporic experience to which Torres-Saillant refers has marked the lives of C.L.R. James, Stuart Hall, Tony Bogues and, indeed, countless other Caribbean figures.

While doing research at the beginning of this century for a political biography of the Trinidadian revolutionary C.L.R. James, I began to notice various points of contact between him and Gramsci. One of these is the way in which young Gramsci and young James articulated their views on colonialism. James was born and raised in a British crown colony, Trinidad, while Gramsci, a Sardinian, was a citizen of the Italian state that was still ruled, at least in formal juridical terms, by the Savoy Monarchy. But quite early in his life, Gramsci began to see the relationship between the Italian state and its Southern territories as essentially 'colonial' in nature, marked by social and economic practices every bit as exploitative as those imposed on their colonies by the European imperialist powers.

For C.L.R. James, a black man born in 1901 in one of the crown colonies of the British Empire, it was natural to express his indignation in racial as well as political terms. But even on this score, we should note that young Gramsci was not indifferent to what W.E.B. Du Bois was later to call 'the color line' separating the world's haves from millions of its have-nots in Africa and Asia. For example, listen to what he had to say about this facet of colonialism in an article of 9 June 1919, in the then-weekly journal *L'Ordine Nuovo*:

> For several years we Europeans have lived at the expense of the death of the colored peoples...But today flames of revolt are being fanned throughout the colonial world. This is the class struggle of the colored peoples against their white exploiters and murderers. It is the vast irresistible drive towards autonomy and independence of a whole world, with all its spiritual riches.[2]

As this article makes clear, Gramsci, like James, thought of racial and class-based exploitation as inseparably intertwined. We should note, also, that the young Gramsci did not conceive of the struggle for independence by oppressed peoples and classes solely from the point of view of political economy. He was eager to emphasise the spiritual and intellectual development of subject peoples. Hence his stress on the expanding 'spiritual riches' that would come with the struggle for autonomy and independence. This idea is one of the animating principles of his 1916 essay 'Socialism and Culture', and it is also what inspired James to think of revolution as an inherently transformational event in every sense, spiritual as well as material.

---

2. Gramsci 1988, p. 113.

I do not mean to imply that there were no differences between the two men in relation to the question of race. James, a Pan-Africanist, consecrated his life to the socialist cause, but he did so as an exponent of black liberation in the Caribbean, in North
America, and in Africa. Gramsci, on the other hand, was for obvious reasons caught up
from the outset of his political life in class struggle, which dominated his consciousness.
The unity of the working class under the leadership of the Communist Party was what
gave his conception of the world its cohesiveness.

A trait common to both James and Gramsci as political thinkers and activists was
their blending of Marxist and radical democratic theory concerning state formation. For
both, the idea of nationhood was a necessary and crucial step along the way to socialism. The phrase 'national-popular' appears almost as often in James's writings as it does
in Gramsci's. In his biography of Arthur Andrew Cipriani, written shortly before he left
Trinidad for England in 1931, James lamented the lack of a strong 'national feeling' among
ordinary Trinidadians, because he saw this lack as an obstacle standing in the way of the
development of what he called 'the idea of a national community'. Socialism could only
emerge, James was convinced, if the people involved in struggle consciously shared a
common unifying patrimony of language, ideas and sentiments.

On a deeper philosophical level, there is a theme that runs through much of James's
and Gramsci's writing, that of organicism, a word that I am using in the sense ascribed
to it by Martin Jay in his book *Marxism and Totality*. It was what gave Gramsci's writings, theoretically and practically speaking, a 'totalising' connective principle; it was also
a way of avoiding the perils of mechanistic and ritualised thinking, of remaining concretely tied to dynamic life processes in all realms of human activity.

For example, the phrase 'organic intellectual', which many people typically associate
with Gramsci, appears once in James's writing as well. I do not know whether he borrowed it from Gramsci. Some years ago I asked James's widow Selma James about this.
All she would say was that James was a diligent reader of Gramsci as he was of other
contemporary Marxists. Nevertheless, its appearance in James's 'Notes on Hamlet', written in 1953, makes one wonder about Gramsci as its possible provenance. James relates
Hamlet's character to the historical moment in which Shakespeare composed the tragedy. In so doing, James observed, Shakespeare fashioned Hamlet's character as typical
of his era. In the Elizabethan age, James observed, 'The intellectual was an organic part
of rationalist society, and Hamlet is the organic intellectual. That is why the character
endures'.[3]

Gramsci's influence on Caribbean intellectuals is exemplified in the writings of two
prominent members of the Jamaican diaspora, Anthony Bogues and Stuart Hall.

As noted above, in *An Intellectual History of the Caribbean* Silvio Torres-Saillant, in
describing exile as the common experience of Caribbean intellectuals, points out that,
because of the region's 'long catastrophic history' of shattered hopes and tragic defeats,

---

3. James 1992, p. 245.

Caribbean intellectuals 'have always spoken about their people's place in the world from abroad'. C.L.R. James is an example of this phenomenon, as are Aimé Césaire, George Lamming, Frantz Fanon, Sylvia Wynter, Marie Chauvet and dozens of others one could mention. But in many cases, after long periods in exile, these intellectuals have also returned home and re-engaged in struggle there. This is the case of Bogues, and it is true of James as well. His return to Trinidad in 1958, after 26 years of living abroad, although cut short in 1962, was marked by intensive involvement in Trinidadian politics. But regardless of whether they developed their ideas at home or abroad, there is no doubt in my mind that their interests, point of view and commitments stem in large part from their roots in their Caribbean homelands.

Tony Bogues is Professor of Africana Studies and Director of the Centre for the Study of Slavery and Justice at Brown University. Before he came to Brown and earned his doctorate in 1994, he worked for many years as an assistant to Prime Minister Michael Manley, a position that reflected his hope to make his native land of Jamaica a place for the development and expansion of democratic socialist politics throughout the Caribbean region. His fortunes followed those of Manley, however, and after Manley was replaced as prime minister by Edward Seaga, Bogues withdrew somewhat from active involvement in Jamaican politics. In addition to his professorship at Brown, he serves on the editorial board of the journal *Small Axe*, in which he has published a number of essays that reveal his indebtedness to Gramsci as a source of insights into popular culture and into the ways in which 'subaltern' classes sometimes produce ideologies that reflect the interests of ruling classes.

Bogues's most important work as far as Gramsci studies are concerned is *Black Heretics and Black Prophets: Radical Political Intellectuals*, published by Routledge in their series on African Thought. This book approaches Gramsci in a respectful but also in a decidedly independent and controversial way.

Bogues brings us into touch with a current of black philosophical thought that insists on its own distinctive style and content vis-à-vis the established Marxist canon. For example, in the first ten pages of his study, while granting that Foucault's 'discussion of the problematic of power' and 'Gramsci's notion of hegemony and its various modes of structuring thought suggest possible directions of how to study black radical thought and black political intellectuals', he argues that neither Foucault nor Gramsci can be considered anything more than 'valuable touchstones for plotting the genealogy of the black radical tradition'. They are by no means, he maintains, complete guides. Various black figures, from Quobna Cugoano to Ida B. Wells-Barnett, from C.L.R. James to W.E.B. Du Bois, from Julius Nyerere to Walter Rodney, in company with what he calls 'the redemptive poetics of Bob Marley', have higher standing in Bogues's hierarchy of influential thinkers than Foucault and Gramsci. These black figures were much closer to the black political experience and much more attuned to some of the intimate rhythms and impulses of black life than were their white counterparts.

Bogues takes issue with Gramsci's concept of 'organic intellectual', which he finds useful, yet ultimately unsatisfactory, at least for his purposes. Here is what he has to say about this particular facet of Gramsci's legacy:

> Without doubt the black radical political intellectual often functions as an 'organic' intellectual. But this is only part of the story. The key question is the nature of his or her political engagements and the character of his or her contributions to radical thought. To call the black radical intellectual an 'organic' intellectual describes only function and relationships, not what that functioning means both for radical thought and for the topography of the black intellectual tradition. Thus, to rely solely on Gramsci in this instance limits our exploration.[4]

Bogues clearly felt the need to demarcate the boundaries of an autonomous black intellectual tradition. The thrust of his thinking is toward a break from the great white fathers of modern radical and Marxist thought. He has his own black thinkers to rely upon, and credits them with having developed a body of thought that reflects the black historical experience.

Two other issues emerge later in Bogues's book that are worthy of note, because they also constitute a kind of declaration of independence from Gramsci and from the dominant schools of western Marxist and radical thought. To do this he calls on the idea of 'heresy' as a more accurate and appropriate marker for the black radical tradition that interests him. The two works that, in his argument, provide examples of a new kind and quality of historical and sociological scholarship are C.L.R. James's *The Black Jacobins* and W.E.B. Dubois's *Black Reconstruction*, which, as Bogues sees it, chart new pathways to historical understanding and 'place before us historical knowledge about two major events [the Haitian Revolution of the 1790s and the crisis of black liberation after the American Civil War] that reorder the narrative structures of Western radical history'. This is a bold argument, no longer entirely new, certainly, but that still retains a sharp cutting edge.

Also worthy of attention is Bogues's chapter on the Guyanese thinker Walter Rodney, who was close to C.L.R. James in the 1960s and considered himself a disciple of the Trinidadian revolutionary. Here, the point Bogues makes concerns the way in which Rodney's conception of political leadership compared with that of Gramsci. The difference between a Gramsci and a Rodney, Bogues argues, stems from how they understood the role of the masses. Rodney expressed himself on this weighty question in a manner that reflects his exposure to the thinking of James, who moved farther and farther away from the idea of a party-led revolutionary movement in favour of one spearheaded by the rising masses:

---

4. Bogues 2003, p. 6.

To state that Rodney's conception of the role of the radical black intellectual was slightly different from that of Gramsci requires us to examine Rodney's statement that the primary task of the radical black intellectual was to 'attach himself to the activity of the masses'.

Now at first blush it might seem that Rodney is arguing for a typical Gramscian intellectual who is integrated into, and represents, the ideational activity of that class. However, there is a difference here. For Rodney the masses were already in motion, and were not in need of any political party through which the intellectuals were organised as representative of the class. Rodney felt that the black intellectual had to learn from the masses, a point he made about learning from Rastafari.[5]

This is a debate that has roiled the Left since Marx and Engels announced in the *Communist Manifesto* that 'modern society as a whole is more and more splitting up into two great hostile camps, into two great classes directly facing each other – bourgeoisie and proletariat'. Gramsci more or less accepted this formulation, but with some cautionary resistance to it when it became more of an impediment than an aid to revolutionary struggle. In any case, James, and with him Rodney, did not see it this way. They believed in the organising and galvanising force of ordinary people whose energy and spiritual resources needed far more space in which to move forward than a party-led or even a worker-led struggle would allow. Bogues seems to have great sympathy for this conception of mass struggle, especially as it expressed itself within the context of black history and culture.

The primary link between Gramsci and James, therefore, was their emphasis on organicism as an indispensable component of effective political struggle. It was through this conceptual lens that the two thinkers understood the need for peoples engaged in struggle to achieve a high level of national cohesion and unity as crucial to the development of a socialist society. This meant that considerable importance must be given by strategists of socialist revolution to the spontaneous surge of rebellion that so often marks the outbreak of virtually all successful revolutions, including socialist revolutions. James moved further towards the primacy of popular mass uprisings than Gramsci, but Gramsci, having observed the ways in which bureaucratic and authoritarian methods could stifle the energy generated by mass upheaval was well aware of the relevance of James's way of thinking to the question of how and why revolutions either succeed or fail in the contemporary world.

Passing now to Stuart Hall, his writings on Gramsci are widely known. For this reason, I will limit what I have to say to a few brief comments on one of his essays, entitled 'Gramsci's Relevance for the Study of Race and Ethnicity',[6] published in the *Journal of Communication Inquiry* in 1986.

---

5. Bogues 2003, p. 134.
6. Hall 1986.

This extraordinary twenty-thousand word essay is one of the most comprehensive overviews of Gramsci's thought and method. In the third section of the essay, Hall identifies eight aspects of Gramsci's distinctive theoretical perspective on racism and related social phenomena. I shall mention several of them here: first, he singles out Gramsci's emphasis on historical specificity as a useful concept for the study of race and ethnicity; second, he focuses on Gramsci's non-reductive approach to questions concerning the inter-relationship between class and race. Third, he notes that whereas the state has been consistently seen by the Left as the site of coercive rule, Gramsci's theory of hegemony, as incorporated in the educative role of both the state and civil society, 'could transform the study, both of the state in relation to racist practices, and the related phenomenon of the 'postcolonial state'. Hall also points to the centrality which Gramsci's analysis always gives to the *cultural* factor in social development.

Hall's essay was designed to clarify Gramsci's distinctive mode of inquiry, which eschews facile generalisations and insists on concreteness and specificity. I am quite sure that Hall's mixed Indian and British ancestry and his formative years in Jamaica prompted his interest in the relevance of Gramsci's method to the study of race and ethnicity.

Gramsci's presence in Cuban cultural and political debates since the 1960s is one of the most interesting chapters in the story of his influence and *rayonnement* in the Caribbean region. It deserves to be examined in far greater detail than is possible for me, here. From what I have been able to ascertain so far, Cuba promises to be the place in the Caribbean region where both the theoretical and the practical significance of Gramsci's ideas has been most keenly felt.

One reason for this, of course, is that the Cuban Revolution was and is about creating a new kind of human being. It was a revolution committed to making equality and justice the foundational principles of a new socialist order. As such, it looked for guidance and inspiration from various sources, one of which, at least among some Cuban intellectuals, writers and cultural workers, was Gramsci.

Let me review briefly several of the attempts by Cubans and Cubanologists to place Gramsci in the context of Cuba's revolutionary origins and objectives. One of them is a 23-page essay by Jorge Luis Acanda González, a political theorist and philosopher, written in 2001.[7]

Acanda Gonzalez not only summarises the debates around Gramsci in Cuba from the 1960s to the beginning of the present century, but also clarifies his own point of view in these debates, a point of view that I think is faithful to what I take to be the authentic aspects of Gramsci's contributions in four areas: 1) Marxism as an integral theory of history and social development; 2) the importance of culture in the building of a socialist society; 3) the concept of civil society; and 4) the theory of hegemony.

---

7. The text of this essay is available on the Internet: <http://vimeo.com/32681058>.

The Cuban scholar identifies three phases of Gramsci's presence in Cuban debates. Phase one was the 1960s when, on the heels of the first Spanish translations of and commentaries on Gramsci's writings published in Argentina, the Cuban government promoted the integration of Gramsci's notes on *Historical Materialism and the Philosophy of Benedetto Croce* into the curriculum of philosophy courses taught at the University of Havana. This set the stage for the appearance in Cuba a few years later of critical essays (in Spanish translations) touching in whole or in part on Gramsci by Cesare Luporini, Louis Althusser, and Nicos Poulantzas. Phase two, across the 1970s and early 1980s, is characterised by Acanda as dominated by the bureaucratisation, ritualisation, and formalisation of Marxist studies that forced Cuban writers into a sort of self-censorship. All use or mention of authors such as Gramsci who were associated with what Acanda calls 'critical communism' were relegated to 'a corner for the forgotten'. Phase three, beginning in the mid-1980s and lasting up to the present (the present, that is, of the early 2000s), was marked by the collapse of the Soviet Union and the widespread sense of crisis that this collapse engendered. In Cuba, this crisis led in turn to a search for a new commitment to socialism marked by three trends: a new appreciation of culture in the building of socialism; a rethinking of Stalinist and economistic models of socialism; and the recovery of the thought of Che Guevara.

On Guevara and Gramsci, in an essay of 2010, Ileanys Mena Fernández argues that

> there is a coincidence between Guevarian thought and Gramscian thought, and various works have been dedicated to it; both are Marxists and in referring to the changes in social relations, they make an interpretation of historical reality and the utilization of the forces that intervene in it, ensuring the role of transformation; the war that Che was waging in the field of the economy was the war of position that Gramsci proclaimed.[8]

This is an observation that cries out for further exploration and investigation, not only because of the intrinsic importance of anything connected to the life of the Argentine revolutionary but also in view of the fact that Guevara's commitments were not always in perfect alignment with the positions taken during his lifetime and after by the Cuban government.

Acanda sees the polemics in Cuba around the notion of civil society in Gramsci and other Marxist thinkers as typical of the 1990s, when the call for a 'rectification' of economic decision-making opened up other opportunities for rethinking the socialist project. Instead of using the concept of civil society in a doctrinaire manner, Cuban intellectuals began to reflect seriously on what the concept really meant in a Cuban context. It may be that another essay by Acanda Gonzalez of 1991 on 'La contemporaneidad de Gramsci' helped some Cubans to think more freely and constructively about Gramsci.

---

8. Fernández 2010, pp. 81–98.

Two articles by Rafael Hernández on Gramsci's concept of civil society, published in *La Gaceta de Cuba* in 1993 and 1994, sparked new debates. In commenting on these two articles, Acanda argues that Cuban intellectuals who had for many years interpreted Gramsci's notes on civil society as designed to privilege the realm of the private over the public, or to discredit the role of the state in building socialism, were wrong in theory and in fact. He attributes this point of view to gross ignorance on the part of many Cuban intellectuals, who claimed erroneously that Gramsci's concept belonged more properly to neo-liberal than to Marxist discourse.

Acanda argues that Gramsci's conception of civil society, and his theory of hegemony, hinged on the inextricable interconnectedness between politics and society, between the state and civil society, not on their separation from each other. Through Acanda's writings and lectures, in tandem with the writings and translations of other Cuban intellectuals – Pablo Pacheco, Manuel Sacristán, Victor Fowler, Fernando Martínez Heredia, Cristina Guerrero, Milena Recio and others – a shift took place back to Gramsci in the late 1990s. This is reflected in the establishment in 1997 of a Chair of Gramsci Studies in the Centre of Development and Investigation of Cuban Culture named after the poet and essayist Juan Marinello, who was among the founding fathers of the Cuban Communist Party. This Chair was given full recognition by the Cuban Ministry of Culture, which led in turn, in that same year, to the publication of selections from the *Prison Notebooks* sponsored by a committee of the social sciences at the University of Havana.

Towards the end of his essay 'Gramsci en Cuba', Acanda made the following statement about Gramsci's fortunes in his country:

> We are in a period of reconstruction of socialism in Cuba. And this implies the need to *rearticulate* socialist hegemony in Cuba and the historical bloc that makes it possible, and to approach this challenge in a creative way. It is here that the theoretical legacy of Gramsci is directly connected to our reality, and that makes our use of this legacy a necessity

On this point, it is encouraging to know that in the above-mentioned article 'Recepción de Gramsci en Cuba', which appeared in 2010 in the journal *Tiempo y sociedad*, Ileanys Mena Fernández felt able to say that, in the future building of Cuban society, 'due attention would be paid to the thought of the philosopher Antonio Gramsci'.

Such a view calls for some commentary by knowledgeable Cubanologists. It also invites us to think of Gramsci as a philosopher, above all in the years that he spent in prison, when concerns about matters of enduring importance were uppermost in his mind.

For his part, Michael Chanan sees the moment in the early 1990s when Cuba could no longer rely on the Soviet Union for vital goods and services as marking a real shift in the Cuban leadership's thinking, away from Marxist-Leninist orthodoxy. This involved 'returning to Gramsci, which means returning to the question of civil society'. Since the mid-1990s, Chanan tells us, Cuba's leading journal of social sciences and the humanities,

Temas, has twice published symposiums on the subject, 'Rereading Gramsci: Hegemony and Civil Society', in 1997, and 'Civil Society in the 1990s: The Cuban Debate', in 1998.[9]

Cuba does not exist in an ideological vacuum. It is influenced by events and personalities in other nations, especially those of South and Central America. This can be seen in the programmes of international conferences to which Cuban political scientists and sociologists have contributed. It was in this way that Cuban intellectuals interested in Gramsci came into contact with Gramsci scholars of international renown, such as the Brazilian Carlos Nelson Coutinho and the Italian Giuseppe Vacca, President of the Gramsci Institute in Rome. Both attended the International Conference of Gramsci Studies held in Mexico City in October 2003 that was organised by the Mexican Gramsci scholar Dora Kanoussi.

---

9. This article is available on the Internet: <http://muse.jhu.edu/login?auth=0&type=summary&url=journals/nepantla/v002/2.chanan.pdf>.

Part Four

Two Protagonists of Gramsci Studies in the United States

Chapter Ten

Gramscian Influences in Robert Dombroski's Critical Engagement with Marxism

I was fortunate to have had a close personal and intellectual relationship with Bob Dombroski, who died in Paris on 10 May 2002. The chance to reappraise some of his critical work gives me the chance to remember him in a way that, I hope, will be worthy of him.

Bob and I had several interests and concerns in common, one of which was our effort to make constructive use of Marxist concepts for the analysis and interpretation of literary texts. We met for the first time in the early 1970s at a session of the Modern Language Association devoted to Antonio Gramsci, whom we both regarded as one of the seminal Marxist thinkers of the twentieth century. We had both found in Gramsci's *Prison Notebooks* new insights not only into problems of political economy, but also into questions such as the relations between literature and society. We were intrigued by Gramsci's arguments concerning the ways in which intellectuals, especially literary intellectuals, 'produce ideology' in forms that often gain a mass following and thereby exert an influence on the way people perceive the society and the larger world in which they live. Bob and I shared a conviction that the labour of literary criticism was intimately bound up with practical worldly matters, that critical commentary on literature was always, to one extent or the other, a vehicle for the expression of a world view, a conception of life, and an ideology. Bob was also keenly interested in the Gramscian notion of hegemony, which he subsequently made the theoretical basis of several of his critical studies.

Dombroski gave a markedly practical turn to the literary-critical enterprise. His emphasis on the worldliness of criticism did not stem only from Marxism. He drew eclectically from a variety of critical methods and approaches. Yet there is little doubt that his primary source was Marxist and historical-materialist. This is evidenced in the concluding paragraph of his 1989 book *Antonio Gramsci*, which ends as follows:

> If Gramsci's work is to have any bearing at all on the way we engage in intellectual or cultural practice, it will do so by developing in us a sense of our own politics: a realization that the actual workings of our critical operations depend on circumstances of which we and the 'text' partake, that we, like Gramsci's intellectuals, are 'agents' working *within* a particular hegemonic or counter-hegemonic process. Therefore, the politics of literature is always a 'politics' of something else – of the control, the power, the dominance, however subtle, that one social group exerts over another. Culture, indeed, is the stuff of which power is made and by which it is maintained.[1]

Taken out of context, this passage, with its blunt references to control, power, and dominance, might lead one to believe that Dombroski conceived of literature and literary criticism as direct outgrowths of socio-political dynamics, and that he thought of culture as a mere instrument for the acquisition and maintenance of political power. But this is not the case. By the time that we reach this passage, we have been amply informed by Dombroski that Gramsci was a dialectical thinker who rejected any and all forms of materialist determinism. The key to Gramsci's thought, Dombroski argued throughout his study, was to be found in the notion of 'historical bloc', which for Gramsci 'involves necessarily the organic unity of base and superstructure'. The economy no longer determines ideology, as in the traditional Marxist view; rather, both spheres are interactive and interdependent.

Within complex processes of class domination and subordination, Dombroski believed, so-called 'superstructural' phenomena – art, literature, philosophy, legal and political thought, historiography and so on – acquire a 'relative autonomy': they circulate within the social organism in ways that are original and unpredictable. Moreover, these superstructural forms of human activity were not only expressions of hegemony, but also of counter-hegemonic processes. Society and history were to be seen as perpetually contested terrain, wherein opposing classes and ideas are engaged in struggles whose ultimate outcome is not predetermined.

Yet at the same time, as Dombroski reminds us forcefully at the end of his Gramsci study, it is theoretically and practically unfeasible to look at the production of art and literature as if it were somehow free of all social, political and economic boundaries and constraints. One needs a comprehensive methodological framework within which to trace the connections between diverse spheres and levels of human activity. Such a

---

1. Dombroski 1989, p. 132.

framework was provided by Marxism, but a Marxism cleansed of its deterministic and reductionist tendencies.

With regard to the Gramscian conception of ideology, Dombroski again brought the theory of historical materialism to bear on his analysis. 'The ideological question in Gramsci', he avers, 'appears the moment the literary work is seen as a practice directed at reforming consciousness'.[2] This is a weighty sentence, deserving of sustained analysis. For our purposes, it will have to suffice to say that for Dombroski, the lesson imparted by Gramsci is that to focus exclusively on the formal qualities of a literary work is to deprive the critical enterprise of its relevance to the great overarching issues and conflicts of contemporary civilisation.

I do not know whether Dombroski ever undertook a systematic study of Marxism. His writings suggest that he considered an understanding of how the capitalist system works, from a Marxist point of view, as indispensable to all critical inquiry, irrespective of one's field of specialisation. What can be said with certainty is that he was indebted intellectually and spiritually to some of Marx's historical-materialist disciples of the mid- to late twentieth century; such names as Luporini, Timpanaro, Williams, Jameson, Eagleton, Lukács, Bakhtin appear and reappear in all of his books and essays. With the exception of Lukács, we should note that these literary theorists and critics have all worked independently of the established Communist power system, that they have all transcended the boundaries of what might be called the dogmatic or doctrinaire Marxism that often typified the cultural policies of the Soviet Union and its allied states.

The demise of the Soviet Union and its accompanying intellectual and moral crisis led Dombroski to question something he had long taken for granted, namely Marxism's claim to universality. He wondered whether the deficiencies of the political system that had been found wanting in the existing Communist societies might not be traceable in some measure to Marxist theory itself. I know from many talks with Bob that he was deeply concerned about this possibility. But in the end, he retained a basically Marxist orientation in his post-1989 writings, while at the same time he continued to make use of disparate schools of philosophical and psychological thought, especially in his studies of Carlo Emilio Gadda and of postmodern currents in the late twentieth-century Italian novel.

What I think Dombroski realised more clearly than ever in the work he did in the 1990s was that literary texts can only be approached, and can never be possessed or definitively appropriated. One finds, in his work of this period, several critical methods drawn from many disciplines: philosophy, linguistics, psychoanalysis (both Freudian and Lacanian), rhetoric, as well as a deepening commitment to relating literary questions to broad historical trends and controversies. It is mainly in this sense that I used the words 'critical engagement' as a marker of Dombroski's attitude toward Marxism. What mattered to him was not only the validity of Marxism as a comprehensive and independent

---

2. Dombroski 1989, p. 124.

body of thought in its own right. He also cared deeply about its ability to accommodate and integrate the contributions made to literary study by other methodologies.

That Dombroski did not abandon his fundamental commitment to a Marxist methodology in the wake of the crisis of the late 1980s and early 1990s is evident from an essay entitled 'Marxism and Literature in the Postmodern Age', which appeared in 2001 in a series of short publications sponsored by the Department of Comparative American Cultures under the editorship of E. San Juan, Jr. at Washington State University. It was published together with another piece on 'Timpanaro in Retrospect', in which Dombroski highlighted the difference between Timpanaro's conception of materialism and that of the group of thinkers associated with 'Western Marxism', which included Gramsci.

On the one hand, these two essays continue the line of reasoning that I outlined above in my comments on the 1989 Gramsci study. We find the same emphasis on the interconnectedness of art and social practice, the same general view of a Marxist approach to literature as one which seeks to understand the origin, make-up and use of culture and cultural artifacts in relation to a particular society in a distinct historical moment. Yet on the other hand, the two essays display some novel features that are important to note, for they bespeak a mind in ferment, and a critical effort, begun years earlier, devoted to the analysis of postmodern theory and fiction. Dombroski had long since branched out beyond the strict confines of Marxist-oriented criticism in an earlier period of his career, an example of which is the brilliant chapters on the Italian writers of the Fascist era in *L'Esistenza ubbidiente – letterati italiani sotto il fascismo*, a 1984 work which I will look at a little later. But the two essays under scrutiny here are even more problematic, more charged with intellectual and moral tension – at least in part a consequence, I am sure, of Dombroski's complex critical response to postmodernism, a response that was far from being entirely inhospitable.

In the first place, as suggested above, in these two essays Dombroski revealed his sensitivity to the crisis of 'actually-existing socialism', and of Marxist theory, which he describes as still 'recoiling from an unexpected ideological defeat'. It is certain, he observed, that the concepts of Marxism and socialism must be rethought in the light of current realities, without, he added, losing sight of the socialist ideal. At the same time, he sprang to the defense of a more traditional version of Marxism, where he seems to return to a viewpoint repudiated in his Gramsci book, namely that in the final instance, superstrucuture is determined by infrastructure, by the socio-economic base of society.

This hardening of position on the level of theory is an interesting moment in Dombroski's development, which may reflect his close working relationship with E. San Juan, Jr., one of the most articulate exponents of a position deeply opposed to the theories and methods underlying postmodernism and postcolonialism. Whatever the case may be, we find Dombroski struggling to keep his critical options open while at the same time retreating to a more rigorous and astringent form of materialism than he had heretofore subscribed to.

A second novel feature of these two essays, especially the one devoted to Timpanaro, is that Dombroski shows marked sympathy for the idea that a clear distinction should be made between historical materialism and materialism *tout court*. The former, he maintains, as seen in the major figures of Western Marxism since the 1960s, is characterised by a belief that mental events and the spheres of the economic, the social and the cultural all have priority in human experience over the natural or biological. A fully materialist orientation, on the other hand, which Timpanaro had found in its purest state in the writings of Giacomo Leopardi and Friedrich Engels, and which he, Timpanaro, had sought to resurrect, takes full account of the element of 'passivity' that exists in all human experience, due to what Timpanaro calls 'the external situation' that humans do not produce for themselves but that is produced for them. In other words, historical materialism is focused on the ways human beings interact with and shape their environments; views nature as a resource to be exploited and dominated; and lays stress on the labour process and on the workings of political economy. The naturalistic and biologically based materialism as expounded by Timpanaro, Dombroski noted, was a healthy corrective to the lingering traces of idealism still found in historical materialism.

Implicit in Dombroski's argument, here, is that, paradoxically, the hubris of many historical-materialist thinkers and that of apologists for the profit-motivated exploitation of nature under capitalism leads to their common tendency to envisage the possibility of total domination by human beings over nature. They both tend to dismiss or deny the primacy of man's biological inheritance, which binds him to all of the Earth's creatures. Moreover, this man-centered conception of reality has the effect of diluting the inherently tragic grandeur of the human experience that a Leopardi and, in his own way, an Engels had conveyed in their writings. Dombroski was also concerned with the problem of bringing Marxist cultural and literary criticism into line with the standards of 'scientific inquiry' established by the various disciplines it needs to utilise, such as linguistics, anthropology, politics, psychology and the like. While acknowledging that criticism could never be an exact science, he maintained that it could adapt itself to the norms accepted by the scientific communities that regulate the development of those fields.

A third new feature of these essays, somewhat surprisingly juxtaposed to the previously mentioned hardening of his materialist position, is Dombroski's response to what he describes as one of the typical current facets of literary study in the West, a concern for polyphony, multilingualism, and heteroglossia, terms popularised by the influential work of the Russian literary theorist Mikhail Bakhtin. We see here that Dombroski wants to connect Bakhtin to a rigorously 'materialist' Marxism, in that, as seen in his *The Formal Method in Literary Scholarship*, the Russian scholar had 'worked within a framework of wholly materialist considerations on language as ideological sign and the class struggle'. Dombroski's main intention, however, was not to secure Bakhtin's place among materialists in the Leopardian and Engelsian sense (evidence for which he does not provide) but rather to rescue his work from the clutches of the postmodernists. Here is the way in which he asserts his belief that Bakhtin had been unjustifiably appropriated by anti- or non-Marxist groups operating mainly in academic settings:

> I mention Bakhtin because he has become a kind of household word in much of post-modern criticism; that is to say, he has been re-fashioned, cleansed of Marxist overtones, to complement postmodernism's obsession with 'difference' in its endless play of voices and forms. He is a good example of how a system of thought and inquiry, which grew out of the Marxist debate on language and ideology and which with a genuinely Marxist purpose placed its emphasis on the social construction of literary speech, has been put into the service of postmodernism, late capitalism's most precious ally.[3]

Dombroski was clearly in a combative mood when he penned this important intervention into the debate over the concepts and categories of postmodernism. He seems to have been anxious, at the turn of the new millennium, to take his stand on behalf of the Marxist intellectual tradition, which found itself heavily under fire. This may be the reason that in this essay he risked defining himself as a 'Marxist humanist'. What this means exactly is a subject for prolonged discussion. My sense of it is drawn from the context in which the risk was taken: it occurs not long after claiming for the Marxist approach to literature something more than a historical perspective, one that in addition to mapping out the relations of power wants to 'probe the texture of language in which those relations are embedded and, therefore, [are] linked inextricably to social situations in culture'. It is at this linguistic level, he argues, 'that art and ideology can be seen to find their articulation and to expand into structure and theme'.

Not long after the passage cited above concerning the postmodern appropriation of Bakhtin, he observes that Marxism is notable for 'its struggle to understand the historical conditions that made its beliefs and doctrines possible', conditions marked predominantly by inequality, injustice, and exploitation. It is in this context that Dombroski speaks of himself as a 'Marxist humanist'.[4] As I see it, he was induced to speak of himself in such personal terms by, first, a consideration of how language expresses the multiple realities of the human condition in historical time, and, second, the fact that Marxism's very origin and development were the result of historically contingent circumstances whose inequities it was committed to understand and eventually to eliminate. An appreciation of language as a quintessentially human attribute, and an awareness of exploitation as a primary aspect of capitalist civilisation, may have combined to elicit Dombroski's self-definition as a 'Marxist humanist'.

Let us look now, in a necessarily cursory fashion, at several of Dombroski's writings in which his theoretical and methodological use of Marxist concepts is put to the test, so to speak, in its application to particular writers and literary texts.

---

3. Dombroski 2001, p. 5.
4. Dombroski 2001, p. 6.

I have selected for comment Chapter Four in *L'Esistenza ubbidiente – letterati italiani sotto il fascismo* ['Obedient Existence – Italian writers under Fascism'], on Giuseppe Ungaretti, published in 1984; Chapter Two on Giovanni Verga in *Properties of Writing – Ideological Discourse in Modern Italian Fiction*, of 1994; and 'Re-writing Sicily: Postmodern Perspectives', an essay which appeared in the volume *Italy's Southern Question – Orientalism in One Country*, published in 1998. I would have liked to include some discussion of *Creative Entanglements – Gadda and the Baroque*, of 1999, a virtuoso performance that drew from the almost three decades of work that Dombroski devoted to the Milanese novelist, beginning with his Harvard dissertation of 1969, *Carlo Emilio Gadda: A Study of His Development*, published in 1974 with the title *Introduzione allo studio di Carlo Emilio Gadda*. But such a discussion would have gone well beyond the boundaries of the present essay.

Three premises underlie the studies just mentioned: first, that literary texts are inextricably inter-related with the society and history of their time; second, that this relationship is not an immediate and direct one, but rather mediated, complex, and discoverable through examining what Dombroski calls the 'mental structures' common to the socio-political order and to literary production at any given moment in time and place; and third, that no literary text, no matter how lyrical, lofty and subjective, should be seen as somehow ideologically innocent.

All three premises are operative in the essays comprising *L'Esistenza ubbidiente*, with particular force in the chapter on Giuseppe Ungaretti, who, as the central figure of the Italian 'hermetic' school of poetry, developed a poetic language whose aim was to reveal privileged but fleeting moments of beauty, insight, and, ultimately, transcendence. His poems were considered emblematic of a state of mind that looked upon the world as an alien place of pain and solitude. The hermetic or closed nature of his early lyrical fragments was due, it was commonly agreed, not only to its Japanese and French sources, but also and principally to Ungaretti's profound discomfort in the face of a pervasive sense of despair in Europe during and after the experiences of World War I, in which he fought and suffered along with his comrades, his 'brothers' in arms.

How, then, in the light of the exquisitely intimate and evocative character of Ungaretti's youthful poetry, and his later appeal for a return to traditional verse forms, can he be connected to the ideological project of Italian Fascism, with its mystique of heroism, its mission of national regeneration, its demand that individuals subordinate their private aspirations to a larger project of human renewal embodied in a vastly strengthened totalitarian state? This is the question that Dombroski poses in regard to Ungaretti's inner life and to the ways in which he chose to express himself poetically.

In the chapter of *L'Esistenza ubbidiente* devoted to Ungaretti, entitled 'Ungaretti between Innocence and Fascism', Dombroski uses several different critical techniques and approaches. His choice of gambit, at once theoretical and historical in nature, connects to the work of Giovanni Raboni in order to pose a two-sided problem: first, the almost total lack of general theoretical supports for the socio-political interpretation of lyric poetry, which he attributes in the main to the overwhelming intellectual influence in Italy of Benedetto Croce's philosophy of aesthetics, virtually unchallenged at the time Ungaretti was at his creative zenith; and second, the fact that Ungaretti was a poet whose ardently pro-Fascist political sentiments and whose poetic *œuvre*, lyrical and elliptical in his crucial early period, seemed to follow completely divergent paths. The burden of Dombroski's argument, therefore, was to show that such a divergence was a mere appearance, and that on a deeper thematic and psychological level Ungaretti's politics and his art were reconcilable with each other. What was needed was a critical reading of Ungaretti that would reveal the 'mental structures' that Fascism and the poetry of Ungaretti had in common.

Dombroski notes, in agreement with Raboni, that Ungaretti's ascent to prominence in the 1920s and early 1930s came after a divisive period of cultural ferment and feverish experimentalism in the arts. The line that Ungaretti took in the years culminating in the volume *Sentimento del tempo*, was that Italian writers, above all its poets, needed to recover a sense of formal discipline and restraint, modeled on the classics of Italian poetry, from Petrarch to Leopardi. This was a position, Dombroski maintains, which arrived almost providentially inasmuch as it was analogous to the Fascist régime's concerted effort to restore order and cultural autarchy, after the years from 1919 to about 1923, when Fascism had advocated a sort of upstart political and cultural radicalism designed to appeal to sectors of the working class and to a disaffected petit-bourgeois intelligentsia. Thus, Ungaretti's call for a restoration of order and authority in the realm of poetry moved along a parallel track with the new authoritarian cultural and educational policies of Mussolini's régime. This was one of the 'correspondences' that Dombroski was after.

But such an analogy was not the most important of the arguments in Dombroski's arsenal. Through artful citation of Ungaretti's prose writings after World War I, he points out the numerous ways in which the poet revealed his need to unite himself with a power greater than himself, whether that power assumed the form of a 'man of destiny' such as Mussolini, whose mere physical presence could 'transform' a victim of alienation into a person of faith and self-confidence, or whether it was a movement of ideas and feelings – the Fascist movement in this case – through which one could change a corrosive sense of separateness into one of cohesive solidarity. In this context, Dombroski argues that it was precisely the 'totalitarian' aspect of Fascism that most appealed to Ungaretti. Fascism provided him with a way to overcome the estrangement that he shared with many of his compatriots in the postwar years. In one important essay, Dombroski notes, Ungaretti turned to two writers, René Johannet and the Dutch Marxist Bernard Groethuysen, to substantiate his conviction that liberal Italy and liberal Europe had run out of ideas in the face of the postwar crisis of bourgeois civilisation. Only Fascism, Ungaretti believed, could slake 'the thirst for the absolute' of contemporary Europeans afflicted by a terrible spiritual void, a sense of aimlessness that, if left uncorrected, could only end in despair.

Ungaretti placed the human search for harmony and order in the world at the summit of human aspirations, an attitude which Dombroski did not fail to link with the socio-political dimension of his thought, and with the 'mystical' kernel of his religious orientation to life, his constant hankering after a sense of oneness with the world and with the cosmos. This complex of feelings expressed itself in some measure in his aesthetics, whose fundamental concept, Dombroski claims, was the myth of renewal, of being reborn into a higher state of consciousness and serenity. Innocence for Ungaretti marked both the beginning and the end of history, a notion tied to the idea of creation, of perfection, of the suspended instant of illumination, of plenitude.

The decisive pages, however, at least as I see the unfolding of Dombroski's argument in this chapter, are those he reserves for a sally into an earlier period of Ungaretti's poetic production, poems written well before the era of *Sentimento del tempo*, which appeared in 1933. In several pages of acute textual analysis, Dombroski demonstrated that during World War I and shortly thereafter, Ungaretti had already articulated states of mind that were manifestly compatible with the kind of impulses that led him, not many years later, into an ardent embrace of the new Fascist order. Such impulses were evidenced in *Allegria di naufragi* (Happiness of the shipwrecked) published in 1919, whose title and whose perspective on life both harked back to the last verse of Leopardi's 'L'infinito': 'E il naufragar m'è dolce in questo mare' ['And shipwreck is sweet in such a sea']. Ungaretti converted this evocative Leopardian verse into the basis of a new spiritual agenda.

The upshot of Dombroski's critical scrutiny of several of the better known poems in *Allegria di naufragi* can be gleaned from the following paragraph, which I have extracted from a much longer passage for the sake of clarity:

> The idea of a plenitude either lost or, at the least, still to be discovered, of a mysterious absence of things, is with difficulty separable from the concept of a national soul or of a Mediterranean race, which remains intact through the vicissitudes of history, just as it is with difficulty separable from the myth of a total society in which isolated individuals become living men in communion with the Absolute. The passage, therefore, from poetry to the apology of the totalitarian program of Fascism, in the young Ungaretti, assumes a total coherence.[5]

At the end of the Ungaretti study, Dombroski assures us that the ideological analysis to which he had just subjected Ungaretti takes nothing away from the value of his poetry. The analysis has traced analogies, correspondences, crossings from one form of expression to another, in search of a common matrix of ideas, ideals, and feelings. It has relied on the commensurability of political and poetic discourse, because the aim is to broaden

---

5. Dombroski 1984, p. 88.

the study of poetry to include its ideological content, or better, its way of 'producing ideology'. The essay ends with the following assertion of confidence in the method or methods that he has employed:

> Ungaretti's poetry, like the work of Pirandello, must be explained in accordance with an internal necessity that possesses, in addition to a specific individual character, a truly social aspect, inasmuch as it is a symbolic answer to a concrete dilemma of historical existence. From this angle of vision the interdependence between artistic and political consciousness is revealed in the most immediate way.[6]

Dombroski's approach to Verga in Chapter Two of *Properties of Writing*, and to the new Sicilian novelists writing in the postmodern mode, shows that he was able to balance traditional components of Marxist literary-critical discourse with the requirements of textual analysis imposed by the new emphasis on difference and undecidability. He was able to make the transition between the two approaches by virtue of his conviction that literary texts are forms of human praxis directed, among other things, at reforming consciousness, and that they are organically related to the fundamental sociopolitical realities of their time of creation. In other words, for Dombroski, there was no escape from history, no return to a golden age of innocence, no road by which writers could somehow deflect attention away from the historical foundation of all literary forms, including those associated with postmodernism.

The Verga essay mixes biographical, anthropological and sociological commentary with an attempt to shed light on the Sicilian writer's highly particularised lyrical voice, especially noteworthy in *I Malavoglia*. The essay situates Verga squarely in the context of an 'emergent capitalism' that began to characterise Italian society of the late Risorgimento and immediate post-Risorgimento periods, from the 1840s to the 1880s.

Dombroski's primary aim was to explore the ethnographic dimension of *I Malavoglia*. The family whose way of life is threatened by the mechanisms of a newly emerging capitalist ethos, whereby financial calculation wins out over devotion to time-honoured principles of faithful labour and familial togetherness, is depicted in its moment of crisis and decline. There seems to be a glimmer of hope for renewal at the end of Verga's narrative, yet the novel leaves us with a sense that the traditional way of life as lived for centuries by Sicily's fishermen had disappeared forever.

In his discussion of this historically grounded aspect of the novel, Dombroski reminds us that *I Malavoglia* was conceived as the first in a series of novels whose aim, in a fashion famously theorised by Émile Zola, was to trace the fortunes, at a decisive turning point in Italian history, of typical people belonging to all of the main social classes; not just to subaltern groups such as fishermen and peasants, but to the rising middle and privileged classes as well. In this sense, Verga saw himself as a social historian who utilised ethnographic techniques to produce an austerely objective and scientifically based narrative,

---

6. Dombroski 1984, p. 90.

marked by its adherence to the principles of scientific positivism. Yet there was more to Verga than positivism, and much more to Dombroski's analysis of the Sicilian novelist than ethnography pure and simple. This something more is detectible in the chapter's sub-title, 'Science and Allegory in *I Malavoglia*'. In addition to its social-scientific aspects Dombroski pays close attention to the novel's rich vein of 'poetic' and 'lyrical' writing, in which certain facets of the family's way of life, especially their home, 'the house by the medlar tree', become 'symbol[s] of a lost plenitude', objects and customs endowed with spiritual significance, what Dombroski calls 'a disappearing structure that can be looked upon only with nostalgia'.[7]

In my view, the insight that distinguishes Dombroski's analysis in this chapter does not lie so much in ethnography or in allegorical reading but rather in the way he examines the components of Verga's conception of life, his 'materialism' and 'pessimism', which stand in sharp contrast to the transcendental Christian belief system that characterised Manzoni's *The Betrothed*. In the chapter on Manzoni which opens *Properties of Writing* and directly precedes the one on Verga, Dombroski highlighted the ways in which Manzoni negotiated the concept of free will and self-determination in relation to the theological constraints imposed by the notion of divine providence, which is operative from beginning to end of *The Betrothed*. Verga's materialism, Dombroski maintains, prevents him from

> envisaging writing as a means of connecting text and context in the Manzonian sense, for there is no basis for such a linkage...The context or situation on which literature acts, for Verga, is a social variable that cannot be integrated into or appropriated by the literary text, only juxtaposed to it. In this sense, it is an alien reality, regulated by its own particular logic, which the literary imagination must approach first and foremost as an object of scientific inquiry.[8]

What Dombroski was saying, although not explicitly, is that these two novels of the nineteenth century, one published in 1827, the other in 1881, express two different moments relevant not only to the authors themselves, but also to two different visions of life incorporated in literary texts that became and remain extraordinarily powerful forces within vast hegemonic and counter-hegemonic processes. The 'ideology' produced by these two works have long pervaded Italian society in ways and with effects difficult to trace in any precise manner yet clearly worth studying for a proper understanding of how and why Italians of differing social and political identities conceive of the world as they do. Gramsci's influence on Dombroski's method is especially noteworthy in his critique of Manzoni and Verga.

The specifically Marxist aspect of Dombroski's critique of *I Malavoglia* flows from the insight just mentioned. Rather than follow the line of thought outlined by Angelo

---

7. Dombroski 1994, p. 30.
8. Dombroski 1994, p. 24.

Marchese, who sees Verga's work as reflecting the crisis of liberal-bourgeois ideology in the wake of Italian unification, Dombroski, always wary of direct causal links between history and literature, prefers to view the novel as expressing what Fredric Jameson describes as 'a socially symbolic strategy', whereby the logic of a capitalist market economy is made visible not through a direct representation of capitalist industry and finance but through the ruminations of a character, young 'Ntoni, who has visited the mainland and observed the new Italy, with its military conscription and additional burdensome forms of taxation imposed mainly on the poor. Dombroski is at his best in those pages of his essay on Verga where he integrates his analysis within a conceptual framework built on the notion of 'capitalist secularisation', the unrecoverable loss of what had been sacred in the Malavoglia family's way of life: honest labour, the sanctity of the home, family solidarity, simple piety. It is the waning of the sacred that accounts, Dombroski thinks, for Verghian lyricism, the particular poetic tonality of Verga's prose in some of the novel's key passages. Poetry is a kind of compensatory refuge amidst the harsh realities of competition and survival that mark the onset of a new historical era.

In the early 1990s, concerned with the question of how to present postmodern thought to university students, and impressed by some of the stunning intellectual performances of postmodern writers and cultural critics, Dombroski turned his attention in particular to comparing the work of a group of contemporary Sicilian novelists – Gesualdo Bufalino, Vincenzo Consolo, Antonio Pizzuto, Leonardo Sciascia – who showed distinctive traces of postmodern perspectives in their writing, with that of earlier generations of Sicilian writers, from the 1880s to the 1950s – Verga, Pirandello, Vittorini, Lampedusa – whose conceptions of the function of prose fiction reflected much older values and attitudes. What Dombroski wanted to accomplish was to clarify precisely what the nature of the new postmodern mode of thinking was in relation to the structures of thought and feeling that had guided the founding generations of Sicilian men of letters.

The tentative title he gave to this study was 'Mythical Tradition and Postmodern Culture in the Contemporary Sicilian Novel', whose central ideas he outlined in 1998 and was working on at the time of his death.

His allusions in this outline to an implicit connection between 'forms of market ideology' and the onset of postmodern paradigms in the contemporary Sicilian novel, his references to 'new cognitive forms and insights' as being enmeshed with the new forms of writing, and the general tenor of the proposal, with its interweaving of literary and social themes, show that Dombroski had not abandoned fundamental aspects of his Marxist approach to criticism. An allusion he makes to Louis Althusser is also significant, because the French philosopher played a major role in propagating a theory of society as ultimately an over-determined 'structural totality', a notion repudiated, even if not always consciously, by the new postmodern perspective governing the novels Dombroski was taking under consideration.

It is not possible for me to say very much that is substantive about Dombroski's approach to postmodernism in his 1998 essay 'Re-writing Sicily: Postmodern Perspectives'.[9] Let it suffice here to say that what he attempted in this essay and elsewhere in his work of the 1990s was to explain and to illustrate how the verities and certainties of an earlier Sicilian fiction were thrown into disarray as a consequence of the postmodern *forma mentis* influencing the works of Consolo, Pizzuto and other Sicilian writers of the 1960s to the 1990s; but not only Sicilian ones, of course. The same postmodern turn, Dombroski indicates, took place in the work of Italo Calvino. The chapter on Calvino in *Properties of Writing*, incidentally, is one of the strongest of the collection.

Dombroski points out how the postmodern vision of the world excludes the kind of focus that had marked earlier prose fiction, where one finds, at the very least, three elements: a single controlling consciousness, a landscape whose identity is clearly marked, and the sense of an unchanging Sicilian essence, whether felt as a positive force, as in Vittorini's *In Sicily*, or as a negative one, as in Lampedusa's *The Leopard*. Even the new historically based novels, such as Consolo's *Il sorriso dell'ignoto marinaio* ['The unknown sailor's smile'], of 1987, lacks a centre of consciousness or a controlling perspective. The narrator is just one of the fragments that constitute his historical account, Dombroski argues, a fragment among fragments. The reader is denied access to any totalising narrative that might claim a comprehensive understanding of a place, a time, a core of meaning.

I am confident that the project that Bob Dombroski outlined in his proposal of 1998, to which I alluded above, would have yielded an important contribution to contemporary Italian literary studies. Yet the essay just mentioned and others that appeared in various periodicals over the past few years already give us a good understanding of what he was aiming to accomplish. So instead of lamenting what was destined not to be, let us take pride and pleasure in the work that Bob *was* able to bring to a successful conclusion.

---

9. Schneider (ed.) 1998, pp. 261–76.

Chapter Eleven

John Cammett's Writings on Antonio Gramsci and the PCI

John McKay Cammett, who died in 2008 at the age of 81, was a history professor and man of the Left who had no patience with historians (or with academics in general) who remained aloof from the struggles and suffering of ordinary humanity. Unpretentious but learned and ready to do battle over issues he cared about, he challenged convention, on and off campus. Alastair Davidson was on target when he observed that John, although a professor by vocation, never forgot his early years as an automobile worker and trade unionist in Detroit, an experience that he brought to bear in his studies of Gramsci and the workers' movement in Turin. I met John in the mid-1950s, when we were both graduate students at Columbia University, he in history and I in Italian. I recall his enthusiasm whenever he spoke to me of his research on Gramsci, to whom he was to dedicate much of his intellectual energy for the rest of his life.

The first part of this essay deals with the intriguing interplay in Cammett's writings between his loyalties to the Old Left and his attraction to the New Left. It then focuses on his work as a bibliographer and editor, the most important aspect of which was his monumental *Bibliografia Gramsciana*, composed of three volumes published in 1991, 1995, and 2001. I will conclude with some remarks on Cammett's work as a professor and academic administrator, and a summary discussion of his 1967 study *Antonio Gramsci and the Origins of Italian Communism.*

Cammett between the Old and New Lefts

In the early to mid-1960s, Cammett teamed up with a group of like-minded friends and colleagues at Rutgers University and Brooklyn Polytechnic Institute to found an organisation they called the Socialist Scholars Conference (SSC: not to be confused with the SSC sponsored a decade later by the Democratic Socialists of America).

The first SSC was an important venture, perhaps unknown by readers of JMIS who were born after 1960. It held six well-attended annual meetings, from 1965 to 1970, when it ceased its activities because of unresolved internal disputes; but not before George Fischer, in partnership with three associate editors, Cammett, Alan Block, and Richard Friedman, published a volume of selected papers of the SSC with the title *The Revival of American Socialism*, which appeared in 1971. The book included essays by a politically disparate group of writers, which reflected their ecumenical approach to the prospects of American socialism. The contributors went from Irving Howe to Harry Magdoff, from Paul Sweezy to James O'Connor and Stanley Aronowitz, from Christopher Lasch to Martin Jay. Cammett presented two papers to the SSC, one, entitled 'Communist Theories of Fascism, 1920–1935', on 11 September 1966, the other, which was anthologised by Fischer, on 9 September 1967, entitled 'Socialism and Participatory Democracy'. His subject in the latter paper was the relation between socialism and democracy; he drew his examples from the factory councils theorised and actuated by Gramsci and several others in 1919 and 1920.

When I began revisiting Cammett's work several months after his death, I was a little surprised to discover that he had been so deeply involved in New Left politics and culture. I had always associated him with an abiding emotional as well as political attachment to the revolutionary accomplishments of the Soviet Union. There were several reasons for my thinking of him in this way. One was his early years as a worker and trade unionist in the automobile plants of Detroit, which influenced his conception of industrial workers as the fullest embodiment of productive labour and as such engaged in a fateful, class-based confrontation with the capitalist system. One of his heroes in the Italian labour movement was Giuseppe Di Vittorio, who with Gramsci and Palmiro Togliatti was among the personalities whose achievements led John to become a member of the Italian Communist Party. The PCI eventually acquired the reputation of being basically a social-democratic party masquerading as a revolutionary one. But on this question we should remember that, when Cammett took this step sometime in the 1950s, the PCI was still a 'Stalinist' party ready to defend the Soviet régime against those who saw Stalin and the Soviet bureaucracy as the antithesis of true communist principles. So his membership in the PCI was an assertion, not a negation, of his Communist ideals.

Cammett's work for the journal *Science and Society* also led me to think of him primarily as a Communist of an older vintage, inasmuch as this journal had many US Communists on its editorial board, and espoused the idea that the Soviet Union, despite the crimes of Stalinism, had always been an irreplaceable contributor to the world socialist revolution. Although he became increasingly critical of the Soviet government and ceased being an active member of the *Science and Society* editorial committee, I can attest to the fact that Cammett saw the collapse of the Soviet Union in the early 1990s as a disaster for socialism, and not, as many in the New Left fervently believed, as a necessary starting point for a renewal of socialism based on radical-democratic rather than authoritarian foundations. Whenever the conversations in which I took part with Cammett turned to our political sentiments and affiliations, he always said of himself: 'I am a Communist', by which I think he meant, among other things, that the existence and example of the Soviet Union was of crucial importance to the worldwide struggle to eliminate poverty, inequality, and racism.

But as I soon realised, there was another side of John's personality and worldview that brought him into close touch with the New Left, and that led to his partnership with a group of left-wing academic intellectuals who had broken away from the old Communism. His feeling of identification with the New Left seems to have developed somewhat before the rise in the mid to late 1960s of a new wave of revolutionary militancy. Riding the crest of this wave were unorthodox, rebellious figures such as Abbie Hoffman who thumbed their noses not only at established authority in bourgeois capitalist societies but, with equal disdain, at the ideologues of Stalinist orthodoxy, whether in the Soviet Union itself or in the Communist Parties of countries such as Britain, France, and the United States. Cammett began to reflect on the fact that the surge of revolutionary activism then in evidence was coming mainly from Asia, Africa, and Latin America, and not from the countries and political parties that had embodied revolutionary Marxism in earlier decades. Ho Chi Minh, Fidel Castro, Che Guevara, Claudia Jones, Frantz Fanon, C.L.R. James, Aimé Césaire, Kwame Nkrumah, and many others, while attempting to integrate Marxist concepts into their politics, were forging new pathways to the goal of liberation from all forms of oppression, domestic and foreign. John had a clear understanding of why American youth in revolt felt much closer to these personalities than to, say, Gus Hall or Norman Thomas.

Concurrent with this change in the configurations of global power relations was the fact that thinkers associated with Marxist and with existential/materialist traditions of thought – such as Herbert Marcuse, Jean-Paul Sartre, Simone de Beauvoir, Gyorgy Lukács, Walter Benjamin, and Antonio Gramsci – were expanding the frontiers of Marxist theory to encompass a broader range of issues and problems than had their more doctrinaire predecessors. I am referring to questions of consciousness and identity, of language and culture, and to issues related to the condition and aspirations of women in modern, male-dominated society. Regrettably, it was typical of the New Left in the 1960s that there was not a single woman among the 16 writers represented in the volume *The Revival of American Socialism*. Still, the fact that new departures from classical Marxism were of major interest to its editors was evident in the sub-titles of the three sections of the book: 'New Paths to Socialism;' 'Late Capitalism', which featured some heavyweight

Marxist economists, namely Harry Magdoff, Norman Birnbaum, Paul Sweezy, and Ernest Mandel; and a third section, entitled 'Neo-Marxism', which focused on the problematic aspects of Herbert Marcuse's influence on radical student movements of the 1960s. Marcuse's critique of Western societies was a major theme of several papers read at the SSC meetings, notably those of Martin Jay, Ronald Aronson, and Paul Breines.

Cammett had no difficulty in associating Gramsci's *Prison Notebooks* with these new departures in historical, sociological, philosophical, and literary-critical thought. He had begun to read Gramsci in the early 1950s. Since he read Italian fluently, he did not have to wait for the first English-language translations of Gramsci, those of Carl Marzani and Louis Marks, both of which appeared in 1957. By the 1960s (recall that his groundbreaking study *Antonio Gramsci and the Origins of Italian Communism* appeared in 1967) he had begun to think about the qualities of Gramsci's mind that justified placing him among other innovative Marxist thinkers who were emerging twenty years after the Italian Communist's death in 1937. Gramsci had paid close attention to the intellectual and creative capacities of human beings as they try to gain a critical understanding of the forces shaping their lives and destinies. Gramsci, after all, had been formed primarily by his studies of history, philosophy, literature and philology; in sum, by the humanities. Cammett was sensitive to the original and provocative dimensions of Gramsci's reflections on how and why human beings think of themselves in a certain manner, and how and why ruling classes exert their authority in society, not only through the exercise of superior force, but through the pervasive diffusion of ideas and values that filter down into the masses of people through myriad channels. These processes, Gramsci thought, were endemic to the struggle for 'hegemony', one of the Gramscian themes that Cammett was attracted to and examined in several of his writings.

In order to illustrate the interplay of old and new in Cammett's conception of the political world from the 1960s to the 1980s, let us look at the above-mentioned essays that he wrote for the second and third meetings of the SSC, in 1966 and 1967, and at another later essay of 1980, his introduction to Carl Marzani's *The Promise of Eurocommunism*.

The Preface to *The Revival of American Socialism* written by Fischer but signed by the Editors, set the tone for the volume's first section, entitled 'New Paths to Socialism'. It was written after the sixth and final conference of the SSC in 1970, which allowed the editors to incorporate the French uprising of May 1968 into their consideration of a socialist revival in the United States.

It is safe to say that the spark of the May 1968 events was ignited by social groups that were largely independent of the French Communist Party and the major labour confederations. They joined in the revolt after the first weeks made it clear that something really significant was taking place in Paris and in other French cities. But, as Daniel Singer shows in his 1970 book *Prelude to Revolution: France in May 1968*, the French CP and the unions did not initiate the revolt. This recent history, I think, was further proof, as far as the SSC organisers were concerned, that the torch of revolution had passed from the Old to the New Left.

Another event of the late 1960s that impelled Cammett and his colleagues to rethink the allegiances they had had earlier in their lives was the struggle in 1968 by Alexander Dubcek and his associates to bring about democratic reforms within the Czechoslovakian Communist Party and open up Czech society to something that Mikhail Gorbachev was later to call *glasnost*. The entrance of Soviet tanks into Prague in August 1968 was a terrible setback to everyone who hoped for reforms in the Soviet Union similar to those advocated by Dubcek.

The phrase 'participatory democracy' that Cammett had in mind when he linked it to socialism in the title of his 1967 essay, was not a theoretical abstraction but rather a reference to a concrete case of a movement for self-management and workplace democracy that Gramsci had helped to set in motion in the years directly following the end of World War I.

The main point of Cammett's commentary on the workers' councils movement in Turin was its relevance to the struggles of the late 1960s. Here is how he formulated this idea in the opening section of his essay:

> The relation between socialism and democracy is not a new concern, either for American Socialism or for socialist movements elsewhere. Nor is the core issue one of direct rule, of self-government at the grass roots. In the socialist tradition, participatory democracy was discussed most often with regard to workers' control. Few have related workers' control to socialism more suggestively, and few today enjoy as much influence on a new generation of socialists, as the great early leader of the Italian Communist Party, Antonio Gramsci. Both in theory and in practice, his work on the creation of 'Italian Soviets' [in 1919] stands out as a notable answer to a most contemporary question: what is the place of working men in a free, non-repressive socialism?[1]

In this passage, several facets of Cammett's personality and political outlook can be discerned without too much difficulty. One is his general concern with the relation between two world-historical movements, socialism and democracy. Another is his insistence on the specificity and originality, within the general history of socialism, of the struggle for workers' self-management, but as it is achieved on the shop floor. He wanted to delimit his remarks, to contain them within a very particular and concrete context. Concreteness of focus is typical of all of Cammett's writing. He was not comfortable with vague propositions and vague conclusions. He was concerned fundamentally with the industrial working class. This differentiates him from figures in the New Left who were more interested in various forms of cultural radicalism than in the fortunes of industrial workers. The New Left was moving away from a politics based on the labor theory of value. Yet at the same time, we should note that Cammett was concerned with finding a place for 'working men' in a 'free, non-repressive socialism'. His reaction to the Stalinist repression of difference and dissent is implicit in this statement. We see right here how different

---

1. Cammett 1971, p. 41.

elements of Cammett's personality were contending for primacy. Still another important theme of this paragraph was the relevance of Gramsci himself, especially to what Cammett called 'a new generation of socialists'. This last point has been substantiated if we can judge by the extraordinary appeal of Gramsci to readers coming from all kinds of political backgrounds. Cammett's bibliographical work is the best source for documenting the worldwide impact of Gramsci's ideas and analyses.

Cammett's awareness of the shifting epicentre of revolutionary insurgency, which he and his colleagues believed called for a new set of theoretical guidelines, appears further on in this same essay. He was asking himself a different set of questions from the ones he had posed earlier in his life, questions pertinent to the 1960s, one of which was the extent to which Gramsci's perspectives could be helpful 'in developing more adequate Marxian ideas on the political and revolutionary possibilities in these newly emerging countries'. The names of Edward Said, Cornel West, Gayatri Spivak, Stuart Hall, José Carlos Mariátegui, and so many others who were influenced by Gramsci and who occupy important places in the intellectual history of the last five decades, attest to Cammett's understanding of Gramsci as a living presence in the minds of radical thinkers coming from diverse backgrounds.

One other aspect of this essay calls for comment: It is Cammett's appreciation of what Gramsci took from Lenin, especially in working out his theory of hegemony. It was Lenin, Cammett argued, who taught Gramsci to avoid economism and a type of 'materialism' that tended to annul the purposive and creative side of human affairs. This is how he summarised his views on this all-important question in Gramsci's writing:

> The fundamental assumption behind Gramsci's view of hegemony is that the working class, before it seizes state power, must establish its claim to be a ruling class in the political, cultural, and 'ethical' fields. The founding of a ruling class is equivalent to the creation of a *Weltanschauung*...Hegemony – rule by consent, the legitimization of revolution by a higher and more comprehensive culture – is the unifying idea of Gramsci's life.[2]

In this dense paragraph, we hear two discordant voices speaking: on the one hand, Cammett spoke of a working class that 'seizes state power'. Were he and his colleagues really thinking in these terms? There had been a seizure of state power in Russia in 1917; but was something analogous to this event possible in the United States, and did it play a major role in the thinking of the New Left? On the other hand, Cammett knew that Gramsci himself saw little possibility of such a seizure after the defeats sustained by the Left in the 1920s and 1930s.

It appears that Cammett, although still in sympathy with the terminology and mentality of the Bolshevik party of the 1920s, particularly its stress on the need for a revolutionary vanguard party, was aware of Gramsci's scepticism about the prospects for such

---

2. Cammett 1971, pp. 52–3.

'seizures of state power', at least in Western Europe. He took due note of the pertinence in the 1960s of what Gramsci had said about the differences between the Russia of 1917 and Western Europe and, implicitly, the United States as well. The difference lay in the highly developed and multi-layered nature of civil society in the West, as compared with the unformed 'gelatinous' nature of civil society in a country like Russia, which had allowed the Bolshevik party to fill a virtual vacuum of power. It followed from this Gramscian distinction, Cammett observed – and here, I am confident in saying that he was thinking of the SSC's potential contribution to the struggle for socialism in the United States – 'the seizure of power by a new class is unlikely to succeed without a prior victory in the area of civil society; hence, the struggle for hegemony, for cultural and moral predominance, is the main task of Marxists in the advanced countries of the West'.[3]

Moving now to Cammett's paper on 'Communist Theories of Fascism, 1920–1935', which he delivered at the SSC conference of 11 September 1966 and published in the Spring 1967 issue of *Science and Society*, we find that his emphasis falls most strongly on problems of historical scholarship and on the need for attention to differences of time, place, and circumstance. Cammett as historian took precedence, in this instance, over Cammett the proponent of a particular political line or position, although in the conclusion of his paper he left no doubt that he was writing in a political context, and that he wanted his analysis to serve the purpose of developing 'a rich, articulate and autonomous socialist culture'.[4] The following passage from the introductory section of his paper is indicative of how seriously Cammett took his job as an independent socialist scholar and critical intellectual. After explaining the sources of his documentation and alluding to the Communist and the bourgeois theories of Fascism, he wrote as follows:

> My plan is to present first a survey of the principal documents of the Comintern on the question of Fascism; then to consider the work of a few Communist scholars and political leaders on more particular aspects of the nature of Fascism; finally, to indicate briefly some of the work which remains to be done in this field. Baldly stated, my thesis in this paper is that from 1920 to 1928 the Communist movement made a good many important contributions to the theory of Fascism, but that after the Sixth World Congress of the Communist International, and including the period of the Popular Front, its work in this field (with a few exceptions) became less and less concrete and more and more adapted to mere political exigencies.[5]

Two things strike me in this passage. First is Cammett's sense that the question of Fascism could not simply be raised and answered in one fell swoop. Like any other complex historical phenomenon, the study and interpretation of Fascism was an ongoing process requiring not only thorough documentation but new and deeper insights commensurate

---

3. Cammett 1971, p. 54.
4. Cammett 1967b, p. 163.
5. Cammett 1967b, pp. 149–50.

with the problems involved. In this connection, his reference to 'particular aspects of the nature of Fascism' was his way of recognising the value of sharply focused studies of a movement that, after all, had won the support of a good part of the Italian population. Second, the distinction that he drew between serious historical scholarship and historical writing 'adapted to mere political exigencies' is also noteworthy. Such 'adaptations' were not methodologically defensible, he thought, as legitimate tools of the responsible historian, whatever his or her aims and point of view.

Cammett then took up one of the perplexing and still controversial questions in the history of Fascism, namely its class constituency. Was it the expression of a disaffected and uprooted petty bourgeoisie? Was it the result of a plot by a group of conspirators drawn mainly from the capitalist and landowning sectors of Italian society? To what extent was it a genuinely popular movement that attracted some workers as well as middle-class strata? In his discussion of these issues, he made it clear that in its reaction to Fascism, the Communist International was often uncertain and befuddled; that the Communist International was not a monolith; that there were different currents flowing within the Comintern, and that Communist theories of Fascism were influenced by changes in the balance of forces in the world at different times. He spoke of the superficiality among prominent Communist theorists of Fascism and cited with approval a speech delivered by Clara Zetkin at the Third Plenum of the Executive Committee of the Comintern in June 1923, when she asserted that 'the mistakes of the CP...lie above all in viewing Fascism only as a military-terrorist movement and not as a mass movement with deep social roots'.[6]

In addition to his many friendships and contacts with people active in the Communist movement, Cammett's exceptional personal library of books and other documents on the history of world communism gave him the ability to utilise materials that were not easily available to most other commentators at the time.[7]

One reason for Cammett's admiration for both Gramsci and Palmiro Togliatti was the part they played, during their periods of residence in the Soviet Union in the 1920s, in resisting a tendency of their fellow Communists to oversimplify and distort the origins and subsequent growth of Fascism because of their 'adaptation to mere political exigencies'. Does theory depend on facts, or do facts depend on theory? Theory, Cammett was convinced, must be nourished and enriched by concrete historical studies. To adhere dogmatically to theoretical constructs unsupported by the evidence of human experience was a formula for failure, as Cammett saw it.

Among the many historians who, in Cammett's opinion, had made useful contributions to the understanding of Fascism, were Rajani Palme Dutt in his *Fascism and Social*

---

6. Cammett 1967b, p. 151.

7. Cammett's widow, Professor Sandi Cooper, donated his entire library to the John D. Calandra Italian American Institute located at 25 West 43rd street (17th floor) in Manhattan. The director of the Institute is Professor Anthony Tamburri.

Revolution, published in 1934, and Frank A. Warren III, in his *Liberals and Communism: The 'Red Decade' Revisited*, published in 1966. Cammett's favourable opinion of these two books exemplify his openness to originality of thought whether it came from an Indian Communist such as Dutt or a left-leaning liberal historian such as Warren. He cited both books as enlightening studies of the contradictions and confusion rife among Communists in defending their sponsorship of the Popular Front.

Cammett waffled here and there in his estimate of Communist theories of Fascism, especially when he dealt with Fascism as an international movement and with the Popular Front era. He is less than persuasive in his consideration of the Comintern slogan in the 1930s concerning what it called 'social fascism', which implied an equivalence or a close similarity between Fascism and social democracy as two faces of the same reactionary phenomenon. He allows that 'social fascism' was an ill-conceived formulation, but that it also had 'a grain of truth'. He agreed with the Italian revolutionary socialist Lelio Basso, who argued that the function of social democracy was not to change the existing situation, but to provide the capitalist system with a mass basis, making the working class the ally and support of big capital.

All in all, this essay was one of the best overviews of its topic to appear in the 1960s, and should be read by everyone interested in what was alive and what was dead in Communist theories of Fascism in the 1920s and 1930s.

It will be worth our while to look at two other essays by Cammett that appeared about a decade later than those just discussed. As far as I know, they were not written expressly for any organisation, although it can be argued that his rather favourable attitude toward Eurocommunism sprang from his membership in the PCI and his desire to be helpful to the Communist Parties of Italy, Spain, and France, all three of which, especially the Italian and Spanish parties, were closely identified with this new political current in the 1970s.

In general, the two essays – an introduction to Carl Marzani's book *The Promise of Eurocommunism*, published in 1980, and an article on 'Communist Women and the Fascist Experience', which appeared in a 1981 volume of essays entitled *European Women on the Left – Socialism, Feminism, and the Problems Faced by Political Women*, reflected Cammett's undogmatic and appreciative response to the political culture of neo-Marxism in its various manifestations.

The official Communist reaction to Eurocommunism in the 1970s was mainly hostile and often dismissive. Cammett, on the other hand, writing in 1980, saw much that was promising in it. On women's issues, it should be remembered that Betty Friedan's *The Feminine Mystique* had been published in 1963, and had sparked a powerful social movement that people on the Left could hardly ignore.

What strikes me most forcefully in Cammett's introduction to Marzani's book *The Promise of Eurocommunism* is its meticulousness and density. In only seven pages, he explains the origins of Eurocommunism, and examines the subtle but theoretically important differences in the interpretations of Eurocommunism as articulated by the three leaders of the Communist Parties in Italy, France, and Spain, respectively Enrico Berlinguer, Georges Marchais, and Santiago Carrillo. It is clear that Cammett's approach to his subject was as much philological as political. He wanted to be as precise as possible in defining his terms and in making distinctions which, if overlooked, could lead to serious errors of judgment.

Cammett is informative also on a problem that Joseph Buttigieg has looked at on a number of occasions, namely right-wing publications' 'uses and misuses' of terms they borrow from Gramsci for the purpose of discrediting them to the general public. In the particular case of the word Eurocommunism, Cammett pointed out the ways in which journals such as *Commentary, Encounter*, and *Foreign Affairs* used some of the arguments of Eurocommunism to denigrate 'actually-existing socialism' in Eastern Europe and the Soviet Union. Their modus vivendi, Cammett thought, was based on the slogan 'The enemy of my enemy is my friend'. At the same time, he expressed his reservations about the ways in which the Left was assimilating the theory underlying Eurocommunism. He took exception to the tendency of some groups on the Left to see the Eurocommunist parties as having been easily integrated into a process of 'social-democratisation'. He then proceeded to argue that, in effect, there was something new and significant occurring within these parties in the 1970s, but the origins of this were to be found much earlier, in the debates on the Popular Front that took place in the 1930s, where one could see that within the Communist movement there had built up 'a resolve to move, somehow or other, beyond the condition of 'vanguard parties' – with their attendant 'purity of doctrine and historical determinism – toward the creation of *mass national parties*'. On this point, Cammett felt that the decision of revolutionary Communist Parties in the 1930s and 1940s to behave 'politically', that is, to participate in the political life of bourgeois states, was a major turning point. Once that happened, 'everything identified with the Eurocommunism of the 1970s became possible'.[8] This is a dubious thesis, because the rethinking of their politics by leaders of the three Communist Parties and their followers in the 1970s was a much more extensive process than what had transpired at the time of the Popular Front. Nevertheless, what Cammett does here is historicise not only a term but a growing tendency of the European Communist movement, over a period of about fifty years, to break out of its protective cocoon and actively engage itself with the prevailing methods and institutions of bourgeois democracy.

Cammett also took up another question often overlooked by students of communism, namely the lessons that Gramsci and Toglatti had learned from the defeat suffered by their Party in the 1920s. Marzani's consciousness of this decisive event and its impact, Cammett observed, was one of the qualities that made his account of Eurocommunism so useful.

---

8. See Marzani 1980.

After a summary account of Marzani's life, Cammett ended his introduction with an acknowledgment of how limited and often wrong our understanding of historical movements can be. Here is the concluding paragraph of the introduction:

> Marzani is, as ever, an optimist and very sympathetic to the Italian Communists, but I do not think he minimises the enormous obstacles which the party has yet to overcome. His book will convince many that the Italian Communists have undertaken one of the nobler political and social tasks of our time – but its ultimate success is far from guaranteed.

We now know the outcome of the PCI effort to reform itself and strengthen its foothold in Italian society through establishing a 'national-popular' strategy. Cammett was well-aware of the pitfalls that his party faced in 1980. He was saddened, but not personally defeated, by the events of the 1990s. Above all, he used the tools of the historian to illuminate the crises of his time and ours, in a remarkably objective manner.

A noteworthy aspect of the volume *European Women and the Left* is that its two editors, Jane Slaughter and Robert Kirn, took a position on the emancipation of women that was strongly anti-capitalist and pro-socialist, and that they looked at women's struggles in historical perspective. For them, 'the emancipation of women will occur only with the socialist revolution, the destruction of private property, and the disappearance of traditional marriage and the family'.[9] It's doubtful that Cammett and most other contributors were willing to unqualifiedly endorse this position, but it's likely that he was not that far away from it either. In any event, the editors acknowledged the 'diversity' of opinion on women's liberation among the contributors.

In this article, true to the historian's craft, Cammett insisted on the importance of archival sources for much of what he felt able to say about the role of Communist women in the anti-fascist movement, especially in Italy. He drew heavily from documents in the Archivio Centrale dello Stato in Rome and from the archive of the PCI, also in the Italian capital. He was anxious to establish the authenticity of the account that he offered on a subject that had not yet been adequately explored by socialist scholars. Probably for the same reason, the article is replete with statistical evidence taken from a large number of secondary sources, which included the testimony of women who had participated in the anti-fascist Union of Italian Women from 1943 to 1945. The article was also a vindication of the role played in the Italian Resistance by Communist women, Cammett stressing the enormous 'sacrifices' made by these women in their dual function as front line members of the Resistance and as wives and mothers who did not want to abandon their responsibilities to their families. He goes into considerable detail to document the social class, political affiliations, work experiences, special 'female' problems, and clandestine activities of the women he was writing about.

---

9. Slaughter and Kern (eds.) 1981, p. 4.

Cammett presented his account of a complex and little known subject in recent Italian and European history with candour and a refreshing lack of self-consciousness. His own experiences as an American historian trained by reputable scholars and as a member of the world Communist movement gave him a freedom of expression that many of his contemporaries did not have when writing about real flesh-and-blood Communists instead of stereotypical images that had been circulating in the United States since the outbreak of the Russian Revolution. Cammett helped to familiarise Americans with the names of Italian Communist women: Camilla Ravera, Cesira Fiori, Adele Bei, Felicita Ferrero, Teresa Noce, and many others whose example opened up new possibilities of self-expression and self assertion for women in Italy and, more generally, in the postwar world.

Cammett as bibliographer and editor

Cammett's bibliographical and editorial work was a primary facet of his self-conception as an 'organic intellectual' in the Gramscian mold. I have already mentioned his work as an editor of the journal *Science and Society*, to which can be added his *Gramsci Bibliography*, his editorship of the sections on 'Italy' and 'The Vatican' in *Soviet Foreign Relations and World Communism – A Selected, Annotated Bibliography of 7,000 Books in 30 Languages* (1965), and his co-editorship, with Shepard B. Clough, Peter Gay, and Charles K. Warner, of *The European Past* (1970). He understood the importance of this kind of work, regarding it as a basic political and philological responsibility, one expression of the debt that he owed to his comrades and colleagues, especially those who shared his interests and point of view.

The eight articles that Cammett contributed to the *Dictionary of Modern Italian History*, published in 1985, exemplify this facet of his intellectual activity.

Perhaps inhibited by the didactic nature and methodology of the Dictionary, Cammett tended at times to avoid difficult critical questions in his entries. Yet he did challenge conventional wisdom in his article on Palmiro Togliatti, whom he defended against charges of his having been an unreconstructed Stalinist; in some of his comments on the history of the PCI; and in his point of view on the Party's intransigent first general secretary, Amadeo Bordiga. In addition to these three topics, Cammett's articles deal with the Socialist newspaper *Avanti!*; with the Socialist Enrico Ferri; with Antonio Gramsci; with the founding father of Italian Marxism, Antonio Labriola; and with Costantino Lazzari, the founder of the Italian Workers' Party.

Cammett's dictionary article on Gramsci goes over some of the same points that I will mention below in my comments on his study of Gramsci and the origins of Italian Communism. But there was something new in what he had to say, not about Gramsci himself, but about the PCI. We should remember that the study of Gramsci was published in 1967, while the article on the PCI under review here was written almost twenty years later.

Therefore, it is necessary to take note of the new perspectives from which Cammett was viewing the PCI at this later stage in his thinking.

First, Cammett highlights the PCI's successful elaboration after World War II of an 'Italian road to socialism', through which it became 'a great mass organisation' and 'an indispensable part of the fabric of Italian social life'. But Cammett did not shrink from saying at the same time that, in its foreign policy positions, the Party 'retained a wholly uncritical attitude toward the USSR'. In this context, he sharpened the critical edge of his remarks by saying that, because of this close to servile relationship with the Soviet Union up to 1956, the Party lost some of its influence on intellectuals and even on sectors of the working class.

Second, he stressed the growing independence of the PCI vis-à-vis the Soviet Union when it rejected the notion that there was only one 'leading Communist state or party'. He credited Togliatti for making this breakthrough in the last political act of his life, known as the Yalta Memorandum written in 1964. Thus the Party moved towards the complete acceptance of political pluralism, which, Cammett believed at the time, assured the Party a prominent role in Italian democratic institutions.

Third, Cammett commented on the new collaborative relationship between the PCI and the Christian Democratic Party in a mildly supportive manner, but without making any pronouncements about its chances for success.

Among the architects of this new collaborative strategy was Palmiro Togliatti, whose accomplishments Cammett always praised, but without taking particular note of the Italian Communist leader's possible complicity in political crimes that, in the final analysis, were attributable to Stalinist methods of dealing with opposing groups and parties. He says nothing about Togliatti's failure to condemn the murder of anarchists by Stalin's agents during the Spanish Civil War, nor does he discuss Togliatti's years of residence in the Soviet Union in the 1930s, during which he consistently 'yielded to the policies of the Communist International'.

Yet if considered from a perspective that encompasses all periods of Togliatti's life, there is little doubt that, as Cammett asserts, he was a skilful tactician and a statesman on a par with any of the other European leaders at the time. The article on Togliatti emphasises his crucial contribution to making the PCI a mass party after World War II, his response to the Khrushchev Report of 1956, which was to call for historical study of 'Stalinist degenerations', and to establish the rationale behind the idea of 'an Italian road to socialism'.

The *Bibliografia Gramsciana* was a singular event in the history of publishing that required Cammett's unflagging devotion to his task, which in its last incarnation of 2001 numbered 14,500 titles of writings of all kinds on Antonio Gramsci, in 33 languages, but also his singular abilities to organise entries under suitable categories, and his wide range of international contacts, which was needed to back up the claim that the volumes were as complete as human energy and intelligence could achieve. Indeed, in order to bring to fruition this Herculean undertaking, Cammett needed to count on assistance from many people and institutions, mainly the Gramsci Institute in Rome, but also groups of scholars and writers in all of the countries represented. The bibliography was an international effort that helped to close the gap in scholarship resulting from the unavailability of writings in languages which most readers in western countries could not be expected to know.[10]

Cammett had a worthy partner in his bibliographical labors in Maria Luisa Righi; he also relied on the support of Elsa Fubini, Giuseppe Vacca, and Antonio Santucci, who afforded him access to the resources of the Gramsci Institute and their insights concerning Gramsci studies in Italy and the world at large.

Professor Cammett

Cammett held the dual positions of Provost and Dean of Faculty at John Jay College of Criminal Justice in New York City from 1969 to 1975, and was Chair of the History Department from 1984 to 1991. He progressed to these academic distinctions in the course of a forty-year teaching career that took him from part-time instructorships at Wayne State University, Columbia College, Middlebury College and Hunter College to an assistant professorship of history at Rutgers University from 1962 to 1967 and to his posts at John Jay. He retired as professor emeritus from John Jay and the Graduate School of the City University of New York in 1991.

At John Jay, Cammett initiated a much broader conception of the kind of education that police officers and others working in the criminal justice system should have available, an education that included the liberal arts, heretofore considered superfluous for a student body composed mainly of police officers and firemen. He believed that members of the citizenry involved in law enforcement must be able to understand the authority invested in them as a means of serving the needs of the community, a role that required rethinking the relationship between the centres of political power and ordinary working people. The strongly democratic and socialist ideals that underlay these efforts at curriculum reform was one of the reasons why Cammett was nicknamed 'The Red Dean'.

Mary Gibson was one of the young PhDs whom Cammett hired at John Jay. She came to the college in 1984. Her remembrances shed light on how Cammett conducted himself as chair of the History Department. Gibson describes him as 'extremely fair-minded and democratic'. With regard to her own career, Gibson notes that 'John was one of the few faculty men in the early 1980s to support women's entrance into academia. He actively fought for my line and was always supportive of my career at John Jay'.[11]

---

10. Among the languages included in the *Bibliografia gramsciana* that are not known by most readers from the United States and West European countries are Japanese, Korean, Chinese, Arabic, Finnish, Catalan, Russian, Slovak and Hungarian.

11. In a letter to me dated 6 October 2009.

Another of Cammett's axccomplishments at John Jay was, as Gibson puts it, 'to make room in the department for two journals, *The Radical History Review*, and *Science and Society*, thereby encouraging leftist research and bringing prestige to the department'. This observation brings us back full circle to the theme highlighted at the beginning of this essay, which was the interplay of the Old and the New Left in Cammett's political sensibilities. He was not one to exclude voices advocating currents of thought and lines of inquiry that he did not entirely agree with. He saw the issues and conflicts of the contemporary world as too complex and multidimensional to allow for arbitrary exclusions.

Some remarks on *Antonio Gramsci and the Origins of Italian Communism*

One of Cammett's closest colleagues at Rutgers University in the 1960s, Eugene Genovese, wrote a frequently cited review of *Antonio Gramsci and the Origins of Italian Communism* that can be read in two keys, one extremely favourable, the other critical of Cammett's 'tendency to avoid a frank discussion of the markedly idealist cast of Gramsci's thought', and his failure 'to develop his criticisms of Gramsci', which forced him 'to restrict himself so much to the task of presenting Gramsci's case'.[12]

Genovese might have put his finger on a weakness of Cammett's book, yet I suspect that at this juncture (in 1968), Genovese was working within a rather restrictive conception of Marxist materialism. All in all, my view is that Cammett succeeded in presenting a well-balanced, thoroughly researched, intellectually engaging portrait of Gramsci in the first three parts of his book: his early years in Sardinia and Turin, his work for the newspaper *L'Ordine Nuovo*, and his role in the founding of the PCd'I and in clarifying the Party's position within the Communist International. Part Four, a discussion of leading themes of the *Prison Notebooks*, is somewhat skimpy, but considering the year in which the book appeared, 1967, Cammett answered the need, especially in the United States, to appreciate Gramsci as a political thinker of formidable powers.

Also essential is Cammett's integration into his study of material related to Gramsci as a proponent of 'open Marxism', a phrase that Carl Marzani, a friend of Cammett's, used in the title of his 1957 English translation of selected passages from the *Prison Notebooks*. I find little evidence of Cammett's desire to soften Gramsci's image or to overemphasise his 'idealist' tendencies. The fact is that Gramsci learned a great deal from the Hegelianised form of Marxism of which Benedetto Croce was a leading exponent. Gramsci did draw inspiration from Antonio Labriola and especially from Croce, whom he credited with initiating the kind of 'moral and intellectual reform' that Gramsci believed was an indispensable element of socialist humanism.[13] Moreover, his understanding of historical

---

12. See Genovese 1970.
13. On this point, see Gramsci's prison letter of 17 August 1931 in Gramsci 1994, Vol. II, pp. 56–7.

materialism was not reductive. Its main feature was his insistence on the primacy of history, not on that of materialism; or better, Gramsci's materialist philosophy was rooted in the unpredictable, infinitely varied and complex nature of history, which comprehended the economic activities and relations of society, without being solely determined by them.

Cammett admired two things in Gramsci's writing: his consistent emphasis on the concrete particulars of whatever phenomenon he was dealing with, combined with his explorations of how and why these particulars formed part of a theoretical position or conception of the world. He shared Gramsci's belief that only by merging these two approaches into an effective unity could a political party striving to insert itself into the unceasing struggle among individuals, groups, classes, and nations achieve predominance and leadership in society. This dialectical component of Gramsci's writings and his work within various social, cultural, economic and industrial organisations, was what sparked Cammett's interest in him.

In his discussions of Gramsci's multifarious activities, Cammett gave rather short shrift to the literary and cultural side of his work, and was also chary of dwelling more than absolutely necessary on the private side of Gramsci's life, except in Part One on his early years in Sardinia. The reason for this imbalance lies in his commitment to writing a primarily political study, focusing on how Gramsci gave his theoretical insights institutional forms, and how he helped to shape several of the newspapers and journals through which he and his comrades expounded their views on the current and future direction of Italian society. To this end, he devoted ample attention precisely to the founding of the PCd'I, and to one of Gramsci's outstanding journalistic accomplishments, the newspaper *L'Ordine Nuovo*. Cammett also describes in considerable detail Gramsci's contributions, both theoretical and practical, to the factory council movement in Turin, and to his assimilation of Lenin's revolutionary leadership, but in the light of Italian conditions, which were in many respects different from those in Russia.

If I had to choose a single word with which to suggest the trait or facet of Gramsci's personality that predominates in Cammett's book, that word would be originality. Each chapter manages to single out examples of Gramsci's way of redefining the issues and problems with which he was concerned. Cammett makes it clear that Gramsci was not bound by convention, that he often moved in directions that were seen by many as deviations from established practices. His refusal to renounce his indebtedness to Benedetto Croce; his reconceptualisation of historical figures, such as Machiavelli, which resulted in the metaphor of the Communist Party as 'a modern prince;' his close working relationship with the Turin liberal thinker Piero Gobetti, whom he honoured in the closing paragraphs of his 1926 essay *Some Aspects of the Southern Question*; and his distinctive way of utilising non-Italian experiences for Italian purposes: these and other expressions of Gramsci's originality are part of what attracted Cammett to the Italian Communist leader, and that gave his account of Gramsci's life and work a unique stamp that endures to this day.

References

Adamson, Walter 1980, *Hegemony and Revolution – Antonio Gramsci's Political and Cultural Theory*, Berkeley, CA: University of California Press.

Aglianò, Sebastiano 1953, *Il Canto di Farinata*, Lucca: Lucentia.

Agosti, Aldo 1974, 'Le sconfitte del 1923 (gennaio-novembre 1923)', *La Terza Internazionale – storia documentaria*, Vol. I, Part 2, Rome: Editori Riuniti.

Alatri, Paolo 1956, *Le origini del fascismo*, Rome: Editori Riuniti.

Alighieri, Dante 1954, *The Inferno*, translated by John Ciardi, New Brunswick: Rutgers University Press.

—— 1978, *La Divina Commedia*, edited by Natalino Sapegno, Florence: La Nuova Italia.

Anderson, Perry 1976, *Considerations on Western Marxism*, London: Verso.

Bergami, Giancarlo 1978, 'Sui rapporti tra Gramsci e Trotsky', *Rivista di Storia Contemporanea*, October: 559–85.

Anglani, Bartolo 1967, 'La critica letteraria in Gramsci', *Critica Marxista*, 3: 208–30.

Berti, Giuseppe (ed.) 1967, *I primi dieci anni di vitu del PCI – documenti inediti dell'Archivio Angelo Tasca*: Milan: Feltrinelli.

Boggs, Grace Lee 1993, 'Thinking and Acting Dialectically: C.L.R. James, the American Years', *Monthly Review* 45, 5: 38–46.

Boggs, Carl 1984, *The Two Revolutions: Gramsci and the Dilemmas of Western Marxism*, Boston: South End Press.

Bogliolo, Enrico 1977, 'Società civile e prassi nelle note gramsciane sulla letteratura', *Annali della Facoltà di Scienze Politiche*, Cagliari: Università di Cagliari.

Bogues, Anthony 1997, *Caliban's Freedom – The Early Political Thought of C.L.R. James*, London: Pluto Press.

—— 2003, *Black Heretics, Black Prophets – Radical Political Intellectuals*, London: Routledge.

Cambria, Adele 1976, *Amore come rivoluzione*, Milan: SugarCo.

Cammett, John M. 1967a, *Antonio Gramsci and the Origins of Italian Communism*, Stanford, CA: Stanford University Press.

—— 1967b, 'Communist Theories of Fascism', *Science and Society* 31 (2): 149–63.

—— 1971, 'Socialism and Participatory Democracy', *The Revival of American Socialism*, edited by George Fischer, Oxford: Oxford University Press.

—— 1991, *Bibliografia gramsciana, 1922–1988*, Rome: Editori Riuniti.

—— 1995, and Maria Luisa Righi, *Bibliografia gramsciana to 1993*, Rome: Fondazione Istituto Gramsci.

Cavalcanti, Pedro and Paul Piccone (eds.) 1975, *History, Philosophy and Culture in the Young Gramsci*, New York: Telos Press.

Coppa, Frank (ed.) 1985, *Dictionary of Modern Italian History*, Westport, CT: Greenwood Press.

Crehan, Kate 2002, *Gramsci, Culture and Anthropology*, London: Pluto Press.

Croce, Benedetto 1940, *La poesia di Dante*, Bari: Laterza.

Degras, Jane (ed.) 1956, *The Communist International, 1919–1922*, Vol. I, Oxford: Oxford University Press.

Del Lungo, Isidoro 1900, *Lectura Dantis – Il Canto X dell'Inferno letto da Isodoro Del Lungo*, Florence: Sansoni.

Delzell, Charles F. 1961, Mussolini's Enemies: The Italian Anti-Fascist Resistance, Princeton: Princeton University Press.

De Sanctis, Francesco 1969, *Scritti critici – antologia*, edited by Mario Puppo, Padua: Edizioni R.A.D.A.R.

Deutscher, Isaac 1965, *The Prophet Unarmed – Trotsky: 1921–1929*, Vol. II, New York: Vintage Books.

Dombroski, Robert 1984, *L'Esistenza ubbidiente – letterati italiani sotto il fascismo*, Naples: Guida Editori.

—— 1989, *Antonio Gramsci*, Boston: G.K. Hall.

—— 1994, *Properties of Writing – Ideological Discourse in Modern Italian Fiction*, Baltimore: Johns Hopkins University Press.

—— 1999, *Creative Entanglements – Gadda and the Baroque*, Toronto: University of Toronto Press.

Farred, Grant 1997, *What's My Name? Organic and Vernacular Intellectuals*, Minneapolis: 2003.

Fernández, Ileanys Mena 2010, 'Recepción de Gramsci en Cuba', *Tiempo y Sociedad*.

Fiori 1973, *Antonio Gramsci: Life of a Revolutionary*, translated by Tom Nairn, New York: Schocken Books.

—— 1977, *Vita di Antonio Gramsci*, Bari: Laterza.

Flynn, Thomas R. 1984, *Sartre and Marxist Existentialism*, Chicago: Chicago University Press.

Forgacs, David (ed.) 1988, *A Gramsci Reader – Selected Writings 1916–1935*, London: Lawrence and Wishart.

Francese, Joseph 2009, 'Thoughts on Gramsci's Need 'To Do Something für ewig,' *Rethinking Marxism*, Vol. 21, No. 1: 54–66.

Francovich, Carlo 1961, *La Resistenza a Firenze*, Florence: La Nuova Italia.

Friedan, Betty 2001, *The Feminine Mystique*, New York: W.W. Norton & Company.

Garosci, Aldo 1951, 'The Italian Communist Party', *Communism in Western Europe*, Ithaca, NY: Cornell University Press.

Genovese, Eugene 1970, 'On Antonio Gramsci', *For a New America: Essays in History and Politics from Studies on the Left, 1959–1967*, edited by James Weinstein and David W. Eakins, New York: Random House.

Germino, Dante 1990, *Antonio Gramsci – Architect of a New Politics*, Baton Rouge: Louisiana State University Press.

Gobetti, Piero 1955, *La rivoluzione liberale*, Turin: Einaudi.

Gramsci, Antonio 1950, *Cartas desde la cárcel*, translated by Gabriela Moner, prologue by Gregorio Bermann, Buenos Aires: Lautaro.

—— 1957, *The Modern Prince & Other Writings*, translated by Louis Marks, New York: International Publishers.

—— 1957, *The Open Marxism of Antonio Gramsci*, edited and translated by Carl Marzani, New York: Cameron Associates.

—— 1964, *2000 pagine di Antonio Gramsci-nel tempo della lotta 1914–1926*, 2 Vols., edited by Giansiro Ferrata and Niccolò Gallo, Milan: Il Saggiatore.

—— 1965, *Lettere dal carcere*, edited by Sergio Caprioglio and Elsa Fubini, Turin: Einaudi.

—— 1967, *Scritti politici*, edited by Paolo Spriano, Rome: Editori Riuniti.

—— 1971, *Selections from the Prison Notebooks*, edited and translated by Quintin Hoare and Geoffrey Nowell Smith, New York: International Publishers

—— 1972, *Briefe aus dem Kerker*, translated by Gerhard Roth,* Frankfurt am Main: S. Fischer Verlag.

—— 1973, *Scritti politici*, edited by Paolo Spriano, Rome: Editori Riuniti

—— 1974, *La questione meridionale*, edited by Franco De Felice and Valentino Parlato, Rome: Editori Riuniti.

—— 1975, *Quaderni del carcere*, 4 Vols., edited by Valentino Gerratana, Turin: Einaudi.

—— 1977, *Selections from Political Writings 1910–1920*, edited by Quintin Hoare, translated by John Mathews, Minneapolis: University of Minnesota Press.

—— 1978, *Selections from Political Writings (1921–1926)*, edited and translated by Quintin Hoare, New York: International Publishers.

—— 1980, *Cronache torinesi*, Turin: Einaudi.

—— 1985, *Selections from Cultural Writings*, edited by David Forgacs and Geoffey Nowell Smith, translated by William Boelhower, Cambridge, MA: Harvard University Press.

—— 1988, *A Gramsci Reader*, edited by David Forgacs, London: Lawrence and Wishart.

—— 1990, *Selections from Political Writings 1910–1920*, edited by Quintin Hoare, translated by John Mathews, Minneapolis: University of Minnesota Press.

—— 1992, *Lettere dal carcere 1908–1926*, edited by Antonio Santucci, Turin: Einaudi.

—— 1992–2007, *Prison Notebooks*, edited and translated by Joseph A. Buttigieg, New York: Columbia University Press.

—— 1994 *Letters from Prison*, 1994, 2 Vols., edited by Frank Rosengarten, translated by Raymond Rosenthal, New York: Columbia University Press.

—— 1995, *Further Selections from the Prison Notebooks*, edited and translated by Derek

Boothman, Minneapolis: University of Minnesota Press.

—— 1996, *Lettere dal carcere*, 2 Vols., edited by Antonio Santucci, Palermo: Sellerio Editore.

Grimshaw, Anna (ed.) 1992, *The C.L.R. James Reader*, Oxford: Blackwell Publishers.

Guglielmi, Armando 1976, *Da De Sanctis a Gramsci: il linguaggio della critica*, Bologna: Il Mulino.

Hobsbawm, Eric and Giorgio Napolitano, 1977, *The Italian Road to Socialism*, translated by John Cammett and Victoria DeGrazia, Westport, CT: Lawrence Hill and Company.

James, C.L.R. 1993, *American Civilizaton*, edited by Anna Grimshaw and Keith Hart, afterword by Robert A. Hill, Cambridge, MA: Blackwell Publishers.

Jameson, Fredric 1971, *Marxism and Form – 20th century dialectical theories of literature*, Princeton: Princeton University Press.

Jay, Martin 1984, *Marxism & Totality – The Adventures of a Concept from Lukács to Habermas*, Berkeley, CA: University of California Press.

Joll, James 1978, *Antonio Gramsci*, New York: The Viking Press.

Kiernan, Victor 1995, *Imperialism and its Contradictions*, edited by Harvey J. Kaye, New York: Routledge.

Lears, Jackson 1985, 'The Concept of Cultural Hegemony: Problems and Possibilities', *The American Historical Review*, 90, 3: 567–93.

Lenin, Vladimir 1975, *The Lenin Anthology*, edited by Robert C. Tucker, New York: W.W. Norton & Company.

Magdoff, Harry 1978, *Imperialism: From the Colonial Age to the Present*, New York: Monthly Review Press.

Mammucari, Mario and Anna Miserocchi (eds.), *Gramsci a Roma, 1924–1926*, Milan: La Pietra.

Mandel, Ernest 1978, *From Stalinism to Eurocommunism*, translated by Jon Rothschild, London: Verso.

Mann, Thomas 1948, *Stories of Three Decades*, translated by H.T. Lowe-Porter, New York: Alfred A. Knopf.

Marx, Karl 1964, *Economic and Philosophic Manuscripts of 1844*, edited by Dirk J. Struik, translated by Martin Milligan, New York: International Publishers.

Marx, Karl 1977, *Capital* Vol. I, introduced by Ernest Mandel, translated by Ben Fowkes, New York: Vintage Books.

Marzani, Carl 1980, *The Promise of Eurocommunism*, New York: J. Hill.

Mattarese, Francesco 1952, *Interpretazioni dantesche*, Bari: Laterza.

Moe, Nelson 2006, *The View from Vesuvius – Italian Culture and the Southern Question*, Berkeley, CA: University of California Press.

Mouffe, Chantal (ed.) 1979, *Gramsci and Marxist Theory*, London: Routledge & Kegan Paul.

Needham, Anurada Dingwaney 2000, *Using the Master's Tools – Resistance and the Literature of the African and South Asian Diasporas*, New York: St. Martin's Press.

Nielsen, Aldon Lynn 1994, *C.L.R. James – A Critical Introduction*, Jackson: University Press of Mississippi.

Ormea, Ferdinando 1975, *Gramsci e il futuro dell'uomo*, Rome: Coines Edizioni.

Ortaggi, Simonetta 1974, 'Gramsci e Trotskij: la lettera del 9 febbraio 1924', *Rivista di Storia Contemporanea*, 4: 478–503.

Padoan, Giorgio 1959, 'Il Canto degli Epicurei', *Convivium*, January–February: 12–39.

Paggi, Leonardo 1984, *Le strategie del potere in Gramsci*, Rome: Editori Riuniti.

Piccone, Paul 1983, *Italian Marxism*, Berkeley: University of California Press.

Quercioli, Mimma Paulesu (ed.) 1977, *Gramsci vivo nelle testimonianze dei suoi contemporanei*, Milan: Feltrinelli.

Rapone, Leonardo 1978, *Trotskij e il fascismo*, Bari: Laterza.

Rastelli, Dario 1948, 'Restauri danteschi', in *Saggi di umanesimo cristiano*, 3.

Ravera, Camilla 1973, *Diario di trent'anni, 1913–1943*, Rome: Editori Riuniti.

Riboldi, Ezio 1964, *Vicende socialiste*, Milan: Edizione Azione Comune.

Rosengarten, Frank 2010, 'On Intellectuals, Engaged and Otherwise', *Italian Culture*, xxvii, 2: 157–67.

Rossi, Cesare 1952, *Il tribunale speciale*, Milan: Ceschina.

Said, Edward 1979, *Orientalism*, New York: Random House.

—— 1979, *The Question of Palestine*, New York: Random House.

—— 1993, *Culture and Imperialism*, New York: Alfred A. Knopf.

—— 2004, *Humanism and Democratic Criticism*, New York: Columbia University Press.

Salvadori, Max 1970, *Gramsci e il problema storico della democrazia*, Turin: Einaudi.

San Juan, Jr., Epifanio 1998, *Beyond Postcolonial Theory*, New York: St. Martin's Press.

Sansone, Mario 1961, *Il Canto X dell'Inferno*, Florence: Le Monnier.

Santucci, Antonio (ed.) 1987, *Letture di Gramsci*, Rome: Editori Riuniti.

—— 1996, *Gramsci*, Rome: Newton and Compton.

Schneider, Jane (ed.) 1998, *Italy's 'Southern Question' – Orientalism in One Country*, New York: Berg.

Schwarz, Bill 1994, 'C.L.R. James in America', *New Formations*, 24: 174–83.

Serge, Victor 1963, *Memoirs of a Revolutionary 1901–1941*, edited and translated by Peter Sedgwick, Oxford: Oxford University Press.

Showstack Sassoon, Anne 1987, *Gramsci's Politics*, Minneapolis: University of Minnesota Press.

Singer, Daniel 1970, *Prelude to Revolution: France in May 1968*, Cambridge, MA: South End Press.

Slaughter, Jane and Robert Kern (eds.) 1981, *European Women on the Left*, Westport, CT: Greenwood Press.

Somai, Giovanni 1979, *Gramsci a Vienna – ricerche e documenti 1922–1924*, Urbino: Argalia.

Spriano, Paolo 1977, *Gramsci in carcere e il partito*, Rome: Editori Riuniti.

Stella, Simonetta Piccone 1962, 'Questioni di estetica nel pensiero di Antonio Gramsci', *Il Contemporaneo*, 44, January: 7–23.

Stipcevic, Niksa 1968, *Gramsci e i problemi letterari*, Milan: Mursia.

Strigelli, Odoardo 1952, 'Il canto di Farinata dopo gli appunti di Gramsci', *Inventario*, 1: 97–104.

Terracini, Umberto 1967, 'Così li ho conosciuti – ricordi dei "cinque" dell'Internazionale: Lenin, Trotsky, Zinoviev, Radek, Bukharin', *Rinascita*, 27 October: 18–20.

Texier, Jacques 1966, *Gramsci*, Paris: Éditions Seghers.

Togliatti, Palmiro 1958, *Il Partito Comunista Italiano*, Milan: Nuova Accademia.

Torres-Saillant, Silvio 2006, *An Intellectual History of the Caribbean*, New York: Palgrave Macmillan.

Trotsky, Leon 1932, *What Next? Vital Questions for the German Proletariat*, translated by Joseph Vanzler, New York: Pioneer Publishers.

—— 1937, *The Revolution Betrayed: What is the Soviet Union, and Where is it Going?*: Garden City: Doubleday.

—— 1969, *The Permanent Revolution and Results and Prospects*, New York: Merit Publishers.

—— 1972, *The First Five Years of the Communist International*, Vol. II, New York: Monad Press.

Young, Robert 2001, *Postcolonialism – An Historical Introduction*, Oxford: Blackwell Publishers.

Index